D1515401

About this Book

This is a practical book, full of advice and suggestions on how to successfully raise debt financing for your business. It covers 373 loan programs, sub-programs and initiatives in both the public and private sectors. It includes 843 contact addresses, phone and fax numbers together with Web sites, where available.

It provides you with a brief history of banking and describes the structure of the Canadian banking industry. It tells you about the types of loans which banks offer. This 2013/2014 Edition has been revised to cover loans and guarantees provided by the federal, provincial and territorial governments and their agencies or private sector partners. It describes loans for exporting and for businesses involved with agriculture, agrifoods, aquaculture and fisheries. It also covers micro loans and loan circles which you can access through a number of non-governmental organizations.

This book also shows you what to do <u>before</u> you approach your bank manager in order to present your business in the best light. It tells you how your bank manager evaluates deals.

Learn how factoring of accounts receivable can be used for financing as well as chattel mortgages. Leasing can help you reduce cash outlay and is considered as a form of debt financing. Find out the advantages and disadvantages.

About the Author

Iain Williamson is an entrepreneur, business consultant and seminar leader. His views have appeared in many newspaper articles. He has also been the guest speaker on a CBC Radio phone-in show on starting a business in a recession. In addition, he has appeared on television shows such as: CBC TV's Venture; TVO's MoneysWorth, and Canada Tonight of BCTV and CHCH Television.

Iain spent five years as a financial analyst and knows what makes business tick. For fourteen years he operated his own businesses in importing, high technology and manufacturing. He now operates Entrepreneurial Business Consultants of Canada and also owns a book publishing business. He holds degrees from Oxford University and from St. Andrew's, Scotland.

Iain writes from firsthand experience which he shares with you. This book is **essential** reading for every entrepreneur and business owner who is seeking debt financing.

OSHAWA PUBLIC LIBRARY

658
.150
971
Wil

Your Guide to Arranging Bank and Debt Financing for Your Own Business in Canada

2013-2014 Edition

Canadian financial institutions, micro-loans and non-traditional lending, "Quasi-Equity" and public sector lending assistance as well as off-balance-sheet financing

IAIN WILLIAMSON

Pr 00885855

OSHAWA PUBLIC LIBRARY

ISBN: 978-1-55270-668-8
ISSN: 1191-0542

This book is dedicated to Vicki for all her help.

Written by:
Iain Williamson
Entrepreneurial Business Consultants of Canada
P.O. Box 7200, Station A
Toronto, ON M5W 1X8
Phone: (416) 322-6171

Published in Canada by:
Productive Publications
P.O. Box 7200, Station A
Toronto, ON M5W 1X8
Phone: (416) 483-0634
Fax: (416) 322-7434
Web site: http://www.productivepublications.ca

Copyright © 2013 by Iain Williamson

National Library of Canada cataloguing

Williamson, Iain

Your guide to arranging bank and debt financing for your own business in Canada

Annual.
1991 ed.-
ISSN 1191-0542
ISBN 978-1-55270-668-8 (2013/2014 ed.)

I. Title

HG4090.W512   658.15   C92-031073-7

All rights reserved. No part of this publication may be reproduced, stored in retrieval system, or transmitted in any form or by any means, electronic, mechanical, photocopying, recording or otherwise, without written permission of the author.

Other Books to Help You Finance Your Business

Your Guide to Starting & Self-Financing Own Business in Canada 2013-2014 Edition has been updated to reflect the many changes that have taken place in the sources of marketing information. Shows you how to operate a business out of your home. How to use computers and the Web to run your business more efficiently. Covers Web authoring software and how to sell online with your own e-commerce site or through eBay; as an Amazon Merchant or through online classifieds. Helps you determine how much money you <u>really</u> need and if you can self-finance your own business to compete in the digital age. 362 pages; ISBN 978-1-55270-665-7; $56.95

Your Guide to Preparing a Plan to Raise Money for Your Own Business: *2013-2014 Edition.* A good business plan is essential to succeed in your quest for financing. Contains a step-by-step guide to create your own winning plan. Computer software you can use to create your plan. Learn how to address the concerns of investors or lenders. Tips on structuring your plan. Contains a sample plan as an example. Reviews some software to help you make great presentations to investors or lenders. The author is a consultant with many years of experience in preparing plans for business clients. 310 pages; ISBN 978-1-55270-666-4; $46.95

Your Guide to Raising Venture Capital for Your Own Business in Canada: 2013-2014 Edition is a gold mine of information if you are trying to raise venture capital in Canada. It shows you how to do it yourself. Learn about the structure of the industry; what venture capitalists are looking for and how they evaluate deals. You are given tips on negotiating with them. It lists 86 conferences and provides 544 addresses. Find out what angel investors are looking for and how they could help. 248 pages; ISBN 978-1-55270-667-1; $74.95

Your Guide to Arranging Bank & Debt Financing for Your Own Business in Canada: *2013-2014 Edition.* Learn the secrets of successful debt financing. Find out who the players are in Canadian lending. Covers 373 loan programs and provides 843 contact addresses. Learn how to prepare your company <u>before</u> you approach lenders. Find out how applications are evaluated. Can factoring or leasing help you? The author has many years of experience in bank financing and leasing. 386 pages; ISBN 978-1-55270-668-8; $81.95

Your Guide to Financing Business Growth by Selling a Piece of the Pie: What's involved in going public; employee share ownership plans and franchising in Canada: *2013-2014 Edition.* Provides a critical examination of three methods of growing your business by using other people's money. How to sell shares to the public or to your employees. How to expand through franchising. The author was formerly a financial analyst in the Canadian stockbrokerage business for five years. 162 pages; ISBN 978-1-55270-669-5; $46.95

Your Guide to Canadian Export Financing: *2013-2014 Edition*. Practical techniques for financing exports. Get details of all provincial, territorial and federal assistance programs that help you export including addresses and phone numbers to steer you in the right direction. Includes a chapter on insurance and another on sources of marketing information. The author is a consultant and entrepreneur who knows the practical side of importing and exporting. 300 pages; ISBN 978-1-55270-670-1; $59.95

Your Guide to Government Financial Assistance for Business **(Separate 2013-2014 Editions-one for each Province & Territory)**. Business financing in Canada is in a constant state of flux. New government programs are continually being introduced. Old ones are often amended or discontinued with little publicity. These books provide you with the latest information on all Federal and Provincial/Territorial programs that specifically relate to each area together with contacts. Specify Province or Territory when ordering. All titles: $89.95 ea.

	ISBN	pages		ISBN	pages
Newfoundland & Labrador	9781552706718	304 pages	**Prince Edward Island**	9781552706725	273 pages
Nova Scotia	9781552706732	308	**New Brunswick**	9781552706749	278
Quebec	9781552706756	312	**Ontario**	9781552706763	376
Manitoba	9781552706770	314	**Saskatchewan**	9781552706787	306
Alberta	9781552706794	306	**British Columbia**	9781552706800	286
The Yukon	9781552706817	256	**The Northwest Territories**	9781552706824	246
The Nunavut	9781552706831	248			

Order securely online at www.ProductivePublications.ca or Place Your Order Overleaf ➜

ORDER FORM

Qty	Title	
	Your Guide to Starting & Self-Financing Your Own Business in Canada $56.95	
	Your Guide to Preparing a Plan to Raise Money for Your Own Business $46.95	
	Your Guide to Raising Venture Capital Your Own Business in Canada $74.95	
	Your Guide to Bank & Debt Financing for Your Own Business in Canada $81.95	
	Your Guide to Financing Business Growth by Selling a Piece of the Pie $46.95	
	Your Guide to Canadian Export Financing $59.95	
	Your Guide to Government Financial Assistance for Business in.... $89.95 ea.	
	PLEASE SPECIFY Province/Territory:	
	Sub-Total	
	Postage/handling $9.95 on first title	$9.95
	Add postage/handling of $2.25 per title thereafter	
	Sub-Total	
	Add HST at 5%	
	TOTAL	

Name_____

Organization_____

Street_____

City/Town_____Prov_____ Postal Code_____

Phone_____Fax_____

Please Indicate Preferred Method of Payment

☐ Cheque   ☐ VISA   ☐ MasterCard   ☐ American Express

Card Number_____

Expiry Date (Month/Year)_____

Cardholder Signature_____

Mail or Fax to: **Productive Publications**
PO Box 7200, Stn. A, Toronto, Ontario M5W 1X8
Phone: (416) 483-0634 Fax: (416) 322-7434
Order online at: *www.productivepublications.ca*
Serving Readers for Over 27 years

STANDING ORDER

Stay Up to Date!

**BUSINESS FINANCING
KEEPS CHANGING**

**Place Your Order Now
to Automatically Receive
the Latest Editions As
Soon As They Become
Available**

Place Your Standing Order Overleaf ➜

STANDING ORDER

Qty	Title
	Your Guide to Starting & Self-Financing Your Own Business in Canada
	Your Guide to Preparing a Plan to Raise Money for Your Own Business
	Your Guide to Raising Venture Capital Your Own Business in Canada
	Your Guide to Bank & Debt Financing for Your Own Business in Canada
	Your Guide to Financing Business Growth by Selling a Piece of the Pie
	Your Guide to Canadian Export Financing
	Your Guide to Government Financial Assistance for Business in....
	PLEASE SPECIFY Province/Territory:

Name_____

Organization_____

Street_____

City/Town_ _____Prov_____ Postal Code_____

Phone_____Fax_____

Please Indicate Preferred Method of Payment

NOTE: Credit Cards will not be charged until date of shipment

☐ Cheque ☐ VISA ☐ MasterCard ☐ American Express

Card Number_____

Expiry Date (Month/Year)_____

Cardholder Signature_____

Mail or fax to: Productive Publications
PO Box 7200, Stn. A, Toronto, Ontario M5W 1X8
Phone: (416) 483-0634 Fax: (416) 322-7434
Serving Readers for Over 27 years

ACKNOWLEDGEMENTS

Thanks are due for the kind assistance given by the librarians at Ryerson, the Canadian Federation of Independent Business and the Business Section of Metro Toronto Reference Library.

Thanks are also due the authors of the many excellent papers and articles on the banking industry which are referred to in the text and which are acknowledged in the notes at the ends of the chapters.

CONTENTS

CHAPTER 1
Introduction

CHAPTER 2
The Role of Banks

Contents

CHAPTER 3
Structure of the
Canadian Banking Industry

CHAPTER 4
Types of Loans

Contents

CHAPTER 5
Loans by the Federal Government or
its Agencies & Private Sector Partners

CHAPTER 6
Loans & Loan Guarantees by Provincial/
Territorial Governments or Their Agencies

Contents

CHAPTER 7
Other Non-conventional Loans

Contents

CHAPTER 8
Loans for Agriculture, Agrifoods, Aquaculture & Fisheries

Contents

CHAPTER 9
Preparations

CHAPTER 10
The Banker's Viewpoint

CHAPTER 11
The True Costs

CHAPTER 12
Factoring

Contents

CHAPTER 13
Export Financing

CHAPTER 14
Leasing

Contents

CHAPTER 15
Mortgaging

CHAPTER 16
Planning and Financing
From the Public & Private Sectors

1

Introduction

Debt as Opposed to Equity

This volume deals with debt financing or the borrowing of money to finance a business or start-up.

Debt financing does not require the giving up of any of the ownership in the business and for that reason, many entrepreneurs prefer it as a form of financing. It is generally easier to obtain than equity financing. The Canadian Chartered Banks operate about 8,000 branches across the country and are well experienced in lending operations.

Venture capitalists, on the other hand, tend to be centred in a few major cities. Informal investors, called "angels" certainly do not advertise because they prefer their privacy, rather than being inundated with hopeful business plans and proposals.

Debt financing is not a panacea. It has costs attached to it, aside from the obvious interest payments. Collateral requirements can be quite onerous which can ultimately make lending a very, very expensive proposition.

Factoring may present a less costly alternative, however, this is a technique largely confined to the textile and clothing trades. It will be examined in some detail.

Leasing as a Form of Debt Financing

Leasing may be considered as a form of debt financing since the product which is leased, is really borrowed against a regular lease payment. Put another way, the use of the product is being loaned (even though there might ultimately be an option to buy it). For that reason, lease financing is included in this volume.

Mortgaging

Mortgaging of property or equipment also presents another way of raising money as debt. A very brief review of mortgaging will be provided in this volume.

2

The Role of Banks

"If it's as easy to borrow money from a bank as its advertising claims, why should anyone want to rob it?" (Evan Esar: 20,000 Quips & Quotes)

Way Back When

Banking has been around for more than 6,000 years. There is evidence that merchants in the ancient Middle Eastern states of Babylonia and Assyria made loans to farmers to enable them to purchase seeds and grow their crops. They also loaned money to traders so they could purchase the crops which the farmers produced and transport them to market.

The first deposit accepting banks didn't appear until ancient Greek and Roman times.

The First Gold Coins

Of course, before you can have banks, you have to have a means of exchange. Initially, "money" was in the form of grain or cattle. Indeed, cattle were still being used as "currency" until very recently by some nomadic tribes such as the Masai in East Africa, but its difficult to carry a goat around in your pocketbook and more practical means of exchange have evolved. I certainly don't find a corral of cattle behind my bank manager's desk! A more practical alternative emerged!

According to the National Mining Association, gold was first used as a currency around 1500 BC when the people in Nubia, in modern-day Egypt, began using gold as a medium for international trade.

Around the same time, a coin made of about 2/3 gold and 1/3 silver made its appearance in the Middle East. This was known as the "Shekel".

In 1091 BC, gold in the form of small square coins, was legalized as a form of money in China.

The first coins of pure gold were made in the ancient Kingdom of Lydia, located in Asia Minor. That was about 610 BC.

In the year 50 BC the Romans began issuing gold coins called the "Aureus".

The Emergence of "Modern Banking"

Jump many centuries later and in 1284 AD, Venice (at that time a major maritime trading power), issued the gold Ducat. The English, not to be outdone, issued the Florin; their first gold coin, in the same year.

Indeed, "Modern Banking" came of age during the Italian Renaissance and then spread rapidly throughout the maritime trading powers of Europe.

The Charging of Interest on Loans

I find it very interesting that in early Judaism, the charging of interest on loans between members of the Jewish faith was forbidden; although interest on loans to those outside of the faith was considered legal. Indeed, in early Christianity "usury" as it was called, was also banned although it became acceptable over time and if you've ever paid interest on an outstanding credit card balance, you'll certainly know that usury is alive and well in our modern society!

The Quran prohibits the charging of interest on money loaned in the Islamic faith and this is still adhered to this very day, and has led to a whole specialized branch of Islamic banking in which a mark-up profit as well as fees are added to financial facilities offered to customers.

The Globalization of World Banking

When I was researching for this book, I tried, without success, to find an all encompassing figure that would give you an idea of the size of the world's commercial banking system, but all I can tell you is that worldwide bank assets run into the hundreds of trillions of dollars.

Size is one thing, but what is very worrying is that the world of banking has become very interconnected and trouble in one area can very quickly spread to other areas, as contagion spreads fear throughout the financial system.

The Near Collapse of the World Banking System

In September 2008, the collapse of US banking giant, Lehman Brothers, sparked a massive credit crunch which spread rapidly across borders and very nearly caused a systemic failure of the entire global banking system. Governments rushed in to prop up ailing banks, businesses found it nearly impossible to get new loans to maintain and grow their operations.

By the time I am writing this in 2012, it seems as politicians have woken up to the hazard of having banks that are "too big to fail" and have instituted a number of measures to try to prevent a repeat of the Lehman Brothers fiasco.

The focus, since 2010, has been on the Eurozone sovereign debt crisis involving Greece, Portugal, Ireland, Spain and to a lesser degree Italy. Harsh austerity measures have been put in place to try and get the national debts of these countries under control, but it remains to be seen whether they will be successful.

All of this makes it abundantly clear that events around the world can affect what happens in Canada. So, bear with me as I briefly cover some of the "outside influences" which have a bearing on domestic banking in Canada.

Changes to the Regulatory Environment Which Will Affect Bank Financing

A number of significant changes have already taken place in the US that are designed to prevent another financial meltdown. These changes will also (hopefully) lead to a better framework in which small business owners can obtain the loans they need in order to grow. First, let's step back and look at how the whole mess started in the first place.

The Repeal of the Glass-Steagall Act

The Glass-Steagall Act came into effect in 1933. It was championed by President Roosevelt as a means of curbing the power of large banks and stop them making investments in one another, in stock brokerage firms and into insurance companies. It was seen as a means of taming the excesses which had led to over 5,000 bank failures in the wake of the 1929 Wall Street Crash.

In 1999, President Clinton and the US Congress passed the Financial Modernization Act which essentially killed the Glass-Steagall Act and abruptly deregulated the US banking industry.

Many critics blame this deregulation for the events which led up to the financial crisis of 2008-2009. Since then, US politicians and regulators have been scrambling to force the deregulation genie back into its bottle.

Dodd Frank Bill

The Dodd-Frank Wall Street Reform and Consumer Protection Act was signed into law by President Obama in 2010. Its stated objectives can be summarized from the text of the Bill, as follows:

To promote the financial stability of the United States by improving accountability and transparency in the financial system, to end "too big to fail", to protect the American taxpayer by ending bailouts, to protect consumers from abusive financial services practices, and for other purposes.

The Volker Rule

The so-called "Volker Rule" named after a former Chairman of the Federal Reserve, is designed to curb proprietary trading and excessive risk taking by US banking giants that are considered "too big to fail". At the time of writing, in early April 2013, the Rule had not been implemented but there has been much heated debate about some of the implications for banks which operate outside of the United States which could get caught up in the web of regulations. A senior official from the US Federal Reserve had expressed hope that the rule would be finished in 2013.

Increasing Scrutiny in the UK

As I mentioned earlier, in the wake of the 2008 financial meltdown, the British Government was forced into taking an 84% interest in Barclays and 43% in Lloyds. As a reluctant stepfather, the British Government now wields a big stick, however, the banks still maintain their independence and this has not been helpful in facilitating small businesses loans in order to grow and create employment.

Canadian Banks Relatively Unscathed

Because banking deregulation was not allowed to proceed to the same degree as in other nations and reserve requirements were maintained, the industry as a whole escaped the carnage which befell the US and UK banks.

The Basel Agreements

Central bankers from around the world met in 1988 to publish a minimum set of capital requirements for banks. The Basel Accord, as it is named, has gone through three iterations; the most recent of which is Basel III. This is designed to strengthen the adequacy of banks by imposing "stress tests" to make sure that they could better withstand another financial crisis.

Now that Big Banks Have Been Brought to Heel
Does it Mean You Can Get a Loan More Easily?

Probably not, but at least it has focussed a lot of attention on the subject! The Obama Administration's Jobs Bill which was designed to help smaller firms gain access the equity markets became ensnared in the political infighting in Congress and never became law.

Insofar as the US, the UK and Canada are concerned, banks still appear to be reluctant to loan money to small businesses unless they obtain some form of government guarantees. The is an irony here. If businesses cannot easily access money to help create jobs, the economy will remain stagnant and banks don't benefit from stagnant economies!

The Banking Function

Banks are in business to make money. They do so simply by using other people's money, which they can obtain at a lower rate of interest, and lending it to other people at a higher rate of interest.

In other words, they use money from your chequing accounts (upon which you pay monthly service and statement charges, as you well know!) and low paying savings accounts to invest in Government of Canada Treasury Bills, commercial paper, mortgages, customer loans or anything else with a higher yield. The difference provides them with their bread and butter or in many cases their champagne and caviar!

According to the latest figures from the Canadian Banker's Association, in October 2012, Canadians had over $2.2 trillion in deposits with Canadian banks.

These sums provide the banks with their play money, since for every dollar they have on deposit or in reserve they can in turn loan out so many dollars. Thus, if a bank operates with a 10% reserve; for every dollar in reserve, it can loan ten dollars out. If it operates with a 5% reserve, it can loan out $20 and so on. Of course, this leaves banks very exposed if the loans they make go bad and they have insufficient reserves as was illustrated in the US financial crisis of 2008 when central banks (especially the US Federal Reserve) had to loan huge amounts of money to the banks to prevent the whole world financial system from total collapse. There have been moves afoot to try to increase the reserve ratios of banks so that they can better withstand future financial shocks but it appears that the banks are putting up stiff resistance since they know full well that the government will come to their rescue again if the mess things up.

These comments are obviously an oversimplification of a sophisticated money machine that has been developed over the years. However, an anonymous statement in Evan Esar's *20,000 Quips and Quotes* claimed that: "when a poor man has too much money, he lends it to the bank; when a rich man hasn't enough, the bank lends it to him". He should have added that the bank lives off the difference in interest rates!

Start-up Financing From Banks

According to the Canadian Banker's Association, at the end of October 2012, Canadian banks had $1.7 trillion in loans outstanding. Of this amount, only a very modest $18 billion was on loan by the major banks to **small** businesses as of June 2012.

How much money do banks and financial institutions supply to companies that are right at the starting gate? Well, they supply only 9% of such additional funding for incorporated start-ups and 7% of that required by unincorporated start-ups. [1]

Studies have shown that by far the greatest bulk of initial start-up financing comes from the owners themselves.

The American experience is somewhat similar. A survey suggested that in the United States, banks provided only 14% of the capital required and that most of it (54%) came from personal savings. [2]

These figures are consistent with the banker's aversion to risk-taking. Banks may be an important source of financing for companies once they are up and running, however, they play a much less significant role at the start-up gate.

In situations where there is no collateral, no receivables, no plant, no real estate and no rich uncles who will guarantee the bank loan, the chances of financing from banks is close to 0% under such circumstances.

If, however, you have personal assets or a spouse who has a steady job, then you may be able to obtain a loan, using personal guarantees. If you can't obtain a business loan, you may at least be able to obtain a personal loan, which in turn, can be used in the business.

Each branch of a bank is a self-contained profit centre which is expected to make money. Since between one quarter and one third of start-up businesses fail within their first two years, start-ups represent a high risk area for the banks to become involved.

In the 1981/82 recession there were approximately 50,000 companies which defaulted on their loans and the banks are anxious to keep this figure to a minimum. This will be especially true in the recession we experienced in the early '90s.

It is much easier for a bank to loan money to a business that has been established for many years and has a visible track record than to one that has just appeared out of the blue. In other words, the twinkle in the start-up entrepreneur's eye is unlikely to impress his steely-eyed bank manager.

The Canadian chartered banks, generally, are not in the business of supplying unsecured credit or venture capital.

It should be noted that most of the major banks operate venture capital subsidiaries, however, almost none of these make investments in start-ups or early stage companies.

It is, therefore, very difficult for the start-up company to raise financing from banking institutions. This is not said to discourage entrepreneurs, but merely to forewarn them about their chances.

Should the start-up company be at the point of introducing its product to market and shortly be in a position of having inventory and accounts receivable then, it may be possible to arrange an operating line with the bank.

If the start-up requires machinery and assets to commence operation, the banks may be willing to lend part of the money in the form of a term loan; using the equipment or assets as collateral for the loan.

In the case of established companies, bank financing is generally much easier to arrange.

Financing for Established Small Businesses

The prime responsibility of chartered banks is the security of the deposits placed with them. Banks should not, therefore, be regarded as sources for risk capital and are generally reluctant to provide funding for high risk situations. Unfortunately, due to high failure rates, most small businesses fall into this category.

When banks do enter high risk situations and are unable to extract themselves gracefully, the results cover the headlines in our daily newspapers; as in the case with the collapse of the Canadian Commercial and the Northland. Similar failures have occurred accompanying the Savings and Loan scandals in the United States.

Bankers took a cautious approach to their profession after the collapses of the Great Depression. During that period over 5,000 bank failures occurred in the United States and although there were none in Canada, a number of banks had to be supported.

Any caution learnt during the depression years was thrown to the wind when a new yuppie generation of MBAs swarmed out of the education system and worked their way into the towers of finance. These managers had been reared by their professors in the importance of the "bottom line" and they aggressively went after higher returns at the expense of caution.

Prior to the mortgage lending crisis in the United States, banks were lending to almost anybody, regardless of their ability to repay. All that changed in 2008 and now that the chickens have come home to roost, the small business owner will find his banker somewhat wiser and a lot more tightfisted than before!

Role of Banks in Small Business Financing

The chartered banks account for 74% of all loans made to small business in Canada according to an independent report prepared by Thompson Lightstone and Company Limited for the Canadian Bankers Association which was released in 1996. It shows that the chartered banks constitute a major source of small business debt financing for small businesses in Canada.

These figures are in line with an earlier survey of newly formed companies in Ontario which found that banks and other financial institutions provided 74% of additional financing required by incorporated companies after they had started. By contrast they supplied a somewhat smaller proportion of 60% of the additional financing required by unincorporated companies. [3]

The same study found that 66% of the owners of incorporated companies were willing to go into debt in order to obtain more capital. In the case of unincorporated companies the figure was in the same order of magnitude at 61%. This suggests that there is an overdependence on the part of small business on bank financing.

Over-dependence on Bank Financing

The over-dependence of small business on banks for financing may be attributable to two reasons.

The first, is a reluctance on the part of many small business owners to give up any interest in their company. They want to be entirely their own boss and run their own show without having to report to any outside shareholders, although they often end up having to report to their banker! In many cases this independence was the very reason the entrepreneur went into business for himself or herself in the first place.

The second, is probably due to a dearth of readily available equity capital and the lack of efficient mechanisms by which it can be obtained.

Relationship Between Small Business Owners and Their Bankers

The relationship between the small business owner and his banker is often "delicate" to say the least. According to Don Allen: "the borrower tends to be too optimistic about his sales and to overstate his assets. His banker tends to have too little knowledge and understanding of the business owner's problems and sometimes pays more attention to collateral than to cash flow. This creates ample opportunity for misunderstanding even though both parties want the business owner to succeed." [4]

These sentiments were echoed by an earlier study by Wyatt, which attributed much dissatisfaction with the reluctance of banks to make high risk loans and their demands for excessive collateral.

In 1994, the House of Commons Small Business Working Committees issued two reports [5] [6], which unleashed an orgy of bank bashing in the press, which suggested that the relationship between small business and their bankers was not even "delicate" - it was downright "hostile"!

The Report of the Standing Committee on Industry [6] recommended that a code of conduct be drawn up which would explain the information that loan applicants must disclose, a clear explanation of the reasons for refusing a loan, a commitment to guide customers to alternative sources of financing and a commitment to provide an internal complaints handling mechanism.

The Committee further recommended that the chartered banks follow the example of the Toronto Dominion Bank in instituting a mediation process that can be evoked by small business borrowers from whom a bank decides to withdraw credit.

Another recommendation by the Committee suggested that the Government establish a Bank Ombudsman to investigate complaints levied against the banks. They recommended that this should be modelled after the Ombudsman in the United Kingdom who has the power to require banks to pay compensation to complainants for financial loss, inconvenience and stress. As might be expected, the banks greeted this suggestion of an "external ombudsman" with predictable hostility and distaste.

At the Committee hearings, it was even suggested that banks be subject to loan quotas that require them to lend to small business. Needless to say that this was greeted with howls of protest from the banking community!

In anticipation of the Committee's reports, the banks announced several new initiatives which were aimed at small business and were obviously designed to quell some of the criticism. In a review entitled: "New Tricks of the Banker's Trade" by Richard Wright, published in Profit Magazine [7] he stated that a "study of these programs indicates there is often less to them than meets the eye - and that the banks' commitment to change is still as much about sound bites as substance".

In an earlier survey, released in December 1985, the Canadian Federation of Independent Business showed that almost 30% of independent business owners were dissatisfied with the service they obtained from their banks.

Only about half of the respondents felt that their bankers knew the local market; understood their business sector; had a high enough lending limit or knew how to put a financing package together. Almost 6 out of 10 considered collateral requirements were too high.

There was some good news however! Nearly three-quarters of the respondents felt that their bankers devoted sufficient time to them!

One recurring problem is the mobility of bank managers in the banking system. This causes constant disruptions for the small business owner who has the constant task of briefing new managers on the business. This mobility also leads to a lack of consistency in the handling of the account. It is possible that the business owner will get on well with one banker; whereas the relationship with a successor may be a total disaster.

The "Jack of All Trades" banker was a criticism raised in the Allen study [4]. The average banker is dealing with car loans; trying to get brownie points by selling banking services and persuading his customers to take out credit cards and so on.

The manager is often too busy and spread too thinly, to be of meaningful assistance to the small business owner. In response to this criticism, the banks (to their credit!) have introduced specialized branches to cater to the needs of business. These will be dealt with in the next chapter.

NOTES

[1] By extrapolating figures in *Newly-Formed Small Businesses in Ontario 1982-1984* - former Ontario Ministry of Industry, Trade and Technology

[2] Venture Magazine, October 1985

[3] *Newly-Formed Small Businesses in Ontario 1982-1984* - Ontario Ministry of Industry, Trade and Technology

[4] *Banking and Small Business* by Don R. Allen & Assoc., prepared for the Canadian Federation of Independent Business, 1982

[5] Small Business Working Committee Report to Ministers entitled: *Breaking Through Barriers - Forging Our Future* 1994

[6] Report of the Standing Committee on Industry: *Taking Care of Small Business*, October 1994

[7] Richard Wright: *New Tricks of the Banker's Trade* published in Profit Magazine, March 1995

Chapter 2
The Role of Banks

3

Structure of the
Canadian Banking Industry

Central Banks

Central Banks are responsible for setting monetary policy and managing a nation's money supply. They do this by setting interest rates, setting the reserve requirements and in a crisis, can act as lender in the last resort. They are also responsible for overseeing the commercial banking system within their jurisdiction.

Central Banks are supposed to be independent of the government or governments of the country or countries which they oversee. With the globalization of world finance, Canada is heavily dependent on events outside of its borders and before discussing the Canadian banking industry, it is useful to take a look at outside influences.

The US Federal Reserve Board

The US Federal Reserve Board (referred to as the "Fed") is made up of twelve Federal Reserve Districts; each of which has a member on the Board.

Chairman, Ben Bernanke, currently rules the roost. Insofar as monetary policy is concerned, he seems to be turning a blind eye to inflation in order to keep rates low in an attempt to ease the pain associated with the collapse of the US housing market and the ensuing credit crunch; while at the same time remaining "vigilant" to guard against inflation. This is "FedSpeak" for saying he will do all he can in an attempt to stop the US economy from spiralling into a second and deeper recession.

The collapse of the US housing bubble and the bankruptcy of Lehman Bros. nearly caused a meltdown of the entire world financial system. The US economy was heading towards the ditch and the Federal Reserve cut borrowing rates to the bone. Fed Chairman, Ben

Bernanke, had a couple of other rabbits to pull out of his hat. The first was to flood the market with money! Indeed he joked that if needed, he would fly around in a helicopter and throw bags of money out of the window.

This became known as "QE I" or the first phase of Quantitive Easing. The stock markets loved it and showed their appreciation by climbing in value. The gold market loved it. Essentially, the money printing press was being cranked up which, in turn, debased the value of the US dollar.

When QE I ran out of steam, Bernanke pulled another rabbit out of his hat: QE II. Here, he set about buying 10 year bonds to help keep yields down and replace them with short-term treasury bills. Again, the gold market loved it.

At the beginning of 2013, the Fed was still purchasing about $85 billion per month in bonds but Chairman Bernanke indicated in June 2013 that he may start to taper off purchases later in 2013 and eliminate them totally in 2014. The gold market hated it, and the stock market took a temporary plunge.

One thing is clear. In spite of Bernanke throwing his figurative bags of money out of his helicopter, which earned him the nickname, "Helicopter Ben", it is apparent that most of it has become stuck in the trees. The banks have benefited from it but very little has floated down to the general public at ground level. In spite of Fed funds rates of between zero percent and 1/4 percent, have you found your "friendly banker" offering you loans carrying interest at 2% or your "friendly credit card company" reducing the interest on your balance from 22% to 2%? I will admit that mortgage rates were very low for a while but were creeping back up again in mid-2013.

Small business lending in mid-2013 remains difficult because of tightened lending standards. Basically, the Federal Reserve is saving the hides of its banking friends with little regard for the "small guy"and that's why QEI and QEII have not been particularly effective at the consumer or small business level in the United States. In Canada, the loan market for small business was still quite tight in mid-2013 although the major banks had been increasing the number of small business loan officers according to a Bloomberg News report in late 2012.

The Bank of Canada

The Bank of Canada is responsible for setting Canadian monetary policy; for issuing currency; for funds management and promoting the safety and efficiency of Canada's financial system. Once again, the Bank offers no direct assistance to small business, however, the actions of its Governor, by raising or lowering the Target for Overnight Rate, can effect interest rates. This Rate is an indicator to financial institutions of what they should be charging other financial institutions for overnight lending. In this way, it influences the rates financial institutions set for loans, mortgages, etc.

In general, the Target for the Overnight Rate is kept high if the Governor of the Bank wants to dampen economic activity and reduce inflation (one of his main mandates) or low if he wants to provide stimulus for economic activity.

One other major consequences of changes to the Target for the Overnight Rate is the change it produces in the value of the Canadian Dollar compared to other currencies, as the Dollar fluctuates on international currency markets. A higher Rate attracts foreign currency buyers since they can get higher interest rates on their money. In this way, high rates relative to those in other countries, will tend to drive up the value of the Canadian Dollar. The converse is true, insofar as low rates will tend to drive down the value.

When the Canadian Dollar has a low value, it makes exports of goods and services less expensive in foreign countries since Canadian goods or services are more competitive in those markets. The converse is also true.

In this way, the Governor of the Bank of Canada can yield tremendous power over the fate of Canadian exporters.

Looking into the past, when John Crow was Governor, he maintained a policy designed to keep inflation as close to zero as possible. In my opinion, this greatly exacerbated the economic downturn of the eighties when those parts of Canada's "branch plant economy" were adjusting to the Free Trade Agreement with the United States.

When Gorden Thiessen assumed the Governorship, he kept interest rates low and the Canadian Dollar stayed at a low level; thereby stimulating exports and the economy.

Unfortunately, the next Governor, David Dodge, raised interest rates in 2003; thereby greatly increasing the value of the Canadian Dollar relative to that of its major trading partner, the United States. This greatly jeopardised the ability of Canada's exporters of manufactured goods to compete in the US market.

Dodge retired and was replaced by Mark Carney on January 31, 2008 and it appears that Governor Carney took a much more pragmatic approach than his predecessor. Like his US counterpart, Ben Bernanke, he turned a blind eye to inflation in order to keep rates low so that the Canadian Dollar trades relatively close to the Greenback; thereby giving Canadian manufacturers a chance to compete on a level playing field.

Mark Carney left his position to join the Bank England and will be replaced in July 2013 by Stephen Poloz, an economist and head of the Export Development Canada (EDC). At the time of writing, it was not clear as to how Governor Poloz will manage Canada's interest rate policy.

The Commercial Banking Function

Banks are in business to make money. They do so simply by using other people's money, which they can obtain at a lower rate of interest, and lending it to other people at a higher rate of interest.

The deposits individuals and businesses make at banks provide them with their play money, since for every dollar they have on deposit or in reserve they can in turn loan out more dollars. Thus, if a bank operates with a 10% reserve; for every dollar in reserve, it can loan ten dollars out. If it operates with a 5% reserve, it can loan out $20 and so on.

These comments are obviously an oversimplification of a sophisticated money machine that has been developed over the years. However, an anonymous statement in Evan Esar's *20,000 Quips and Quotes* claimed that: "when a poor man has too much money, he lends it to the bank; when a rich man hasn't enough, the bank lends it to him". He should have added that the bank lives off the difference in interest rates!

Canada's Chartered Banks

Canada's chartered banking system is characterized by its branch networks. Thus, there are over 8,000 bank branches and over 17,000 Automated Banking Machines (ABMs). Total assets amount to over $3.6 trillion in October 2012, according to the Canadian Bankers Association. They serve 93% of the market, representing over 915,000 small business customers. As such, they clearly represent a very important source of financing for Canadians. Banks are classified on the basis of how widely their shares are held. Thus, the shares of what are termed "Schedule I Banks" are widely held but with restrictions on foreign ownership. In contrast, the shares of Schedule II Banks are tightly held.

Canada's Domestic Banks

There are 23 domestic banks in Canada. These are also referred to as "Schedule I Banks" and the maximum ownership by any one shareholder is limited to a maximum of 10%. The largest of these banks; known as "The Big Six" are as follows:

> The Royal Bank of Canada
> The Canadian Imperial Bank of Commerce
> The Bank of Montreal
> The Bank of Nova Scotia (Scotiabank)
> TD Bank Financial Group (includes the Canada Trust merger)
> The National Bank of Canada

A survey conducted in 1985 by the Canadian Federation of Independent Business found that 78.1% of their respondents banked with the largest five of the "Big Six". A Carleton University Working Paper, revealed these hold more than 80% of all small business loans.

Commercial Banking Units

Commercial Banking Units are specialized branches established by the major Schedule I Banks to cater to the business customers in their area. Essentially, the managers of these branches are trained in the needs of small business and to be able to evaluate business plans, cash flow projections, etc. All the major six banks are in the business of commercial banking and have either established special branches, or have divisions within their regular branches to deal with the small business owner. Several have set up teams of account managers to look after business clients so that there is some continuity in account coverage.

Foreign Banks in Canada

In mid-2013, there were 25 foreign bank subsidiaries operating in Canada (also known as "Schedule II Banks") however, three of these were in the process of licquidation at the time of writing. There are 23 foreign banks which offer full service.

A number of restrictions apply to non-American foreign banks with regard to size and the number of branches they can open. These limitations were removed from American banks under the Canada-US Free Trade Agreement.

The number of foreign banks has declined over the years due to poor profit performance and amalgamations. Although foreign banks may be small in size in Canada, they usually have large, powerful organizations standing behind them in their home countries.

By far the largest foreign bank is HSBC Bank Canada (formerly the "Hong Kong Bank of Canada") which acquired Lloyds Bank Canada in February 1990 to bring its total assets in Canada to $7.6 billion with 104 branches. The HSBC Bank Canada moved closer to the activities of the domestic banks by acquiring branch networks in Canada. Thus, it purchased 58 branches of the Bank of British Columbia in 1986, followed by a further 54 branches owned by Lloyds Bank (formerly the Continental Bank of Canada) in early 1990. HSBC Bank Canada specializes in trade financing for medium-sized businesses, in addition to offering retail banking.

Other foreign banks, such as CitiBank, make loans to small businesses in specialized areas. Some, such as the Korean Exchange Bank, have been successful in providing business loans for former citizens of their countries who are now resident in Canada.

Canadian Credit Unions & Caisses Populaires

Initially, credit unions and caisses populaires (their Québec equivalents) were cooperative associations which provided limited financial services to certain employee groups, such as teachers, government workers etc. Since then, they have expanded so as to allow persons within a certain geographical area to become members. They have over $110 billion in assets; equivalent to about 12% of the domestic assets of Canadian financial institutions.

Approximately one-third of Canadian individuals use a credit union or caisses populaires as their main financial institution. They have approximately 10 million members. In Québec and Saskatchewan they account for about 40% of the market share for consumer financial services and 20% in British Columbia.

They differ from banks in that all are controlled by provincial regulations and in the manner in which they treat their profits. Usually these are returned to their members in the form of dividends, bonuses etc. Having said this, there are six credit union centrals that have opted to register under federal legislation as well as being regulated provincially.

Credit unions are restricted by provincial and internal regulations in the amount of money they can lend to businesses. This is usually a small percentage of their total assets. Thus, in Ontario commercial loans are restricted to 15% of the total loan portfolio. In Manitoba, they are limited to 10% of their shares and deposits. Having said this, credit unions and caisses populaires are starting to play an increasingly important role in small business financing.

As mentioned in the introduction to this section, the Québec equivalent of credit unions is the caisse populaires. They have total assets of about $70 billion. These operate under an umbrella group called the Desjardins Group which was named in honour of Alphonse Desjardins who established the first credit union in North America in 1900. There are no limits on lending to small business by these institutions in the Province of Québec. Indeed Desjardins has established over 90 Desjardins Corporate Financial Centres (CFCs) in

Québec together with four in Ontario which are designed to assist in small business financing.

Government Owned Banks

There are several government owned banks in Canada. The most obvious one is the Bank of Canada, which is the country's Central Bank which was discussed previously and which is not involved in commercial lending.

Both the Business Development Bank of Canada and Farm Credit Canada are not deposit taking institutions but do make loans. These will be covered in more detail in Chapters 5 and 8 respectively.

ABT Financial: 4-H Loan Program

The Alberta Treasury Branches are provincially owned institutions which provide banking services in Alberta even though they are not classified as "banks". They were created during the Great Depression during a time of very strong anti-bank sentiment fuelled by the provincial government which was in power at the time.

Through the 4-H Loan Program, ATB provides support to members of the 4-H Program by loaning money for the purchase of marketable livestock: beef, swine, sheep, meat goats, and horses, or other approved projects. Loans can be for up to a maximum of $5,000 with interest as low as prime. No fees are charges but co-signature from a parent or guardian is required. Information can be obtained at any of the branches across the Province.

Canadian Aboriginal and Métis Banks

Northern development together with the settlement of land claims have helped fuel the demand for banking services which are geared toward the needs of peoples of Aboriginal and Métis ancestry. To cater to this market, two of Canada's largest banks, The Royal Bank of Canada and CIBC have established special Aboriginal banking units. In addition, a number of smaller banks and trust companies have been established which cater to this market and the better known ones are the First Nations Bank and Peacehills Trust. The latter has outlets in the four Western Provinces and one branch in Fredericton, New Brunswick.

Merchant Banks

Merchant banks are unlike your typical street corner bank, insofar as they do not perform the usual chequing and bank deposit functions; but confine themselves to medium and long-term lending and to taking equity positions in companies. Equity participation is frequently on a short-term basis to facilitate mergers, acquisitions and public stock issues. They also provide project financing, syndicated lending and venture capital financing. Most merchant banking business is done with medium and larger-sized companies.

Merchant Banks in Canada

Up until recent years, merchant banking was not generally recognized as a banking function in Canada. The Federal Government prohibits merchant bankers from using the title "bank" however, they do exist! In fact, many of the major banks perform merchant banking functions as a part of their everyday business. Many foreign banks are also heavily into this field. In addition, there are "merchant banks" which are divisions of non-financial companies, such as conglomerates.

Subordinate Financing

Subordinate financing is a hybrid between debt and equity and often falls within the realm of merchant banking. It has also been referred to as "subordinated debt", "mezzanine financing", "structured equity", "equity linked notes" and "quasi-equity financing". The debt usually ranks behind secured creditors. Subordinate financing could also involve the grant of stock options and royalties; or both.

In this type of financing, a merchant bank may act as the lead investor in a syndicate of lenders. It is often used to help senior managers buy out business owners who wish to retire.

US Investment Banks

US Merchant Banks can also be involved in managing portfolios, and acceptance credits (mostly used in foreign trade).

Canadian Trust Companies

There are about 20 deposit taking trust companies in Canada. Trust companies are involved in the real estate brokerage business, investment counselling, mutual fund sales and some (such as Power Financial Corp.) also offer insurance coverage.

Trust companies are active in the area of secured loans, usually for such things as real estate, mortgages etc. Up until recently they have been limited in the extent to which they could make commercial loans to 7% of their total assets. Under regulations introduced in 1988, provincially chartered trust companies in Ontario and Québec could make commercial loans of up to 20% of their total assets. The May 1994 Ontario Budget announced further new legislation to eliminate the 20% limit; to allow the issuing of letters of credit; to permit investments in start-ups and newly formed businesses and permit long-term commercial lending (previously limited to one year).

4

Types of Loans

Types of Small Business Loans

There are a variety of different ways of borrowing money from a bank. The following summarizes some of the more common types of loans and includes many of the "quasi-government" programs that are available. It does not cover direct government loan programs which are dealt with in the volumes in this series on government assistance in each of the ten provinces and two territories.

Operating Lines

Operating lines of credit are used by businesses to provide working capital for their day-to-day operations. This is particularly so when supplier credit and operating cash flows are insufficient to cover the company" need for cash in order to grow.

Basically, an operating line of credit allows the small business owner to borrow funds; as and when required; up to a certain specified limit. Repayment can be made of money not required.

Some bankers like to be involved directly in these transactions; whereas others will allow you to phone in directly to the department that deals with this matter.

The various loans are filled out on a series of pre-signed promissory notes. Your banker will normally request that a whole stack of these be signed when the loan arrangement is entered into.

Some banks have replaced the operating line with an operating account which provides overdraft or line of credit privileges. Interest is calculated daily and deposits made by the business owner are used to automatically draw down the line of credit, thereby reducing interest costs.

The interest charged on operating lines is at a premium to the official Bank Rate and usually varies in accordance with it.

As a general guideline, banks are prepared to finance anywhere from 60% to 90% of accounts receivable under 90 days old. This range will vary according to the quality of the receivables but, in practice, will be in the range of 60% - 75%. The figure is often negotiable.

Banks may also grant operating lines on the basis of inventory. Since this is more difficult to dispose of, should things go wrong, it is usually discounted to anywhere between 25% and 50% of its value. If inventory is of a specialized nature without much marketability, the bank may simply not be interested in talking at all.

Theoretically (as in school text books), operating lines may be secured or unsecured. In practice, however, most small business people can expect accounts receivable or inventory (or both) to be assigned to the bank and can expect to be required to post personal guarantees as well. In other words, if the business goes sour, the bank may place the business in receivership and collect all the money still owing. If that is insufficient, your "friendly" banker may come pounding on the door and want to sell your house and everything else you have pledged.

It should be pointed out that the bank has the option to "call" a loan at any time and demand immediate payment. This may happen if there is a drop in the value of receivables or inventory to support the loan. It can also happen if the bank manager starts to feel nervous about the company, the economy or any number of things. Horror stories abound in the small business community about loans that have been "called"; forcing the small business owner (usually at a time when his swamp is already full of alligators) to scuttle around for alternate financing or get his receivables in as fast as possible.

Term Loans

Term loans may be of medium duration - two to seven years; or long term - over seven years. Interest rates may be fixed for the life of the loan at the time it is negotiated. When interest rates are high, there is a tendency for shorter and longer term rates to be much the same. When rates are low, there is a tendency for the banks to want a premium on longer terms. Some term loans may have floating interest rates.

Term loans may be paid off in instalments or in one lump sum at the end. They are generally used to purchase equipment, machinery or fixed assets such as buildings. They may also be used for renovations or expansions.

As a rule of thumb, banks will finance up to about 75% of the amount for buildings based on a recent evaluation. In the case of equipment, it may be 50% of the value or more. You can also expect the assets to be used as collateral for the loan together with the bank's old favourite - the personal guarantee of the business owners.

It should be noted that term lending is not the exclusive domain of the banks. Insurance, trust, acceptance and commercial finance houses are also active in this area.

Floor Plan Loans

Some banks offer floor planning. This is used by manufacturers to finance the goods in the retailer's or distributor's premises. Cars, trucks and seasonal items are frequently financed in this manner. This activity is not confined to banks. Acceptance companies are also active in this field.

The arrangement allows the retailer or distributor to stock up on inventory and have it available in time for the commencement of the selling season. He then pays back the loan arranged by the manufacturer as the product is sold.

Warehouse Receipts

Warehouse receipts are frequently used to finance inventories of finished goods and possibly for raw materials. These are normally stored in a public or controlled warehouse and banks (or others) will provide a greater level of financing than if the goods are located on the business owner's premises. Financing of up to 80% of the value of the merchandise or raw materials may be possible.

The rationale behind this type of financing is that the goods or materials are readily marketable and can be readily seized by the creditor in the event of trouble.

Again, this is not an exclusive domain of the banks, however, others in the area are relatively rare. I would suggest that the business owner contact some local public warehouses who may be able to steer him or her in the right direction.

Overdraft Facilities

For businesses with a good credit standing, most banks will offer overdraft facilities to allow for an account to become overdrawn for a short period of time. It is usually necessary to pay down the overdraft on a periodic basis; usually every 30 days. While this does not represent a long-term financing solution, it can help a business avoid short-term cash shortages.

Letters of Credit

Letters of credit are used widely for importing and exporting. This topic is covered in more detail later in this book. However, letters of credit may also be used in other instances.

Standby Letters of Credit (SLC): can be used in cases where a business makes a bid and contract security is required. Alternatively, SLCs can be used in cases where suppliers require security of payment. The maximum term is usually one year.

Standby Letter of Credit Facility: often has terms of 5 years and features an aggregate dollar limit. Commission of between 2% and 4% is usually charged, depending on the risk.

Personal Loans and Credit Cards

Frequently, in the case of start-ups, bank managers may show a reluctance to loan money to the company, however, they will often consider a personal loan based on the small business owner's credit rating and the assets which can be offered for security.

Quite a number of entrepreneurs, who have been turned down by banks, have successfully financed their businesses by using cash advances on the credit cards issued by the same banks! There is even a story of a 21 year old musician who managed to raise $160,000 in this manner!

In an effort to legitimize this use of credit cards by entrepreneurs, some banks now offer small business cards. For example, in Canada, The Bank's "CreditLine" offers business lines of credit of up to $35,000 and Bank of Montreal's "mbanx" offers a business MasterCard card with credit of up to $50,000. A satisfactory credit history and ability to repay are the main considerations in establishing credit limits and not collateral. Just don't forget that the money has to be paid back and carries with it, some pretty hefty interest rates!

Commercial Mortgaging

The banks are also heavily into the mortgage market. This will be discussed in a later Chapter.

Chapter 4
Types of Loans

5

Loans by the Federal Government or its Agencies & Private Sector Partners

The Canada Small Business Financing (CSBF) Program

The Canada Small Business Financing (CSBF) Program was created to help small businesses reach their potential by making it easier for them to get term business improvement loans to finance the purchase or improvement of fixed assets for new or expanded operations. Administered under the **Canada Small Business Financing Act (CSBFA)**, the Program is a joint initiative between the Government of Canada and private sector lenders.

The Government Web site boasts that it has helped more than 120,000 businesses since 1999 with loans totalling over $1 billion per annum, however, a more detailed examination shows that although about 18,000 loans were authorized in 1999, the number has since declined sharply to under 7,500 during the 2011-2012 period.. According to a Canadian Press Report, published in The Globe & Mail on October 15, 2012, private sector lenders have been reluctant to participate because of the burden of red tape and also because the loans offered them little opportunity to profit from the program. As a consequence, business owners may find that their banks are reluctant to promote the program although changes have been proposed to make the program more profitable for the banks but such changes will also make it more expensive for small businesses.

The private sector lenders are authorized to make loans directly to small business owners. Lenders are required to make CSBFA loans with the same care as in the conduct of their ordinary business, that is: to assess credit worthiness and draw up agreements following normal lending practice and to administer the loans in accordance with specific program requirements.

Those interested in the CSBF loans should approach the lender of their choice. In all, there are over 1,350 private sector lenders with over 15,000 outlets across Canada. These lenders are responsible for making all credit decisions; providing the loans and administering them. In 2012, the CSBF Web site provided the following list; each of which has numerous branches:

- ATB Financial
- Bank of Montreal
- Caisses populaires Acadiennes
- Caisses populaires de l'Ontario
- Canadian Imperial Bank of Commerce
- Canadian Western Bank
- Canada's Credit Unions
- GE Capital Financial Services
- HSBC Bank Canada
- Industrial and Commercial Bank of China (Canada)
- Laurentian Bank of Canada
- Mouvement des caisses Desjardins
- National Bank of Canada
- Royal Bank of Canada
- Scotiabank
- TD Canada Trust.

The program recognizes that the owners of small businesses frequently lack the funds they need to pay for business improvement or expansion. Financing may not be available to them unless they are willing to include their personal assets as loan security. Those wanting to start up new businesses face similar problems.

Under the CSBFA, if a borrower defaults on a loan, the Federal Government will cover the lender for 85% of any loss suffered by the lender, with the lender taking responsibility for the remaining 15%. The loss claims incurred by the Program during 2010-2012 amounted to about $80 million and, according to a Canadian Press Report, only about 60% of the losses are recovered in the form of fees charged. To help stem the losses, the Government proposed to increase loan interest charged by 0.75% to 3.75% over prime effective April 1, 2013. It also proposed to allow private sector lenders to charge the same fees that they charge on regular commercial loans, however, this move has been severely criticized by the

Canadian Federation of Independent Business as favouring profits for the banks at the expense of small businesses and the jobs which they create.

Most small businesses starting up or operating in Canada are eligible for CSBFA loans, as long as their estimated annual gross revenues do not exceed $5 million during the fiscal year in which they apply for a loan. For new businesses, gross revenues must not be expected to exceed $5 million during the first 52 weeks of operation. Farming, charitable, non-profit or religious enterprises, however, are not considered eligible businesses. Businesses may be operated as sole proprietorships, partnerships or incorporated companies.

Loan proceeds may be used to finance up to 90% of the cost of:

- the purchase or improvement of real property or immovables;
- the purchase of leasehold improvements or improvements to leased property;
- the purchase or improvement of new or used equipment; necessary for the operation of the business, and,
- registration fees.

In fiscal 2009-2011, 46% of loans were used for purchasing equipment; leasehold improvements accounted for 31% and real property for 23%.

Loan proceeds cannot be used to finance:

- goodwill
- working capital
- inventories
- franchise fees
- the purchase of shares in a corporation operating as a small business
- research and development.

The maximum value of loans a borrower may have outstanding under the CSBFA is $500,000 and the maximum amount that can be used to purchase or improve the finance of equipment is $350,000. This same $350,000 maximum also applies to freehold improvements.

The period during which a loan must be repaid will generally coincide with the expected economic life of the asset being financed, up to a maximum of 10 years. Instalment payments on the loan principal must be scheduled at least annually, but monthly payments are usually called for depending upon arrangements between the borrower and the lender.

Under the CSBFA, borrowers may choose between:

- floating rate loans, where the interest rate fluctuates with changes in the lender's prime lending rate over the term of the loan, but cannot be more than 3.75% over the lender's prime lending rate; and,
- fixed rate loans, where the interest rate is fixed for the term of the loan, but cannot be more than 3.75% over the lender's residential mortgage rate for the applicable term.

A loan can be prepaid or the interest rate can be converted to a fixed or floating rate. The lender may charge a penalty for the prepayment or conversion of the loan.

Lenders are obligated to take security in the assets financed. When financing leasehold improvements or computer software, the lender may take security in other business assets. The lender may take personal guarantees or suretyships not exceeding, in aggregate, 25% of the original amount of the loan. Corporate guarantees are optional, however, these guarantees or suretyships cannot be secured with personal assets.

The Program makes financing more accessible to small business owners since it reduces the personal assets that are required to be posted as security to support their business financing requirements.

Lenders are required to pay a one-time loan registration fee to the government equal to 2% of the amount loaned. The fee is recoverable from borrowers who may reimburse the lenders when their loans are advanced or have the amount of the fee added to their loan balances, provided that the individual borrower's loan maximum of $500,000 in total is not exceeded.

In addition there is an annual administration fee of 1.25% payable by the lender to the government. This fee is included in the 3.75% interest rate charged to the business.

According to the Program's 2010-2011 Annual Report, over 7,466 small businesses took out loans during that fiscal year for a total of $1.03 billion. The average loan size was $137,521. The report also indicated that start-ups and new businesses in operation for under one year accounted for about 57% of total loan value. It also noted that companies operating in the food and beverage service industry accounted for 27% of the total loan value.

In October 2012, the Government announced that it was nearing completion of an information and technology system which would enable electronic registration with; and fee payments to financial institutions.

One of the biggest advantages of obtaining funding under the Canada Small Business Financing Program is that personal guarantees or suretyships may not exceed, in aggregate, 25% of the original amount of the loan. This is in contrast to the very high collateral requirements required by many traditional bank lenders.

Another advantage is that interest on floating rate loans is relatively low; being set at up to 3.75% above a bank's prime lending rate. At the time of writing, all the banks I looked at had their prime rates set at 3.75%; meaning that interest would be 6.75%.

The advantage in the case of fixed rate loans is that the interest rate cannot be more than 3.75% over the lender's residential mortgage rate for the applicable term. At the time of writing, CIBC's residential mortgage rate varied from 3.0% for one year which would translate into an interest rate of 6.75% fixed interest rate on a one year loan. In the case of a 10 year loan, the residential mortgage rate was 6.75% which would translate into an interest rate of 10.50%.

Obviously the rates quoted above, will vary from time-to-time and readers should check with their financial institution to find out the rates at the time of application.

Canada Small Business Financing Program Directorate, Industry Canada
C.D. Howe Building, 235 Queen Street, 5 West, Ottawa ON K1A 0H5
Phone: (613) 954-5540   Fax: (613) 952-0290
Toll-free phone: 1-(866) 959-1699
E-mail: csbfp-pfpec@ic.gc.ca   Web Site: www.ic.gc.ca/csbfa

Business Development Bank of Canada (BDC)

The Business Development Bank of Canada (BDC) is a financial institution wholly owned by the Government of Canada. BDC offers a wide range of business solutions for small businesses. BDC's 2012 Annual Report indicated that it had total assets of $17.2 billion. It had loans outstanding in the amount of $14.7 billion and, as such, it is an important provider of capital to small and mid-sized businesses in Canada.

The figures for fiscal 2012 were not published but during the course of fiscal 2011, 60.2% of money loaned was for the purchase of fixed assets; 15.7% for working capital and 12.6% for refinancing. Financing to assist in the change of ownership accounted for 7.8%. That left a balance of 3.8% relating to other forms of loan assistance.

During fiscal 2012, BDC provided financing of $3.6 billion with an average level of assistance of about $1.2 million. This assistance was directed to businesses at different levels of development as follows:

Start-up:	6.9%
Development	5.5%
Expansion	57.6%
Turnaround	3.5%
Mature	26.5%

By way of comment, even though BDC claims that it is assisting early stage businesses, their own track record indicates that start-ups and companies at the development stage only receive 12.4% of the available funding compared to 87.6% received by more mature companies at the Expansion, Turnaround and Mature stages of development.

Financing Solutions

BDC's financing solutions complement products available from other institutions. It can also arrange subordinate financing and venture capital. These solutions are discussed in detail in the text below.

Term Financing

BDC provides flexible term financing for expansion projects, plant overhauls, the purchase of existing businesses, the acquisition of fixed assets, etc. In some cases, financing may be used to reconstitute working capital depleted by capital expenditures or to finance sales growth.

Refinancing

BDC can refinance commercial mortgages or equipment in cases where commercial banks will no longer provide adequate financing. It can also provide refinancing for a BDC-financed expansion project such as the construction, acquisition of a building or for the purchase of equipment.

Interest may be at fixed or floating rates. Loan repayment can be made over 4 to 6 years and principal payments may not be required in the first year. Payments may be based on the projected cash flow of the business.

Business Credit Availability Program (BCAP)

The Business Credit Availability Program (BCAP) was announced in the 2009 Federal Budget. It was designed to improve access to financing during this period of economic uncertainty through enhanced cooperation between private sector financial institutions and the financial Crown corporations such as Export Development Canada (EDC). BDC's 2012 Annual Report indicated that BCAP's activities had been wound down and that lending has since returned to pre-recession levels.

Multi Seller Program for Small Organizations (MSPSO)

BDC has partnered with TAO Asset Management which is part of the TAO Group, a Canadian owned and operated group of companies established with the purpose of providing a range of services to participants in the Canadian financial and credit markets.

The Multi Seller Program for Small Organizations (MSPSO) had $150 million authorized in BDC's fiscal 2011 for the purchase of asset-backed securities. BDC's 2012 Annual Report indicated that $440 million had been provided in revolving fixed securitisation facilities. The program operates in conjunction with the Vehicle and Equipment Financing partnership (VEFP) which was announced in the Federal Budget of 2010. In this way, MSPSO helps to facilitate equipment and vehicle leasing at a time when credit markets are extremely tight.

Financing for Working Capital

BDC can complement an existing line of credit and provide the cash flow needed for business growth. It offers flexible repayment terms and long-term financing can be arranged for up to $250,000. Working capital financing can be used to:

- develop new products
- launch new products
- adding e-commerce capabilities
- upgrade marketing and promotion strategies.

Repayments can be made for up to 8 years and BDC offers an option to defer payments on principal during the first 12 months after the loan has been authorized. No penalty is applied for repaying up to 15% of the remaining balance per year.

In order to qualify for working capital financing, applicants should have:

- an existing line of credit with a chartered bank or credit union/caisse populaire;
- a normal level of working capital assistance from conventional sources;

- an experienced management team and solid profit history;
- projected growth of sales and good profit potential; and,
- an accounting review engagement or audited year-end financial statements.

Economic Recovery Loan (Working Capital)

BDC claims that its Economic Recovery Loan has assisted 3,700 in the post-recession recovery. In terms of value it represented $246 million to assist with working capital requirements during fiscal 2011.

Market Xpansion Loan

The Market Xpansion Loan can provide loans of up to $100,000 for any of the following activities:

- to participate in prospecting initiatives (e.g., to visit overseas trade shows);
- to develop export plans;
- to develop e-commerce plans;
- to provide an advance on Scientific Research & Experimental Development (SR&ED) refunds to replenish working capital;
- to cover SR&ED consulting costs;
- to conduct product development and R&D; or,
- to purchase additional inventory for export.

In the event that parts of the loan have been repaid and a need later occurs for additional financing, a portion of the paid-off loan can be re-advanced. In this way, the loan gives the borrower added flexibility when money is required.

Financing New or Used Equipment Purchases

BDC can supply long-term financing of up to five years for:

- purchasing a production line
- automating an existing production line
- purchasing equipment
- retooling
- purchasing commercial vehicles
- replenishing working capital depleted by equipment-related purchases
- consulting services for increasing productivity or implementing quality solutions.

Long-term financing can be for 125% to cover additional costs (such as the refurbishing of used equipment) and carry flexible repayment schedules which can allow deferral of principal payments until after the equipment is installed and performing optimally.

Business Transition Financing

For those who wish to retire or sell their business, BDC can provide consulting services and financing solutions to assist in selling a business to children, other family members, outsiders or to sell to management or employees. Financing is available as follows.

Long-Term Loans: based on the fixed assets of the business, such as land, building, equipment, etc.

Unsecured Term Loans: based on intangible assets such as goodwill, intellectual property, employee skills, management expertise etc.

Subordinate Financing: usually brings together some of the features of both debt (in the form of fixed interest on the amount financed) and equity financing (with repayments based on the cash flow of the business which could be in the form of stock options or royalties on sales). The loan portion is usually secured by a lien on assets but has a lower priority than the liens of other secured lenders (in the event of default); hence the name "subordinate".

Vendor Take-Back Financing: in which the financing is provided by the seller (as opposed to a financial institution).

Financing the Purchase of Land or Buildings

BDC may offer term financing for buying land or a building. Assistance is in the form of standard mortgages or term financing.

Total loan amounts are not predetermined and repayment options are flexible. Financing is granted for a specific term which cannot be cancelled without a valid reason. BDC takes into account the growth potential for the business which could allow for greater financing.

Financing Building Construction

BDC can provide financing for the following:

- construction of new premises
- expansion of existing premises
- replenishment of working capital depleted by current construction costs
- consulting services.

Term financing can be for up to 20 years and can be used to fund construction projects from start to finish. In addition, bridge financing may be available to cover initial planning costs as well as design costs. Loans can carry floating or fixed interest rates and cannot be called without due cause.

Flexible repayment schedules may allow deferral of principal payments until after the new building has been occupied. Repayment options can be arranged on a progressive or seasonal basis and tailored to the cash flow of the business. In addition, repayment options can be arranged to repay up to 15% of the remaining balance per year without any penalties.

ITC Solutions

Independent and experienced professional advice, together with flexible financing from BDC is available for Information and Communications Technology (ICT). The program provides consulting, web site diagnostics and assistance with developing an Internet strategy. It can include a coaching progam.

BDC is prepared to offer financing to upgrade or purchase ITC equipment. This can include purchases of:

- hardware (servers, network, telephony, computers and accessories);
- Software (ERP, CRM, human resources, supply chain, finance and accounting); and,
- Consulting services (IT planning, strategy, security, online sales, Internet marketing, social media).

Term loans can be arranged with beneficial terms. During fiscal 2012, the percentages of financing acceptances were as follows:

Hardware:	36%
Software:	26%
Internet:	19%
Services:	12%
Other:	7%

Financing for Starting a Business

BDC can offer financing in the following areas:

- working capital to supplement an existing line of credit;
- the acquisition of fixed assets;
- marketing;
- start-up fees; and,
- the purchase of a franchise.

BDC may provide long-term financing and consulting services to support the goals of the business. Financing can be arranged for up to $100,000 with repayment terms of up to 6 years.

Repayments can be progressive or seasonal and geared to the expected cash flow of the business. It may be possible to defer capital payments. Loans have a guaranteed term and cannot be called without due cause. Interest rates may be floating or fixed and no penalty is applied for repaying up to 15% of the remaining balance per year.

In order to qualify, entrepreneurs should:

- be at the start-up or early growth phase (first 12 months of sales);
- have a business that can demonstrate realistic market and sales potential;
- have experience or expertise in their chosen field;
- demonstrate the personal attributes of a successful entrepreneur;
- have a competent management team in place;
- have invested reasonable financial resources in the enterprise; and,
- be able to provide personal and credit references.

It should be noted that BDC start-up financing is generally not available to start a retail business.

Financing the Acquisition of a Business

BDC can offer a number of financing options for the acquisition of an existing business through a Management Buy Out (MBO). Financing can be long-term financing and could include subordinate financing. Flexible repayment terms are available. No penalty is applied for repaying up to 15% of the remaining balance per year.

Aboriginal Business Development Fund (ABDF)

In February 2006, a new Aboriginal Business Development Fund (ABDF) of $250,000 was established to provide micro loans of between $2,000 and $20,000. The loans are fully repayable with terms varying from two to three years depending upon the cash flow expectations of the applicant. All applicants are required to complete a business plan and be prepared to attend information sessions on starting a business and workshops on marketing, office management and account control.

BDC also helps to organize E-Spirit, which is an Aboriginal youth business plan competition in which 5,900 students had participated up to the end of March 2013..

Peer Lending

BDC has provided $40,000 to establish a loan fund, which is administered and promoted by North Central Community Futures Development Corporation. This offers loans of $500 to $1,500 on a peer lending basis. Loans can be used to purchase raw materials like beads, sewing machines and other material required to produce the crafts. Usually, a 10% holdback is applied to cover possible loan interest payment delinquencies.

Growth Capital for Aboriginal Business (GCAB)

Loans of up to $100,000 can be provided to Aboriginal business people who want to expand an existing business operating on or off a reserve in Canada. Start-ups are eligible for financing of up to $25,000.

Interest rates and security requirements are determined on a case-by-case basis. Loans have flexible repayment terms and are based on anticipated future cash flow. Payments of principal may be deferred for the first year. Stepped up seasonal payments may be permitted in appropriate circumstances.

To be eligible, Aboriginal entrepreneurs must:

- have a commercially viable business proposal;
- have an acceptable level of management expertise;
- be able to demonstrate financial commitment;
- be willing to take part in a mentorship program; and,
- operate on or off reserve in any area of Canada.

Financing can also be made available for acquiring land, buildings or equipment or to provide working capital. Financing can also be arranged to explore export markets, develop e-commerce initiatives and adopt quality management standards such as ISO and HACCP certification.

Business management coaching is provided by Canadian Executive Service Organization (CESO) Aboriginal Services. This is a not-for-profit organization which supplies volunteer advisors to Aboriginal entrepreneurs.

Pros and Cons of BDC Debt Financing

Probably the biggest advantages of dealing with BDC are that personal assets are excluded from collateral requirements, loan repayments can be customized to your business cycle and early pay-downs can be made without penalty. On the flip side, I have heard of complaints about loan application fees and pressure to take on the services of consultants; the costs of which can, of course, be added on to any loan amount!

Total Care Program

At BDC, all employees are expected to support quality customer service. To uphold this commitment, BDC has developed the Total Care Program which contains a detailed Charter of Client Rights which the Bank has vowed to meet in terms of accountability, openness, fairness, confidentiality and process. In addition, a BDC Ombudsman has been appointed to monitor the application of the Charter. BDC has also instituted a complaint handling process and can call upon the help of an independent mediator in instances where adverse changes can result in a loan being called.

Office of the Ombudsman
Business Development Bank of Canada
5 Place Ville Marie, Suite 400
Montréal, QC H3B 5E7
Toll-free phone: 1-(800) 232-1150
Toll-free fax: 1-(877) 283-7676

Subordinate Financing

BDC can supply subordinate financing which is a hybrid between debt and equity. The debt usually ranks behind secured creditors. Subordinate financing could also involve the grant of stock options and royalties; or both.

Subordinate financing has also been referred to as "subordinated debt", "mezzanine financing", "structured equity", "equity linked notes" and "quasi-equity financing".

Financing is usually in the range of $250,000 to $6 million with terms of three to seven years. BDC's 2012 Annual report indicated that $163.8 million was offered by way of subordinate financing during 2012; a small portion of which ($1.7 million) was provided by the Caisse de dépôt et placement du Québec.

Repayment is usually tied to cash flow projections and can be a combination of interest, royalties on sales or warrants. Bonus interest can apply when certain pre-established milestones are reached.

Conditional guarantees are required from key shareholders. In this type of financing BDC will often act as the lead investor in a syndicate of lenders and BDC's security is usually subordinate to that of other lenders.

This type of subordinate financing is often used to help senior managers buy out business owners who wish to retire. It should be noted that BDC does not offer subordinate financing to companies that are in distress or those at the start-up stage.

The contact addresses, phone and fax numbers for Subordinate Financing are as follows:

Montréal:
5 Place Ville Marie
Suite 500
Montréal, QC H3B 5E7
Phone: (514) 496-0626
Fax: (514) 496-1020

Eastern Québec:
1134 Grande Allée Ouest
Ground floor
Québec, QC G1S 1E5
Phone: (418) 648-5517
Fax: (418) 649-6301

North-Shore/South-Shore:
5 Place Ville Marie, Suite 500
Montréal, QC H3B 5E7
Phone: (514) 283-8265
Fax: (514) 496-1020

South Western Ontario
148 Fullarton, Suite 1000
London, ON N6A 5P3
Phone: (519) 675-3114
Fax: (519) 645-5989

Greater Toronto Area
121 King St W. Suite 1200
Toronto, ON M5H 3T9
Phone: (416) 952-6291
Fax: (416) 954-2630

Ottawa & Atlantic
55 Metcalfe Street
Suite 1400
Ottawa, ON K1P 6L5
Phone: (613) 995-4084
Fax: (613) 943-9866

Prairies & Northwest Territories
444 7th Avenue SW, Suite 110
Calgary, AB T2P 0X8
Phone: (403) 292-5112
Phone toll-free: (403) 292-5000
Fax: (403) 292-5862

British Columbia and Yukon
One Bentall Center
505 Burrard Street
Suite 2100, P.O. Box 6
Vancouver, BC V7X 1M3
Phone: (604) 666-7875
Fax: (604) 666-8482

GO Capital L.P.

The GO Capital Fund supports the creation of Québec-based companies in all sectors of science and technology. This includes life sciences, natural sciences and information technology.

It is a partnership between the following:

- FIER Partners
- BDC
- Caisse de dépôt et placement du Québec (Caisse)
- Solidarity Fund
- Fondaction CSN.

BDC has matched the direct investments of the other participants to increase the total funding for seed capital investments up to $100 million.

Alliance Between the
Caisse de dépôt et placement du Québec (Caisse) and BDC

In December 2006, the Caisse de dépôt et placement du Québec (Caisse) and BDC announced the creation of a $330 million fund to be invested in small and medium-sized businesses. According to the 2012 BDC Annual Report, the participation of the Caisse is gradually being wound down.

BDC Web Conferencing

In fiscal 2012, BDC began to invest in Web conferencing technology to help their staff with assisting business clients across Canada. This technology is expected to become fully operational during 2013.

Further Information

Head Office:
5 Place Ville Marie
BDC Building, Suite 400
Montreal, QC H3B 5E7
Toll-free phone: 1-(877) 232-2269
Toll-free fax: 1-(877) 329-9232
E-mail: info@bdc.ca
Web site: www.bdc.ca

Branches

BDC operates through a network of more than 100 branches across the country.

Newfoundland and Labrador

Fortis Tower, 4 Herald Avenue, 1st Floor
Corner Brook, NF A2H 4B4
Phone: (709) 637-4515
Fax: (709) 637-4522

42 High Street, P.O. Box 744
Grand Falls-Windsor, NF A2A 2M4
Phone: (709) 489-2181
Fax: (709) 489-6569

Atlantic Place
215 Water Street, Main Floor
St. John's, NF A1C 5K4
Phone: (709) 772-7320
Fax: (709) 772-2516

Prince Edward Island

BDC Place, 119 Kent Street
PO Box 488
Charlottetown, PE C1A 7L1
Phone: (902) 566-7454
Fax: (902) 566-7459

Nova Scotia

Cogswell Tower - Scotia Square
2000 Barrington Street Suite 1400
Halifax, NS B3J 2Z7
Phone: (902) 426-7850
Fax: (902) 426-6783

275 Charlotte Street, Suite 117
Sydney, NS B1P 1C6
Phone: (902) 564-7700
Fax: (902) 564-3975

622 Prince Street, P.O. Box 1378
Truro, NS B2N 5N2
Phone: (902) 895-6377
Fax: (902) 893-7957

103 Water St., PO Box 98
Yarmouth, NS B5A 4B1
Phone: (902) 742-7119
Fax: (902) 742-8180

New Brunswick

Harbourview Place
275 Main Street, Suite 205
Bathurst, NB E2A 4W1
Phone: (506) 548-7360
Fax: (506) 548-7381

Carrefour Assomption
121 de L'Église Street, Suite 405
Edmundston, NB E3V 1J9
Phone: (506) 739-8311
Fax: (506) 735-0019

The Barker House
570 Queen Street, Suite 504
P.O. Box 754
Fredericton, NB E3B 5B4
Phone: (506) 452-3030
Fax: (506) 452-2416

766 Main Street
Moncton, NB E1C 1E6
Phone: (506) 851-6120
Fax: (506) 851-6033

53 King Street
Saint John, NB E2L 1G5
Phone: (506) 636-4751
Fax: (506) 636-3892

Québec

65 Saint-Joseph Street South, Suite 101
Alma, QC G8B 6V4
Phone: (418) 698-2254
Fax: (418) 698-5678

1570 Ampère Street, Suite 300
Boucherville, QC J4B 7L4
Phone: (450) 645-2000
Fax: (450) 645-2055

1175 boul. de la Rive-Sud, Suite 100
St-Romuald QC G6W 5M6
Phone: (418) 834-5144
Fax: (418) 834-1855

2785 Claude Léveillée Avenue
Terrebonne, QC J6X 4J9
Phone: (450) 964-8778
Fax: (450) 964-8773

4255, Lapinière, Suite 200
Brossard, QC J4Z 0C7
Phone: (450) 926-7220
Fax: (450) 926-7221

1134 Grande Allée Ouest.
Ground Floor
Québec, QC G1S 1E5
Phone: (418) 649-6198
Fax: (418) 648-5525

345 des Saguenéens Street, Suite 210
Chicoutimi, QC G7H 6K9
Phone: (418) 698-2254
Fax: (418) 698-5678

1010 René-Lévesque Blvd.
Drummondville, QC J2C 5W4
Phone: (819) 478-4951
Fax: (819) 478-5864

90 Robinson Street South, Suite 102
Granby, QC J2G 7L4
Phone: (450) 372-5202
Fax: (450) 372-2423

259 St-Joseph Blvd., Suite 104
Gatineau, QC J8Y 6T1
Phone: (819) 997-4434
Fax: (819) 997-4435

2525 Daniel-Johnson, Suite 100
Laval, QC H7T 1S8
Phone: (450) 973-3727
Fax: (450) 973-6860

450 Aimé-Vincent Street
Vaudreuil-Dorion, QC J7V 5V5
Phone: (450) 455-9370
Fax: (450) 455-8126

3000 Cours Le Corbusier Street
Boisbriand, QC J7G 3E8
Phone: (450) 420-4900
Fax: (450) 420-4904

BDC Building, 5 Place Ville Marie
Plaza Level, Suite 12525
Montréal, QC H3B 2G2
Phone: (514) 496-7966
Fax: (514) 496-7974

6500 Trans-Canada, Suite 210
Pointe-Claire, QC H9R 0A5
Phone: (514) 697-8014
Fax: (514) 697-3160

1134 St-Louis Road, Ground Floor
Québec, QC G1S 1E5
Phone: (418) 649-6188
Fax: (418) 648-5525

391 Jessop Blvd., Ground Floor
Rimouski, QC G5L 1M9
Phone: (418) 722-3300
Fax: (418) 722-3362

139 Québec Blvd., Suite 301
Rouyn-Noranda, QC J9X 6M8
Phone: (819) 764-6701
Fax: (819) 764-5472

55 Castonguay Street, Suite 102
Saint-Jérôme, QC J7Y 2H9
Phone: (450) 432-7111
Fax: (450) 432-8366

3100 Côte-Vertu, Suite 160
Saint-Laurent, QC H4R 2J8
Phone: (514) 496-7502
Fax: (514) 496-7510

6347 Jean-Talon Street E.
Saint-Léonard, QC H1S 3E7
Phone: (514) 251-2818
Fax: (514) 251-2758

1802 King Street West
Sherbrooke, QC J1J 0A2
Phone: (819) 564-5700
Fax: (819) 564-4276

1500 Royale Street, #150
Trois-Rivières, QC G9A 6E6
Phone: (819) 371-5632
Fax: (819) 371-5220

Ontario

151 Ferris Lane, P.O. Box 876
Barrie, ON L4M 4Y6
Phone: (705) 725-2533
Fax: (705) 739-0467

284B Wallbridge-Loyalist Road
Belleville, ON K8N 5B3
Phone: (613) 969-4009
Fax: (613) 969-4018

24 Queen Street East Suite 100
Brampton, ON L6V 1A3
Phone: (905) 450-9845
Fax: (905) 450-7514

4145 North Service Road, Suite 101
Burlington, ON L7L 6A3
Phone: (905) 315-9590
Fax: (905) 315-9243

400 Dundas St. W.
Whitby, ON L1N 2M7
Phone: (905) 666-6694
Fax: (905) 665-1059

1243 Islington Avenue
Suite 1001
Toronto, ON M8X 1Y9
Phone: (416) 954-2604
Fax: (416) 954-2631

120 Research Lane, Suite 100
Guelph, ON N1G 0B5
Phone: (519) 826-2663
Fax: (519) 826-2662

25 Main Street West, Suite 101
Hamilton, ON L8P 1H1
Phone: (905) 572-2954
Fax: (905) 572-4282

519 Main Street East
Hawkesbury, ON K6A 1B3
Phone: (613) 995-0234
Fax: (613) 995-9045

227 Second Street South
Kenora, ON P9N 1G1
Phone: (807) 467-3525
Fax: (807) 467-3533

1000 Gadiners Rd, #201
Kingston, ON   K7P 3C4
Phone: (613) 389-0999
Fax: (613) 389-2543

Commerce House Building
50 Queen Street North Suite 110
Kitchener, ON N2H 6P4
Phone: (519) 571-6676
Fax: (519) 571-6685

148 Fullarton, Suite 1000
London, ON N6A 5P3
Phone: (519) 645-4229
Fax: (519) 645-5450

3965 Highway 7 East
Markham, ON L3R 2A2
Phone: (905) 305-6867
Fax: (905) 305-1969

4310 Sherwoodtowne Blvd., Suite 100
Mississauga, ON L4Z 4C4
Phone: (905) 566-6499
Fax: (905) 566-6425

222 McIntyre Street West
North Bay, ON P1B 2Y8
Phone: (705) 495-5700
Fax: (705) 495-5707

1120, Finch Avenue West
Suite 502
North York, ON M3J 3H7
Phone: (416) 736-3420
Fax: (416) 736-3425

Manulife Place
55 Metcalfe Street, Ground Floor
Ottawa, ON   K1P 6L5
Phone: (613) 995-9754
Fax: (613) 995-9045

700 Silver Seven Road, Suite 100
Kanata, ON K2V 1C3
Phone: (613) 592-5592
Fax: (613) 592-5053

Peterborough Square Tower
340 George Street North, 4th Floor
P.O. Box 1419
Peterborough, ON K9J 7H6
Phone: (705) 750-4800
Fax: (705) 750-4808

153 Great Northern Road
Sault Ste. Marie, ON P6B 4Y9
Phone: (705) 941-2006
Fax: (705) 941-3040

1086 Modeland Road
Sarnia, ON N7S 6L2
Phone: (519) 383-1848
Fax: (519) 383-1849

Metro East Corporate Centre
305 Milner Avenue , Suite 112
Scarborough, ON M1B 3V4
Phone: (416) 954-0709
Fax: (416) 954-0716

39 Queen Street, Suite 100
P.O. Box 1193
St. Catharines, ON L2R 7A7
Phone: (905) 988-2874
Fax: (905) 988-2890

516 Huron Street
Stratford, ON N5A 5T7
Phone: (519) 271-5177
Fax: (519) 271-8472

Brady Square, 233 Brady Street, Unit 10
Sudbury, ON P3B 4H5
Phone: (705) 670-6482
Fax: (705) 670-6387

1136 Alloy Drive, Suite 102
Thunder Bay, ON   P7B 6M9
Phone: (807) 346-1780
Fax: (807) 346-1790

85 Pine Street South, Suite 202
Timmins, ON P4N 2K1
Phone: (705) 267-6416
Fax: (705) 268-5437

121 King Street West
Suite 1200
Toronto, ON M5H 3T9
Phone: (416) 952-6094
Fax: (416) 954-5009

3901 Highway 7 West, Suite 600
Vaughan, ON L4L 8L5
Phone: (905) 264-0623
Fax: (905) 264-2122

2485 Ouellette Avenue
Suite 200
Windsor, ON N8X 1L5
Phone: (519) 257-6808
Fax: (519) 257-6811

Manitoba

940 Princess Avenue, Suite 10
Brandon, MB R7A 0P6
Phone: (204) 726-7939
Fax: (204) 726-7555

155 Carlton Street, Suite 1100
Winnipeg, MB R3C 3H8
Phone: (204) 983-7900
Fax: (204) 983-0870

1655 Kenaston Blvd. Suite 200
Winnipeg, MB R3P 2M4
Phone: (204) 983-6530
Fax: (204) 983-6531

Saskatchewan

Bank of Canada Building
2220 - 12th Avenue, Suite 320
Regina, SK S4P 0M8
Phone: (306) 780-6478
Fax: (306) 780-7516

135 - 21st Street East
Saskatoon, SK S7K 0B4
Phone: (306) 975-4822
Fax: (306) 975-5955

1499 10th Avenue East
Suite 1
Prince Albert, SK   S6V 7S6
Phone: (306) 953-8599
Fax: (306) 953-1343

Alberta

444 - 7th Avenue SW., Suite 110
Calgary, AB   T2P 0X8
Phone: (403) 292-5600
Fax: (403) 292-6616

1935 - 32 Avenue NE., Suite 100
Calgary, AB   T2E 7C8
Phone: (403) 292-5590
Fax: (403) 292-6651

Sovereign Building,
6700 Macleod Trail SE, Suite 200
Calgary, AB   T2H 0L3
Phone: (403) 292-8882
Fax: (403) 292-4345

First Edmonton Place
200 - 10665 Jasper Avenue
Edmonton, AB   T5J 3S9
Phone: (780) 495-3388
Fax: (780) 495-6616

201 Huntington Galleria
4628 Calgary Trail N.W.
Edmonton, AB   T6H 6A1
Phone: (780) 495-7200
Fax: (780) 495-7198

236 Mayfield Common
Edmonton, AB   T5P 4B3
Phone: (780) 442-7312
Fax: (780) 495-3102

10625, West Side Drive, Suite 203
Grande Prairie, AB   T8V 8E6
Phone: (780) 532-8875
Fax: (780) 539-5130

520 - 5th Avenue South
Lethbridge, AB   T1J 0T8
Phone: (403) 382-3000
Fax: (403) 382-3162

4815 - 50th Avenue, Suite 107
Red Deer, AB   T4N 4A5
Phone: (403) 340-4203
Fax: (403) 340-4243

2248 13th Avenue SE, Suite 101
Medicine Hat, AB   T1A 8G6
Phone: (403) 527-2601
Fax: (403) 528-6899

British Columbia

6581 Aulds Road, Unit 500
Nanaimo, BC   V9T 6J6
Phone: (250) 390-5757
Fax: (250) 390-5753

205-B Cranbrook Street North
Cranbrook, BC   V1C 3R1
Phone: (250) 417-2200
Fax: (250) 417-2213

10230 - 100th Street, Suite 7
Fort St-John, BC V1J 3Y9
Phone: (250) 787-0622
Fax: (250) 787-9423

205 Victoria Street
Kamloops, BC V2C 2A1
Phone: (250) 851-4900
Fax: (250) 851-4925

313 Bernard Avenue
Kelowna, BC V1Y 6N6
Phone: (250) 470-4802
Fax: (250) 470-4832

619B Front Street
Suite 1
Nelson, BC V1L 4B6
Phone: (250) 352-3837
Fax: (250) 352-3809

221 West Esplanade, Suite 6
North Vancouver, BC V7M 3J3
Phone: (604) 666-7703
Fax: (604) 666-1957

177 Victoria Street, Suite 100
Prince George, BC V2L 5R8
Phone: (250) 561-5323
Fax: (250) 561-5512

5577 - 105A Street Suite 301
Surrey, BC V3S 5K7
Phone: (604) 586-2410
Fax: (604) 586-2430

3233 Emerson Street
Terrace, BC V8G 5L2
Phone: (250) 615-5300
Fax: (250) 615-5320

Suite 370 - 2755 Lougheed Hwy.
Port Coquitlam, BC V3B 5Y9
Phone: (604) 927-1400
Fax: (604) 927-1415

BDC Tower - Bentall Centre
1 - 505 Burrard Street
Main Floor, P.O. Box 6
Vancouver, BC V7X 1V3
Phone: (604) 666-7850
Fax: (604) 666-1068

221 West Esplanade
Suite 3
North Vancouver, BC V7M 3J3
Phone: (604) 666-7703
Fax: (604) 666-1957

990 Fort Street
Victoria, BC V8V 3K2
Phone: (250) 363-0163
Fax: (250) 363-8029

The Yukon

2237 2nd. Avenue, Suite 210
Whitehorse, YT Y1A 0K7
Phone: (867) 633-7511
Fax: (867) 667-4058

Northwest Territories & Nunavut

4912 - 49th Street
Yellowknife, NT X1A 1P3
Phone: (867) 873-3565
Fax: (867) 873-3501

Canadian Youth Business Foundation (CYBF)

The Canadian Youth Business Foundation (CYBF) is a non-profit, private-sector initiative formed to provide business support, financing, and mentoring to young Canadian entrepreneurs (aged 18-34) who are creating new businesses. The founding partners were The Royal Bank of Canada, The Canadian Imperial Bank of Commerce and The Canadian Youth Foundation. CYBF delivers its program coast to coast to coast through a national network of more than 160 community partners and 3,660 volunteers including business mentors.

The Business Development Bank of Canada (BDC) co-finances business ventures and during fiscal 2012, it provided 260 loans with a total of $6 million.

The programs offered by CYBF are as follows.

CFYB Start-Up Loan

Loans of up to $15,000 are available to qualified candidates who have been in business for less than 12 months and who are unable to raise funding elsewhere.

The eligibility criteria for applicants for a CYBF Start-Up Loan are as follows:

* must be between 18-34 years old;
* must be eligible to work in Canada (work permit holders are not eligible);
* produce a complete and viable business plan;

- in business, fully operating, for less than 12 months;
- live in or operates the business in the community which offers the CYBF program;
- have some training / experience related to their business idea;
- agrees to work with mentor for a period of two years;
- have a business idea that creates full-time sustainable employment;
- must hold at least 51% voting share in the business (if a partnership);
- must not be full-time students;
- loan proceeds may not be used for refinancing of existing debt;
- loan proceeds may not be used to fund businesses that are sexually exploitive or that are inconsistent with generally accepted community standards of conduct and propriety, including those that feature sexually explicit entertainment, products or services; businesses that are engaged in or associated with illegal activities; businesses trading in countries that are proscribed by the Federal Government; and any other commercial activities inappropriate for government funding.

If the business is a partnership, and only one partner meets the CYBF age criteria he/she must hold at minimum 51% of the partnership and meet all other CYBF criteria and be subject to the CYBF application process. If all partners meet the CYBF age criteria, then all are subject to the CYBF application process. If any partner is a minority shareholder and is over the CYBF age limit, they are not subject to the application process.

If the business is incorporated, the applicant must be the majority shareholder, having at least 51% of the voting shares and be involved in the day-to-day management of the business. The applicant must also meet CYBF's age and all other criteria. If the business is incorporated and there are two or more shareholders and not one person holds the majority of the shares, then the shareholders who meet the CYBF age and all other criteria must hold the majority of the voting shares and are subject to the same application process. Any shareholder who meets the CYBF age criteria must be subject to the CYBF application process.

Through the partnership with the Business Development Bank of Canada (BDC) the loan amount can be doubled for a grand total of $45,000; $30,000 of which would come from BDC.

CYBF Spin Master Innovation Fund

The Spin Master Innovation Fund offers an opportunity for innovative entrepreneurs that are launching or building exciting start-ups with national and international expansion potential. Up to $50,000 in start-up financing provided by CYBF and its affiliate, Entrepreneur Gateway Canada. No collateral is required. Successful applicants receive low interest rates with no principal repayment in the first year and are matched with a mentor from CYBF.

Successful applicants also get a paid trip to Toronto to attend the two-day Innovation Launch Pad Workshop where they will meet one-on-one with Spin Master executives to get advice, guidance and contacts help to launch or grow their business. Six months later, they will be invited to attend the Acceleration Workshop to reconnect with experts and peers and discuss their progress so far.

The Prince's Operation Entrepreneur

The Prince's Operation Entrepreneur is an exclusive program for recently retired and transitioning Canadian Forces members interested in entrepreneurship. The program provides:

- entrepreneurial education and business plan support;
- start-up and growth financing;
- specialized business mentoring;
- "Based in Business" boot camp; and,
- networking and community support.

The program is open to transitioned or transitioning Canadian Forces members who:

- are Canadian citizens or permanent residents of Canada;
- have a business idea that creates full-time sustainable employment for the applicant; and,
- agree to work with a mentor.

Successful applicants will qualify to participate in the CYBF Start-up Program; which was described previously. In addition, they can attend a "Based in Business" boot camp which is a free one-week in-class session to develop entrepreneurship skills of selected transitioning CF members.

CFYB Newcomer Entrepreneur Program

In March 2011, the Business Development Bank of Canada (BDC) and the Canadian Youth Business Foundation (CYBF) announced the Newcomer Entrepreneur Program which recognizes that recent immigrants may require targeted support to start their own businesses. In addition to offering flexible financing, the program is designed to overcome the difficulty many young, newly arrived immigrants have in accessing credit because they do not have a Canadian credit history. The program also offers mentoring and business resources so newcomers can learn about operating a business in Canada and improve their chances of success.

Newcomer Entrepreneur Program offers flexible loan assessments that don't require a credit history. Successful applicants may receive up to $15,000 in start-up financing to a maximum of $7,500 from CYBF, matched with a maximum amount of $7,500 from the Business Development Bank of Canada (BDC).

With regard to business mentoring, CYBF will match successful applicants with an experienced business mentor who can provide guidance and thus make better decisions for a new career in Canada.

To be eligible for the CYBF Newcomer Entrepreneur Program, applicants must:

- be a permanent resident of Canada;
- have lived in Canada for less than 36 months from application date;
- have a Social Insurance Number that does not begin with '9';
- be between 18 and 34 years old;
- possess a solid working knowledge of English or French; and,

- provide three character-based references of which at least two must be from Canadian citizens.

Expansion Financing Loan Program

CYBF now offers Expansion Loans for those who have been in businesses for more than three years but less than five years. Loans can be for up to $10,000 for existing CYBF Entrepreneurs who are aged 18 to 34. Additional funding of up to $10,000 may be available from the Business Development Bank of Canada.

Expansion Loans are available to CYBF businesses who have been in operation between 36 to 60 months from the date of the CYBF advance. Loan proceeds cannot be used to refinance existing debt. It should be noted that no funding can go beyond the 60th month of the original loan disbursement and clients who paid off their loans are also eligible.

The applicant must work full time in the business and be legally eligible to work in Canada. Full business and operating plans must be submitted together with a description of the expansion project.

A marketing plan should be submitted which defines the market opportunity and which provides a competitive analysis.

Cash flow forecasts for 2 years must be submitted which indicate a positive position and project the profitability of the expansion project.

Quarterly reports are required.

Partnerships are eligible provided the applicants meet the age criteria and they should have at least 51% of the voting shares and be involved in the day-to-day management of the business. Incorporated businesses with more than two shareholders and no single majority shareholder are eligible provided they meet the age criteria and must collectively hold the majority of the voting shares, be involved in the day-to-day management of the business, and take direct responsibility for the liability.

CYBF will add any outstanding loan balance (if any), to the new Expansion Financing Loan and re-amortize for a maximum term of 48 months.

An initial $50 loan administration fee is charged by CYBF together with a $15 monthly administration fee.

Mentoring through "CYBF moMENTum"

CYBF provides a structured mentoring program (referred to as "moMENTum") for young entrepreneurs who receive a start-up loan. Volunteer mentors are experienced managers and business owners from the community. A training program and resource materials provide a foundation for the mentor and young entrepreneur to establish and maintain a successful mentoring relationship.

At the time of writing, no more applications were being accepted from the Toronto GTA, Hamilton or the Lower Mainland of British Columbia.

Business Resources

CYBF's Web site is a resource for entrepreneurs seeking advice on business plans, financing and growing a business.

Further Information

Loan terms, conditions, eligibility and application documents can be obtained at 180 locations across Canada. The contact information for these locations can be obtained from CYBF's Web site.

NATIONAL OFFICE:
Canadian Youth Business Foundation
133 Richmond Street West, Suite 700
Toronto, ON M5H 2L3
Phone toll-free: 1-(866) 464-2922
Fax toll-free: 1-(877) 408-3234
Web site: www.cybf.ca

Business Credit Availability Program (BCAP)

The Business Credit Availability Program (BCAP) is designed to help businesses find financing solutions to preserve jobs and fund growth. As of the end of January 2010, Export Development Canada (EDC) and the Business Development Bank of Canada (BDC) reported total activity under the Business Credit Availability Program of about $5 billion, assisting almost 9,000 businesses (which equates to over half a million dollars per business). The financial Crown corporations have provided assistance in regions all across the country and in all sectors of the economy, with a particular focus on small businesses.

BCAP provides direct lending and other types of support and facilitation at market rates to businesses with viable business models whose access to financing would otherwise be restricted. By working in close cooperation with private sector lenders, this program will fill gaps in market access and lever additional lending by private sector institutions in cases where joint participation facilitates private action. Participating private sector lenders have committed to:

- work with the financial Crown corporations to find solutions for creditworthy business clients who would otherwise have insufficient access to credit;
- ensure that the extension of credit by financial Crown corporations is incremental for Canadian businesses and does not displace or substitute for private credit in aggregate.

The Canadian Bankers Association (CBA) has entered the scene and is supposed to be working with both the EDC and BDC and the banks to promote BCAP. More information is available from the following banks; however, business readers may find some of the information of little value or the patronage to be offensive.

- BMO Bank of Montreal
- Canadian Western Bank
- CIBC
- HSBC
- Laurentian Bank
- National Bank of Canada
- RBC
- Scotiabank
- TD Canada Trust

Business Development Bank of Canada:
Toll-free phone: 1-(877) 232-2269

Export Development Canada:
Toll-free phone: 1-(866) 283-2957

Western Economic Diversification Canada (WD)

Western Economic Diversification Canada (WD) was established in 1987 with a mandate to promote the development and diversification of Western Canada's economy and ensure that the interests of the region are represented in national economic policy.

Entrepreneurs with Disabilities Program (EDP)

Entrepreneurs with Disabilities Program (EDP) is designed to improve access to business services and other support mechanisms to entrepreneurs with disabilities to help them start or expand small businesses. The program operates in different Western cities and rural communities with different program supporters, as follows.

Vancouver and Victoria: Advice and Business Loans for Entrepreneurs with Disabilities (ABLED)

This Program is open to persons with disability who are interested in self-employment by starting or expanding a small business and who are located in the Greater Vancouver Regional District and the Greater Victoria District. ABLED offers flexible loans that provide individual business loans of up to $35,000 with terms of up to 5 years to:

*   start or expand a business;
*   purchase and apply new technology;
*   upgrade facilities and equipment;
*   develop marketing and promotional activities; and,
*   establish working capital.

ABLED is delivered by VanCity Savings Credit Union and Coast Capital Savings Credit Union. The contact phone numbers are as follows:

VanCity Savings Credit Union
Phone: (604) 709-6930

Coast Capital Savings Credit Union
Phone: Lower Mainland (604) 517-7637

Edmonton: Entrepreneurs with Disabilities Program (EDP)

The Edmonton Entrepreneurs with Disabilities Program (EDP) is funded by Western Economic Diversification (WD). It is designed to help applicants with a disability. It provides business loans of up to $20,000 to help entrepreneurs with disabilities start or expand their own business. The program is in effect until March 2011. Loans can be used for the following purposes:

*   start or expand a business;
*   purchase and apply new technology;

- upgrade facilities and equipment;
- develop marketing and promotional activities; and,
- establish working capital.

For more information on the Edmonton Entrepreneurs with Disabilities Initiative, contact:

Distinctive Employment Counselling Services of Alberta
11515 - 71 Street, Edmonton, AB T5B 1W1
Phone: (780) 471-9621
Phone TTY: (780) 471-9635
Fax: (780) 474-7765
Web site: www.decsa.com

Calgary: Entrepreneurs with Disabilities Program (EDP)

The Calgary Entrepreneurs with Disabilities Program (EDP) is funded by Western Economic Diversification (WD). It is designed to help applicants with a disability. It provides business loans of up to $10,000 to help entrepreneurs with disabilities start or expand their own business.

Loans can be used for the following purposes:

- start or expand a business;
- purchase and apply new technology;
- upgrade facilities and equipment;
- develop marketing and promotional activities; and,
- establish working capital.

Momentum
Room 16, 2936 Radcliffe Drive South East
Calgary, AB T2A 6M8
Phone: (403) 204-2671   Fax: (403) 235-4646
Web site: www.momentum.org

Saskatoon and Regina: Entrepreneurs with Disabilities Program (EDP)

The Saskatoon and Regina Entrepreneurs with Disabilities Program (EDP) is funded by Western Economic Diversification (WD). It is designed to help applicants with a disability. It provides business loans to help entrepreneurs with disabilities start or expand their own business. Loans can be used for the following purposes:

- start or expand a business;
- purchase and apply new technology;
- upgrade facilities and equipment;
- develop marketing and promotional activities; and,
- establish working capital.

The North Saskatchewan Independent Living Centre in Saskatoon and the South Saskatchewan Independent Living Centre in Regina manage this program. The centres take a lead role in providing mentoring and counselling services, support in business development stages, as well as providing business loans to people with disabilities who wish to start or expand their business.

Through the EDP, the Independent Living Centres:

- promote entrepreneurship and self-employment as an option for people with disabilities exploring employment;
- provide mentorship and peer support;
- provide access to information resources and community services;
- provide access to support in the development stages of business in areas such as developing a business plan, financial forecasts and researching capital options;
- provide a mechanism for follow-up and aftercare; and,
- provide an option for capital (and the possibility of leveraging additional money) through the investment fund to people with disabilities wanting to start or expand their business.

South Saskatchewan Independent Living Centre
2220 Albert Street
Regina, SK S4P 2V2
Phone: (306) 757-7452
Fax: (306) 757-5892
TTY: (306) 757-7452
Web site: http://www.ssilc.ca

North Saskatchewan Independent Living Centre
237 - 5th Avenue North
Saskatoon, SK S7K 2P2
Phone: (306) 665-5508
Fax: (306) 244-2453
E-mail: uedp@nsilc.com
Web site: www.nsilc.com

Winnipeg: Entrepreneurs with Disabilities Program (EDP)

The Winnipeg Entrepreneurs with Disabilities Program (EDP) is funded by Western Economic Diversification (WD). It is designed to help applicants with a disability. It provides business loans of up to $75,000 to help entrepreneurs with disabilities start or expand their own business.

The Independent Living Resource Centre (ILRC) was contracted by WD to deliver this initiative.

ILRC can provide:

*   coordinate and facilitate partnerships of cross disability organizations in support of entrepreneurs with disabilities;
*   assist in preparing business plans;
*   provide peer support and networking;

- facilitate partnerships to assist clients to access financing to help start or expand a business;
- provide access to entrepreneurial training; and,
- provide one-on-one consulting services for both start-up and existing businesses.

Independent Living Resource Centre (ILRC)
Suite 311A, 393 Portage Avenue
Winnipeg, MB R3B 3H6
Phone: (204) 947-0194
Fax: (204) 943-6625
TTY: (204) 947-0194
Web site: www.ilrc.mb.ca

Community Futures Development Corporations (CFDCs)

The Community Futures Development Corporations (CFDCs) provide assistance to small, remote, rural, northern and Aboriginal communities to help them identify and address regional economic opportunities. They focus on specific local investment opportunities and provide counselling, mentoring and financial assistance to small business and start-up entrepreneurs. The CFDC initiative addresses high unemployment rates in remote communities.

In addition, CFDCs provide a focal point for local community economic development planning and local based information on other government employment initiatives.

The CFDCs are run by local boards of volunteer directors which tailor service delivery according to local needs. They work with local small and medium-sized businesses to assist in creating job opportunities.

Loans: CFDCs offer loans to new and start-up businesses from locally managed investment funds. The average loan size is about $25,000 with a maximum of $150,000. These loans are offered at commercial rates and repayment terms are negotiated on a case-by-case basis.

Applicants should be operating or about to operate in a rural area of one of the Western Provinces and application should be made at their local CFDC office.

CFDCs have business advisors whose job is to:

*   council start-up entrepreneurs;
*   assist businesses through tough times; and,
*   claim any security pledged for the loans only in the last resort.

There are approximately 90 CFDCs located in Western Canada. Further information on the location of the nearest CFDC office can be obtained toll-free at: 1-888-338-WEST.

MANITOBA

Community Futures Cedar Lake
Box 569
#1 St. Godard Street
The Pas, MB R9A 1K6
Phone: (204) 627-5450
Phone toll-free: 1-(888) 303-2232
Fax: (204) 627-5460

Community Futures Manitoba
559 - 167 Lombard Ave
Winnipeg, MB R3B 0V3
Phone: (204) 943-2905
Fax: (204) 956-9363

Community Futures Dakota Ojibway
4820 Portage Ave
Headingley, MB R4H 18
Phone: (204) 988-5373
Fax: (204) 988-5365

Community Futures Greenstone
228 - 35 Main St. Flin Flon, MB R8A 1J7
Phone: (204) 687-6967
Fax: (204) 687-4456

Community Futures Heartland
11 - 2nd Street N.W.
Portage la Prairie, MB R1N 1R8
Phone: (204) 239-0135
Phone toll-free: 1-(888) 303-2232
Fax: (204) 239-0176

Community Futures Kitayan
4-846 Marion Street Avenue
Winnipeg, MB R3J 0K4
Phone toll-free: 1-(888) 303-2232
Fax: (204) 943-3412

Community Futures East Interlake
PO Box 10, 12 Main Street North
Riverton, MB R0C 2R0
Phone: (204) 378-5106
Phone toll-free: 1-(888) 303-2232
Fax: (204) 378-5192

Community Futures North Central Development
P.O. Box 1208, #2 - 3 Station Rd.
Thompson, MB R8N 1P1
Phone: (204) 677-1490
Phone toll-free: 1-(888) 303-2232
Fax: (204) 778-5672

Community Futures North Red
18 Main Street
Selkirk, MB R1A 1P5
Phone: (204) 482-2020
Phone toll-free: 1-(888) 303-2232
Fax: (204) 482-2033

Community Futures Northwest
PO Box 188
499 Sheritt Ave.
Lynn Lake, MB R0B 0W0
Phone: (204) 356-2489
Phone toll-free: 1-(888) 303-2232
Fax: (204) 356-2785

Community Futures Parkland
P.O. Box 516
421 Main Street
Grandview, MB R0L 0Y0
Phone: (204) 546-5100
Phone toll-free: 1-(888) 303-2232
Fax: (204) 546-5107

Community Futures Southeast
200 - 208 Edmonton Street
Winnipeg, MB R3C 1R7
Phone: (204) 943-1656
Phone toll-free: 1-(888) 303-2232
Fax: (204) 943-1735

Community Futures West Interlake
P.O. Box 68
TBJ Mall Main Street
Ashern, MB R0C 0E0
Phone: (204) 768-3351
Phone toll-free: 1-(888) 496-8932
Fax: (204) 768-3489

Community Futures Triple R
PO Box 190
220 Main Street North
Morris, MB R0G 1K0
Phone: (204) 746-6180
Phone toll-free: 1-(888) 303-2232
Fax: (204) 746-2035

Community Futures Westman
217-10th Street #5
Brandon MB R7A 4E9
Phone: (204) 726-1513
Phone toll-free: 1-(888) 347-4342
Fax: (204) 727-5832

Community Futures White Horse Plains
56 Royal Road North
Portage la Prairie, MB R1N 1V1
Phone: (204) 856-5000
Phone toll-free: 1-(888) 947-2332
Fax: (204) 856-5006

Community Futures Winnipeg River
Box 505
4 Park Avenue
Lac du Bonnet, MB R0E 1A0
Phone: (204) 345-2514
Phone toll-free: 1-(888) 298-9023
Fax: (204) 345-6334

SASKATCHEWAN

Community Futures Beaver River
PO Box 2678
106 - 1st Street East
Meadow Lake, SK S9X 1Z6
Phone: (306) 236-4422
Fax: (306) 236-5818

Community Futures Saskatchewan
207-120 Sonnenschein Way
Saskatoon, SK S7M 1M8
Phone: (306) 477-3030
Cell: (306) 717-4002

Community Futures East Central
PO Box 727
601 Edmonton Street
Broadview, SK S0G 0K0
Phone: (306) 696-2443
Fax: (306) 696-2508

Community Futures Meridian
P.O. Box 2167
125 - 1st Avenue East
Kindersley, SK S0L 1S0
Phone: (306) 463-1850
Phone toll-free: 1-(888) 919-3800
Fax: (306) 463-1855

Community Futures Mid-Sask/REDA
PO Box 176
500 Progress Avenue
Outlook, SK S0L 2N0
Phone: (306) 867-9566
Phone toll-free: 1-(888) 929-9990
Fax: (306) 867-9559

Community Futures Newsask
PO Box 357
903 - 99th Avenue
Tisdale Civic Centre
Tisdale, SK S0E 1T0
Phone: (306) 873-4449
Phone toll-free: 1-(888) 586-9855
Fax: (306) 873-4645

Community Futures Northwest
761 C 106 Street
North Battleford, SK S9A 1V9
Phone: (306) 446-3200
Phone toll-free: 1-(877) 446-2332
Fax: (306) 445-8076

Community Futures Prince Albert and District
#1 - 1499 - 10th Avenue East
Prince Albert, SK S6V 7S6
Phone: (306) 763-8125
Fax: (306) 763-8127

Community Futures Sagehill
P.O. Box 10, 515 Mayer Street
Bruno, SK S0K 0S0
Phone: (306) 369-2610
Phone toll-free: 1-(888) 732-8999
Fax: (306) 369-4142

Community Futures South Central
88 Saskatchewan Ave.
Moose Jaw, SK S6H 0V4
Phone: (306) 692-6525
Phone toll-free: 1-(800) 329-1479
Fax: (306) 694-1728

Community Futures Southwest
885 6th Avenue NE
Swift Current, SK S9H 3V5
Phone: (306) 773-0900
Fax: (306) 773-0906

Community Futures Sunrise
11 - 3rd. Street NE
Weyburn, SK S4H 2K1
Phone: (306) 842-8803
Phone toll-free: 1-(800) 699-0533
Fax: (306) 842-4069

Community Futures Ventures
204 Smith Street East
Yorkton, SK S3N 3S6
Phone: (306) 782-0255
Phone toll-free: 1-(877) 851-9997
Fax: (306) 783-2590

ALBERTA

Community Futures Centre West
228 River Avenue
Cochrane, AB T4C 2C1
Phone: (403) 932-5220
Phone toll-free: 1-(877) 603-2329
Fax: (403) 932-6824

Community Futures Chinook
5324-48th Avenue
Taber, AB T1G 1S2
Phone: (403) 388–2926
Phone toll-free: 1-(888) 223-3330
Fax: (403) 223-2096

Community Futures Alberta
#4, 205 First Street East
Cochrane, AB T4C 1A5
Phone: (403) 851-9995
Fax: (403) 851-9905

Community Futures Crowsnest Pass
P.O. Box 818
Room 180, 12501 - 20 Avenue
Blairmore, AB T0K 0E0
Phone: (403) 562-8858
Fax: (403) 562-7252

Community Futures Big Country
PO Box 610
181 North Railway Avenue
Drumheller, AB T0J 0Y0
Phone: (403) 823-7703
Fax: (403) 823-7753

Community Futures East Central
P.O. Box 5000
5104 - 53 Avenue
Viking, AB T0B 4N0
Phone toll-free: 1-(877) 336-3497
Fax: (403) 336-2266

Community Futures East Parkland
P.O. Box 250, 5020 - 50 Avenue
Mirror, AB T0B 3C0
Phone: (403) 788-2212
Phone toll-free: 1-(888) 788-2829
Fax: (403) 788-2199

Community Futures Entre-Corp
Business Development
#202, 556 - 4th Street, SE
Medicine Hat, AB T1A 0K8
Phone: (403) 528-2824
Phone toll-free: 1-(888) 528-2824
Fax: (403) 527-3596

Community Futures Wood Buffalo
100B, 9816 Hardin St.
Fort McMurray, AB T9H 4K3
Phone: (780) 791-0330
Fax: (780) 791-0086

Community Futures Highwood
14 McRae St. PO Box 1599
Okotoks, AB T1S 1B5
Phone: (403) 995-4151
Fax: (403) 995-3760

Community Futures Lac La Biche
Box 2188; 10106 - 102 Ave
Lac La Biche, AB T0A 2C0
Phone: (780) 623-2662
Fax: (780) 623-2671

Community Futures Lakeland
PO Box 8114, 5010 - 50 Avenue
Bonnyville, AB T9N 2J4
Phone: (780) 826-3858
Fax: (780) 826-7330

Community Futures Lethbridge Region
2626 - South Parkside Drive
Lethbridge, AB T1K 0C4
Phone: (403) 320-6044
Fax: (403) 327-8476

Community Futures Elk Island Region
Box 547, #4 - 5002 Diefenbaker Avenue
Two Hills, AB T0B 4K0
Phone: (780) 657-3512
Phone toll-free: 1-(888) 526-6689
Fax: (780) 657-2359

Community Futures Lesser Slave Lake Region
PO Box 2100
Suite 1, 100 Poplar Lane
Slave Lake, AB T0G 2A0
Phone: (780) 849-3232
Fax: (780) 849-3360

Community Futures Lloydminster
#5 4010-50th Ave.
Lloydminster, AB T9V 1B2
Phone: (780) 875-5458
Phone toll-free: 1-(888) 875-5458
Fax: (780) 875-8026

Community Futures Northwest Alberta
P.O. Box 210; 9810-99 Street
High Level, AB T0H 1Z0
Phone: (780) 926-4233
Phone toll-free: 1-(888) 922-4233
Fax: (780) 926-2162

Community Futures Peace Country
9816-98 Avenue
Peace River, AB T8S 1J5
Phone: (780) 624-1161
Fax: (780) 624-1308

Community Futures Central Alberta
5013 - 49th Avenue
Red Deer, AB T4N 3X1
Phone: (403) 342-2055
Phone toll-free: 1-(888) 343-2055
Fax: (403) 347-6980

Community Futures Grande Prairie and Region
104, 9817 - 101 Avenue
Grande Prairie, AB T8V 0X6
Phone: (780) 814-5340
Phone toll-free: 1-(877) 402-3198
Fax: (780) 532-5129

Community Futures Alberta Southwest
PO Box 1568, 659 Main St.
Pincher Creek, AB T0K 1W0
Phone: (403) 627-3020
Fax: (403) 627-3035

Community Futures St. Paul/Smoky
Lake (Smoky Lake)
4802 - 50 Avenue, Box 1484
Smoky Lake, AB T0A 3A0
Phone: (780) 645-5782
Fax: (780) 645-1811

Community Futures St Paul/
Smoky Lake (St.Paul)
PO Box 1484, 4802 - 50 Avenue
St. Paul, AB T0A 3A4
Phone: (780) 656-5782
Fax: (780) 645-1811

Community Futures Tawatinaw
10611 - 100 Avenue
Westlock, AB T7P 2J4
Phone: (780) 349-2903
Phone toll-free: 1-(888) 349-2903
Fax: (780) 6542

Community Futures Treaty Seven
300 - 6011 - 1 A Street SW
Tsuu T'ina (Sarcee), AB T2W 0G5
Phone: (780) 251-9242
Fax: (403) 251-9750

Community Futures Capital Region
5006-50 St., PO Box 3175
Stony Plain, AB T7Z 1Y4
Phone: (780) 968-7013
Phone toll-free: 1-(800) 848-2285
Fax: (780) 968-7048

Community Futures West Yellowhead
221 Pembina Ave.
Hinton, AB T7V 2B3
Phone: (780) 865-1224
Phone toll-free: 1-(800) 263-1716
Fax: (780) 865-1227

Community Futures Yellowhead East
4926 - 51st Avenue
P.O. Box 2185
Whitecourt AB T7S 1P8
Phone: (780) 706-3500
Phone toll-free: 1-(877) 706-3500
Fax: (780) 706-3501

Community Futures Wild Rose
Box 2159, #101, 331-3rd Avenue
Strathmore, AB T1P 1K2
Phone: (403) 934-6488
Phone toll-free: 1-(888) 556-0328
Fax: (403) 934-6492

Community Futures Peace River
9816 - 98 Avenue
Peace River AB T5S 1J6
Phone: (780) 1161
Fax: (780) 624-1308

BRITISH COLUMBIA

CFDC of 16-37
101 - 4734 Lazelle Avenue
Terrace, BC V8G 1T2
Phone: (250) 635-5449
Fax: (250) 635-2698

CFDC of Alberni Clayoquot
4757 Tebo Avenue
Port Alberni, BC V9Y 8A9
Phone: (250) 724-1241
Phone toll-free: 1-(877) 724-1241
Fax: (250) 724-1028

CFDC of Cariboo - Chilcotin
266 Oliver Street
Williams Lake, BC V2G 1M1
Phone: (250) 392-3626
Phone toll-free: 1-(888) 879-5399
Fax: (604) 392-4813

CFDC of Central Interior First Nations
#215 - 345 Yellowhead Highway
Kamloops, BC V2H 1H1
Phone: (250) 828-9833
Fax: (250) 828-9972

CFDC of Central Island
#104 - 5070 Uplands Drive
Nanaimo, BC V9T 6N1
Phone: (250) 585-5585
Phone toll-free: 1-(877) 585-5385
Fax: (250) 585-5584

CFDC of Central Kootenay
201, 514 Vernon Street
Nelson, BC V1L 4E7
Phone: (250) 352-1933
Fax: (250) 352-5926

CFDC of Central Okanagan
110-1632 Dickson Ave.
Kelowna, BC V1Y 9T5
Phone: (250) 868-2132
Fax: (250) 868-2173

CFDC of Cowichan Region
135 Third Street
Duncan, BC V9L 1R9
Phone: (250) 746-1004
Fax: (250) 746-8819

CFDC of Fraser Fort George
1566 - 7th Avenue
Prince George, BC V2L 3P4
Phone: (250) 562-9622
Fax: (250) 562-9119

CFDC of Greater Trail
825 Spokane Street
Trail, BC V1R 3W4
Phone: (250) 364-2595
Fax: (250) 364-2728

CFDC of Haida Gwaii
P.O. Box 40
1730 Hodges Avenue
Massett, BC V0T 1M0
Phone: (250) 626-5594
Phone toll-free: 1-(888) 328-5594
Fax: (250) 626-5693

CFDC of Howe Sound
Suite 102 - 1909 Maple Drive
Squamish, BC V8B 0T1
Phone: (604) 892-5467
Fax: (604) 892-5227

CFDC of Mount Waddington
PO Box 458
8, 311 Hemlock Street
Port McNeill, BC V0N 2R0
Phone toll-free: 1-(877) 956-2220
Fax: (250) 956-2221

CFDC of Nadina (Houston)
P.O. Box 236
2430 Butler Ave. Unit A
Houston, BC V0J 1Z0
Phone: (250) 945-2522
Phone toll-free: 1-(800) 556-5539
Fax: (604) 845-2528

CFDC of Nadina (Smithers)
P.O. Box 2319
1164 Main St.
Smithers, BC V0J 2N0
Phone: (250) 847-1389
Phone toll-free: 1-(800) 556-5539
Fax: (604) 845-1860

CFDC of Nicola Valley
PO Box 159
2099 Quilchena Avenue
Merritt, BC V1K 1B8
Phone: (250) 378-3923
Fax: (250) 378-3924

CFDC of North Fraser
32386 Fletcher Avenue
Mission, BC V2V-5T1
Phone: 604) 826-6252
Fax: (604) 826-0052

CFDC of North Okanagan
302, 3105 33rd St.
Vernon, BC V1T 9P7
Phone: (250) 545-2215
Fax: (250) 545-6447

CFDC of Okanagan - Similkameen
102, 3115 Skaha Lake Road
Penticton, BC V2A 6G5
Phone: (250) 493-2566
Phone toll-free: 1-(877) 493-5566
Fax: (250) 493-7966

CFDC of Pacific Northwest
#200 - 515 3rd Avenue West
Prince Rupert, BC V8J 1L9
Phone: (250) 622-2332
Phone toll-free: 1-(877) 622-8288
Fax: (250) 622-2334

CFDC of Peace Liard (Dawson Creek)
904-102nd Avenue
Dawson Creek, BC V1G 2B7
Phone: (250) 782-8748
Phone toll-free: 1-(877) 296-5888
Fax: (250) 782-8770

CFDC of Powell River Region
2 flr, 4717 Marine Avenue
Powell River, BC V8A 4Z2
Phone: (604) 485-7901
Fax: (604) 485-4897

CFDC of Revelstoke
PO Box 2398
204 Campbell Avenue
Revelstoke, BC V0E 2S0
Phone: (604) 837-5345
Fax: (604) 837-4223

CFDC of Shuswap
Box 1930
101, 160 Harbourfront Drive NE
Salmon Arm, BC V1E 4P9
Phone: (250) 803-0156
Fax: (250) 803-0157

CFDC of South Fraser
1 - 31726 South Fraser Way
Abbotsford, BC V2T 1T9
Phone: (604) 864-5770
Phone toll-free: 1-(877) 827-8249
Fax: (604) 864-5769

CFDC of Sto:Lo
7201 Vedder Road
Chilliwack, BC V2R 4G5
Phone: (604) 858-0009
Fax: (604) 858-3829

CFDC of Strathcona - Campbell River
PO Box 160
900 Alder Street
Courtenay, BC V9W 2P6
Phone: (250) 830-0999
Fax: (250) 830-1189

CFDC of Stuart - Nechako
P.O. Box 1078
2750 Burrard St.
Vanderhoof, BC V0J 3A0
Phone: (250) 567-5219
Phone toll-free: 1-(800) 266-0611
Fax: (250) 567-5224

CFDC of Sun Country
P.O. Box 1480
203 Railway Avenue
Ashcroft, BC V0K 1A0
Phone: (604) 453-9165
Phone toll-free: 1-(800) 567-9911
Fax: (604) 453-9500

CFDC of Sunshine Coast
PO Box 128
301-5500 Wharf Avenue
Sechelt, BC V0N 3A0
Phone: (640) 885-1959
Phone toll-free: 1-(800) 886-2332
Fax: (604) 885-2707

CFDC of the Boundary Area
P.O. Box 459
245 South Copper Street
Greenwood, BC V0H 1J0
Phone: (604) 445-6618
Fax: (604) 445-6765

CFDC of the North Cariboo
335 A Vaughan Street
Quesnel, BC V2J 2T1
Phone: (250) 992-2322
Phone toll-free: 1-(877) 992-2332
Fax: (604) 997-7700

CFDC of the S.E. Region of BC
110A Slater Rd. NW
Cranbrook, BC V1C 5P8
Phone: (250) 489-4356
Phone toll-free: 1-(800) 661-2293
Fax: (250) 489-1886

CFDC of Thompson Country
230 - 301 Victoria Avenue
Kamloops, BC V2C 2A3
Phone: (250) 828-8772
Phone toll-free: 1-(877) 335-2950
Fax: (250) 828-6861

Nuu Chah Nulth CFDC
P.O. Box 1384
7563 Pacific Rim Highway
Port Alberni, BC V9Y 7M2
Phone: (250) 724-3131
Phone toll-free: 1-(866) 444-6332
Fax: (250) 724-9967

Community Futures Development
Association of B.C.
Suite 1056 - 409 Granville Street
Vancouver, BC V6C 1T2
Phone: (604) 685-2332
Fax: (604) 681-6575

Women's Enterprise Initiative

Studies have indicated that women face gender-specific barriers especially in obtaining access to capital, training, information, networks, contacts and mentors; not to mention the conflict of family responsibilities. It is to address issues such as these that the Women's Enterprise Initiative has been established. The WEI's offer the following:

Women's Enterprise Initiative Loan Program: each western province has set up its own component of this pan-western initiative. The non-profit groups offer access to a loan fund, advisory services, path finding to existing services plus a host of unique products and services tailored to meet the needs of women entrepreneurs in their province.

In general, to access the loan fund, applicants must be:

- a legal entity 51% owned or controlled by a woman or women;
- operating, or about to operate, in one of the four Western Provinces;
- be able to submit a business plan that indicates a viable business (WEI will provide counselling on the development of the business plan);
- seeking debt financing up to a maximum of $150,000; and,
- seeking financing for start-up or expansion of the business.

WEI will also provide assistance in accessing traditional bank financing, through the relationships that have been established with local financial institutions.

The WEI office in each province has established it's own lending criteria and loan program details and further information is provided in the following sections.

Women's Enterprise Centre of Manitoba/
Centre d'entreprise des femmes du Manitoba

The Women's Enterprise Centre is a Manitoba non-profit organization dedicated to helping entrepreneurial women address the unique challenges facing them as they build their businesses. The Centre offers innovative supports that can help change these challenges into opportunities.

Loans: for start-up or expansion of women owned businesses (at least 50%) in Manitoba. There is no minimum loan size, but the maximum is set at $150,000. Terms can be for up to five years.

The interest charged on start-up loans is prime plus 3% and prime plus 1% for expansion loans. There is no fee to apply and no penalties or fees for pre-payment or partial payment.

A business plan is required to apply and business advisors are available at no cost to assist in its preparation.

Security is required but it does not have to be for the full value of the loan.

Loans can be used for the following:

* purchase of an existing business;
* leasehold improvements;
* purchase of inventory;
* purchase of equipment;
* advertising and marketing costs; or,
* one-time or part-time projects will be evaluated on a case-by-case basis.

Loans cannot be used for the following:

* the purchase of goodwill;
* owner's draw or salary;
* the purchase of land or buildings; or,
* investments in real estate for speculative purposes.

Loan applications are assessed on the following:

* a business plan that demonstrates a reasonable potential for success and ability to repay the loan;
* credit worthiness and stability of the applicant;
* the cash or equity contribution committed by the applicant;
* ability to provide security for the loan (on a case-by-case basis).

It should be noted that loan applications for amounts of less than $10,000 do not require a business plan.

Business Analysis: business appointments can be made, on site or by phone, with a business advisor, free of charge, to discuss business plans, expansion plans, marketing plans or any business issues on which feedback is needed.

Training: business seminars are offered on different topics of interest to women starting or operating a business. Also, a business-to-business linking program has been designed to put entrepreneurs in touch with a similar, non competing business in Western Canada. This service is open only to clients of the Women's Enterprise Centre.

Further information: services are available throughout Manitoba.

Manitoba Women's Enterprise Centre
100-207 Donald St.
Winnipeg, MB R3C 1M5
Phone: (204) 988-1860
Fax: (204) 988-1871
Toll-free: 1-(800) 203-2343
E-mail: wecinfo@wecm.ca
Web site: http://www.wecm.ca

Women Entrepreneurs of Saskatchewan Inc.

Women Entrepreneurs of Saskatchewan Inc. (W.E.) is a non-profit membership organization formed to provide support to women entrepreneurs throughout the Province. Services include training seminars, business advising, a loan fund, networking, mentoring and publication of a bulletin and a newsletter.

Advising Services: covers business management and development for start-up and expansion and includes advice on how to assess product and market opportunities or develop a business plan.

Training: business development workshops are provided in partnership with other community and service organizations throughout the Province.

General Loans: W.E. offers loans of up to $150,000 from its loan fund with interest rates set at bank prime plus 3% to businesses that are 51% or more owned by women. Funds can be for the purchase of tangible and/or intangible assets; working capital for inventory or start up costs. Applicants must contribute 20% to 25% equity towards the project.

John and Bernice Williams and North Prairie Developments Angel Investment Fund: is administered by the Women Entrepreneurs of Saskatchewan. Potential applicants will be identified at the business advisory stage. All applicants must provide a completed loan application, a personal financial statement, and business plan. To be eligible, the applicant must be a member of W.E. and a current business advising client. The client must be able to contribute 10% of the required equity, as well as seeking a loan through W.E. The business must be viable and demonstrate the ability to repay the required debt, as well as the equity contribution. The maximum amount available per applicant is $10,000.

Membership: is offered at a full membership rate of $100.00 plus GST and associate membership at $50.00 plus GST. Membership is a requirement to access business advising and loans, and there are many other benefits to being a member.

Publications: consists of a bi-monthly "Bulletin" containing news about training, trade shows, conferences, service organizations and the activities at W.E. In addition, there is a semi-annual newsletter called "Women in Business", which covers different business topics.

Pathfinding and Information: in the form of a small resource library is available in Saskatoon and Regina. Clients needing specific information can receive advice on where to obtain it.

Annual Business Conference: provides the opportunity for women in business to come together to gain business knowledge and network in an environment of mutual support.

W.E. Mentoring Circles: consisting of a group of 10-15 women which generally includes a lawyer, accountant and financial representative with content determined by the needs of the group.

Youth Initiatives: in which W.E. works closely with high schools and other youth institutions to encourage young women and girls to consider entrepreneurship as a career option.

Women Entrepreneurs of Saskatchewan Inc.
108 - 502 Cope Way, Saskatoon, SK S7T 0G3
Phone: (306) 477-7173
Fax: (306) 477-7175

Woman Entrepreneurs of Saskatchewan Inc.
100 - 1919 Rose Street
Regina, SK S4P 3P1
Phone: (306) 359-9732
Fax: (306) 359-9739

Province-wide toll-free: 1-(800) 879-6331
E-mail: info@womenentrepreneurs.sk.ca
Web site: www.womenentrepreneurs.sk.ca

Alberta Women Entrepreneurs (AWE)

Alberta Women Entrepreneurs (AWE) helps Alberta women start and expand businesses. This non-profit corporation is led by an independent Board of Alberta business people and is funded by Western Economic Diversification and corporate sponsors.

AWE works with committed Alberta women to help them turn their business idea into a successful reality. Services are confidential and many are sponsored on a minimal cost recovery basis. They include:

* linking to people and business information that serve as a business source;
* guidance with business plan development;
* information sessions, workshops and networking;
* one-on-one business coaching;

- access to volunteer experts; and,
- assistance in accessing financing.

AWE Business Loan

The AWE Loan Program provides small business start-up and expansion loans of up to $150,000. Loans are open to majority-women owned businesses in Alberta.

Applicants must present a business plan and pay a non-refundable application fee of $100. Once approved, there is an administration of 1% of the amount of the loan to a maximum of $500.

The criteria for loan applications is as follows:

- the business owner must be 18 years or older;
- the business must be 50% owned by a woman or women;
- the business operations must be controlled 51% by a woman or women;
- the woman or women owners must live in the Province of Alberta;
- the business must operate within the Province of Alberta;
- the business must have a satisfactory credit rating; and
- a business plan must have been prepared and a marketing strategy must be in place.

Loan interest is charged at TD Bank Prime plus 3%. Terms for loans are typically for 5 years with no penalty for early repayment.

An equity contribution is required and is generally as follows:

- no minimum equity required on loans of under $5,000;
- 10% on loans of between $5,000 and $25,000;
- 15% on loans of between $25,000 and $50,000;
- 20% on loans of between $50,000 and $75,000;
- 25% on loans of between $75,000 and $100,000.

It should be noted that AWA Loans cannot be used for any of the following:

- to pay back existing debts;
- multi-level marketing ventures;
- franchise fees;
- independent agents and or direct sellers;
- tuition/educational training;
- goodwill on purchasing a business;
- owners' salaries;
- to re-finance existing debt.

Further information

AWE is part of the Pan-Western Women's Initiative. Similar centres are active in Manitoba, Saskatchewan and British Columbia. AWE has offices in Edmonton, Calgary and Lethbridge and its services may be accessed province-wide through the toll-free number listed below and through its Web site.

Web site: www.awebusiness.com
Phone toll-free: 1-(800) 713-3558

Alberta Women Entrepreneurs (AWE)
370, 105 12 Avenue SE
Calgary, AB T2G 1A1
Phone: (403) 777-4250
Fax: (403) 777-4258

Alberta Women Entrepreneurs (AWE)
308, 10310 Jasper Avenue (Melton Building)
Edmonton, AB T5J 2W4
Phone: (780) 422-7784
Fax: (780) 422-0756

Women's Enterprise Centre

The Women's Enterprise Society of B.C. (WESBC) was formed in May 1995, to respond to gaps that previous research had identified in financing and services for women entrepreneurs. It is now called the "Women's Enterprise Centre".

The mission of the Centre is to encourage the establishment and growth of women-owned and controlled businesses in British Columbia, in order to strengthen and diversify the British Columbia economy, encourage job creation through self-employment and business development, and promote economic equality between men and women.

The goals of Centre are to assist women in starting, purchasing or growing a business. to offer services that are accessible to all women in British Columbia, including those dealing with special circumstances, such as immigrant and visible minority women, or women facing socio-economic, physical, and emotional/mental challenges; and, to raise awareness of entrepreneurship and self-employment as career options. Services include:

Professional Guidance: advice for business challenges and growth strategies, as well as marketing and financial issues. Offer tools to assist in the development of a business plan and provides assessment of plans for financing.

Business Loans: can help start a business or assist with the growth of a business and blends business planning, training, guidance and advice with financing up to $150,000.00 for new and existing businesses.

Practical Skills Development: provides "real-world" training and workshops in a number of essential subject areas required to run a successful business, and in a variety of formats to suit busy entrepreneurs. The do-it-yourself training is a handy way to learn tips.

Networking Connections: to connect women to other business service providers throughout the Province, as well as to networking and peer learning opportunities.

Resource Library: is full of information and resource guides to start or grow a business.

Events and Workshops: often feature guest women entrepreneurs relating their stories and lessons.

Eligibility for Loans

To be eligible for WESBC business loans, applicants must be:

- an operation that is 51% owned and controlled by a woman or women; who reside in BC and plan to operate the business in BC;
- a Canadian citizen or landed immigrant;
- a resident of British Columbia; and,
- in good financial standing with respect to any existing assistance.

Applicants must submit a comprehensive business plan. Plans must contain financial projections that can be substantiated. Management overviews must show that the woman or women involved possess the knowledge and skills to carry out the plan.

Applicants are generally required to provide 30% security and 25% equity.

Loan Features

As mentioned, the Women's Enterprise Centre can provide loans of up to $150,000 for BC women according to the following criteria:

- loans can be for market-ready start-ups, business expansion projects and business purchases;
- loans can be used for leaseholds, equipment, operating capital etc.,
- flexible repayment options and terms up to 5 years;
- lower security and equity requirements than many other lenders;
- lower fees than many other lenders; and,
- competitive interest rates.

It should be noted that the loan fund is not intended to compete with other financial institutions and is designed only for women who are unable to secure traditional financing.

Generally, loans are for between $2,000 and $150,000 and carry interest rates that are competitive with those charged by major banks and credit unions. They can carry terms of a few months, up to a maximum of five years.

Projects are eligible for loans, provided that:

- they meet loan criteria;
- they have the potential to lead to one or more profitable operations; and,
- they show reasonable potential to repay the loan.

It should be noted that speculative investments in real estate and the purchase of shares, stocks and other so-called "non-productive investments" are not eligible for loan assistance. Also, loans are not available for businesses at the pre-start-up stage.

Further Information

The Women's Enterprise Centre
Suite 201, 1726 Dolphin Ave.
Kelowna, BC V1Y 9R9
Phone: (250) 868-3454
Fax: (250) 868-2709
Toll-free in B.C. at: 1-(800) 643-7014
E-mail: inquiry@womensenterprise.ca
Web site: http://www.womensenterprise.ca

Satellite offices:

82-601 West Cordova St., Suite 82
Vancouver, BC V6B 1G1
Toll-free in B.C. at: 1-(800) 643-7014
Fax: (250) 868-2709

2659 Douglas Street, Suite 2
Victoria, BC V8T 5M2
Phone: 1-(800) 643-7014
Fax: (250) 868-2709

Francophone Economic Development Organizations (FEDO)

WD supplies support to four provincial organizations to help them provide services to Francophone entrepreneurs. These services include:

- small business information for francophone entrepreneurs;
- referral to government programs;
- information sessions, workshops, and exhibits to strengthen the skills of francophone entrepreneurs and to allow them to explore business opportunities;
- business management skills development for francophone businesses, including marketing and bookkeeping;
- business counselling and access to financing for business development and expansion;
- community economic development.

La Société de développement
économiquede la Colombie-Britannique
220-1555 7th Avenue West
Vancouver, BC V6J 1S1
Phone: (604) 732-3534
Toll-free phone: 1-(877) 732-3534
Fax: (604) 732-3516
Web site: www.sdecb.com

Conseil de développement
économique de l'Alberta
8929 - 82 Ave
Edmonton, AB T6C 0Z2
Phone: (780) 414-6125
Toll-free phone: 1-(888) 414-6123
Fax: (780) 414-2885
Web site: www.lacdea.ca

Conseil de la Coopération
de la Saskatchewan (CCS)
300-2114 - 11th Avenue
Regina, SK S4P 0J5
Phone: (306) 566-6000
Phone toll-free: 1-(800) 670-0879
Fax: (306) 757-4322
Web site: http://www.ccs-sk.ca

Conseil de développement économique
des municipalités bilingues
du Manitoba (CDEM)
200 - 614, rue Des Meurons
Saint-Boniface MB R2H 2P9
Manitoba Toll Free: 1-(800) 990-2332
Phone: (204) 925-2320
Fax: (204) 237-4618
Web site: www.cdem.com

Further Information

WD is also involved in delivery of information services with the western branches of the Canada Business Service Centres. Further information may also be obtained from any of the Department's regional offices in Winnipeg, Saskatoon, Edmonton and Vancouver together with satellite offices in Calgary and Regina:

Western Economic Diversification Canada
Suite 1500, Canada Place
9700 Jasper Avenue
Edmonton, AB T5J 4H7
Phone: (403) 495-4164
Fax: (413) 495-4557
Toll-Free: 1-(888) 338-9378

Western Economic Diversification
Canada - Satellite Office:
Room 300, 639 - 5th Avenue S.W.
Calgary, AB T3P 0M9
Phone: (403) 292-5458
Fax: (403) 292-5487
Toll-free: 1-(888) 338-9378

Western Economic Diversification Canada
P.O. Box 2025
Suite 601, S.J. Cohen Bldg.
119 - 4th Ave. South
Saskatoon, SK S7K 3S7
Phone: (306) 975-4373
Fax: (306) 975-5484
Toll-free: 1-(888) 338-9378

Western Economic Diversification Canada
700 – 333 Seymour Street
Price Waterhouse Building
Vancouver, BC V6B 5G9
Phone: (604) 666-6256
Fax: (614) 666-2353
Toll-free: 1-(888) 338-9378

Western Economic Diversification Canada
240 Graham Avenue, Room 620
Winnipeg, MB R3C 0J7
Phone: (204) 983-4472
Fax: (204) 983-3852
Toll-free phone: 1-(888) 338-9378

WD Ottawa
Gillin Building
141 Laurier Avenue West, Suite 500
Ottawa, ON K1P 5J3
Phone: (613) 952-2768
Fax (613) 952-9384

Web Site: http://www.wd.gc.ca
Toll free phone number: 1-(888) 338-WEST

FedNor (Federal Economic Development Initiative for Northern Ontario)

FedNor, the Federal Economic Development Initiative for Northern Ontario, is a federal agency designed to strengthen and diversify the economies of Northern Ontario communities. It contributes toward community economic development initiatives, and improves the availability of capital for northern not-for-profit organizations and small business in partnership with lending institutions.

FedNor's mission is to promote economic growth, diversification, job creation and sustainable, self-reliant communities in Northern Ontario by working with community partners and other organizations to improve small business access to capital, information and markets. In support of its mission, FedNor directs its efforts toward planning, developing and implementing innovative strategies designed to meet the needs of Northern Ontario. In addition, FedNor maintains responsibility for delivery of the Community Futures Program throughout Northern and rural Southern Ontario.

FedNor's activities are concentrated in the following areas.

Northern Ontario Development Program

FedNor's Northern Ontario Development Program (NODP) is designed to promote economic growth by supporting projects focussed on the following.

Community Economic Development

Community economic development supports community based planning and assisting in implementing strategic plans. No direct financial assistance is provided to small businesses.

Business Growth and Competitiveness

Business Growth and Competitiveness is designed to foster economic growth and increased competitiveness of Northern Ontario's businesses by working with community and industry stakeholders to invest in projects that improve productivity, reach new markets, facilitate access to capital, foster investment, encourage entrepreneurship and cultivate industry collaboration. The only direct financial assistance to small businesses of under 500 employees is the Youth Internship Program.

Youth Internships - Private Sector Program: supports full-time internships within private sector businesses involved in activities related to:

- innovation (the identification of new products or processes and the evaluation; research and development; and commercialization or implementation of new processes);
- connectedness (enhancing telecommunications capacity and information and communications technology); and,
- trade (improving access to both foreign and domestic markets).

Assistance is provided for up to 50% (to a maximum of $27,500) of salary and benefits for a period of one year. Agreements for periods of less than 52 weeks are pro-rated. In the case of not-for-profit organizations, assistance will cover 90% with the same maximum. **Financial assistance received under Youth Internships is non-repayable.**

Innovation

Innovation is designed to increase the number of businesses in Northern Ontario that are engaged in the applied research and innovation process; and to increase the number of value-added products, processes or services developed and commercialized to enhance productivity and competitiveness in key sectors in Northern Ontario. It is open to not-for-profit organizations, municipalities and small and medium-sized businesses with fewer than 500 employees.

Applied Research and Development (R&D): includes the following:

- proof of concept;
- engineering design;
- prototype development;
- product testing;
- patent registration;
- early stage marketing;
- outreach and promotional initiatives;
- product, process and service certifications;
- market research and technical studies to determine needs and direct future R&D and other related R&D studies; and,
- youth internships (see above) to assist with projects related to R&D for a period of 12 months.

To increase the Level of Innovation, Productivity, Quality and Competitiveness: in

- biotechnology;
- the mining industry;

- the forest industry;
- agri-food;
- information and communications technology;
- renewable energy; and,
- manufacturing.

FedNor states that eligible activities include:

- technology development and acceleration;
- commercialization of intellectual property;
- creating, acquiring or enhancing assets and capacity to support technological innovation, industrial R&D, and creation, adoption or adaptation of technology;
- linking stakeholders in the innovation system to create synergies, optimize information sharing and collaborative working relationships and create or strengthen technology and research clusters;
- acquiring the services of a consultant, accountant or other expertise to complete complex funding applications and proposals to government or other research granting/funding programs;
- training on new equipment or process enhancements in support of technology innovation and transfer;
- completing studies, assessments, analyses and plans of management and operations;
- undertaking feasibility studies, project plans, business plans/strategies, cluster and competitiveness studies; and,
- youth internships (see above) to assist with projects related to innovation for a period of 12 months.

FedNor states that non-capital costs may be covered for up to 50% and include:

- fees for professional and technical services, including technology implementation, engineering services;
- costs related to training on new technology;
- costs related to securing intellectual property, licensing and patent registration;
- costs related to producing and disseminating results of study/plans;

- marketing costs, including design, promotional materials, advertising, product demonstrations and participation at trade shows; and,
- travel expenses and labour costs.

Capital costs may receive up to 33% financial support and may include:

- applied research (**not** basic research) and development needs, such as a laboratory modification;
- servicing of industrial lands;
- leasehold improvements; and,
- machinery, equipment and technology.

All financial assistance (other than Youth Internships) is repayable and applicants are expected to contribute to at least 10% of project costs.

Community Futures Development Corporations (CFDCs)

The Community Futures (CF) Program supports 61 Community Futures Development Corporations (CFDCs) in Ontario with FedNor in charge of 24 in the North. The remaining 37 CFDCs located in the South and East are served by FedDev Ontario. (See below)

Community Futures Development Corporations (CFDCs) offer services that help Ontario's rural and northern communities expand their economies. As a community-based, non-profit organization, each CFDC is run by a board of local volunteers. It is staffed by professionals who encourage entrepreneurship and the pursuit of economic opportunity.

Through Industry Canada and FedNor, the Federal Government provides funding, advice and support to a network of CFDCs across Ontario who carry out the following services:

- strategic community planning and socio-economic development;
- support for community-based projects;
- business information and planning services; and,
- access to capital for small and medium-sized businesses and social enterprises.

The CFDCs offer financing of up to $150,000 in the form of loans, loan guarantees and equity investments. Decisions are made at the local level. Readers should contact their nearest CFDC for details. The list is available at the following Web site: http://www.ontcfdc.com.

Greenstone Economic
Development Corporation
1409 Main Street
Geraldton, ON P0T 1M0
Phone: (807) 854-2273
Fax: (807) 854-2474

Rainy River Future
Development Corporation
608 Scott Street
Fort Frances, ON P9A 1H6
Phone: (807) 274-3276
Fax: (807) 274-6989

Chukuni Communities
Development Corp.
P. O. Box 250
Red Lake, ON P0V 2M0
Phone: (807) 727-3275
Fax: (807) 727-3285

Patricia Area Community Endeavours Inc.
P.O. Box 668
66 Keith Avenue, Unit 2
Dryden, ON P8N 2Z3
Phone: (807) 221-3293
Fax: (807) 221-3294

Atikokan Economic
Development Corporation
P. O. Box 218
Atikokan, ON P0T 1C0
Phone: (807) 597-2757
Fax: (807) 597-2726

Economic Partners / Partenaires dans l'économie
30 rue Front Street, Unit A
Sturgeon Falls, ON P2B 3L4
Phone: (705) 753-5450
Fax: (705) 753-3456

East Algoma CFDC
P.O. Box 398, 1 Industrial Road
Blind River, ON P0R 1B0
Phone: (705) 356-1152
Fax: (705) 356-1711

Superior North Community
Futures Development Corp.
P.O. Box 716, 7 Mill Road
Terrace Bay, ON P0T 2W0
Phone: (807) 825-4505 ext 1
Fax: (807) 825-9664

Nishnawbe Aski Development Fund
106 Centennial Square, 2nd Floor
Thunder Bay, ON P7E 1H3
Phone: (807) 623-5397
Fax: (807) 622-8271

Thunder Bay Ventures
1294 Balmoral Street, Suite 140
P.O. Box 10116
Thunder Bay, ON P7B 6T6
Phone: (807) 768-6650
Fax: (807) 768-6655

Lake of the Woods Business
Incentives Corp.
Bannister Centre, Second Floor
301 First Avenue South
Kenora, ON P9N 1W2
Phone: (807) 467-4640
Fax: (807) 467-4645

Superior East Community
Development Corp.
P.O. Box 709
Wawa, ON P0S 1K0
Phone: (705) 856-1105
Fax: (705) 856-1107

Community Development Corp.
of Sault Ste Marie & Area
672 Queen Street East
Sault Ste Marie, ON P6A 2A4
Phone: (705) 942-9000
Fax: (705) 942-0274

Nord-Aski Regional Economic
Development Corporation
P.O. Box 6000
Hearst, ON P0L 1N0
Phone: (705) 362-7355
Fax: (705) 362-8246

NECO Community Futures
Development Corporation
250 First Ave. W
North Bay ON P1B 3C1
Phone: (705) 476-8822
Fax: (705) 495-6038

Nickel Basin Federal Development Corp.
200 Brady Street Tom Davies Square
Sudbury, ON P3E 5K3
Phone: (705) 673-9802
Fax: (705) 673-7722

North Claybelt Community
Futures Development Corp.
6 Ash Street
Kapuskasing, ON P5N 2C8
Phone: (705) 337-1407
Fax: (705) 337-6285

Waubetek Business
Development Corp.
6 Rainbow Valley Rd.
Birch Island, ON P0P 1A0
Phone: (705) 285-4275
Fax: (705) 285-4584

LAMBAC
P.O. Box 130,
30 Meridith St.
Gore Bay, ON P0P 1H0
Phone: (705) 282-3215
Fax: (705) 282-2989

Kirkland & District
Community Business Corp.
P.O. Box 128
23 Government Road East
Kirkland Lake, ON P2N 3M6
Phone: (705) 567-3331
Fax: (705) 567-6565

Parry Sound Area Community Business &
Development Centre Inc.
1 - A Church Street
Parry Sound, ON P2A 1Y2
Phone: (705) 746-4455
Fax: (705) 746-4435

Muskoka Community Futures
Development Corporation
111 Manitoba Street
Bracebridge, ON P1LH 2B6
Phone: (705) 646-9511
Fax: (705) 646-9522

Wakenagun Community Futures
Development Corp.
28 Amisk, P.O. Box 308
Moose Cree First Nation Reserve #1
Moose Factory, ON P0L 1W0
Phone: (705) 658-4428
Fax: (705) 658-4672

The Venture Centre
38 Pine Street North
Suite 134, 101 Mall
Timmins, ON P4N 6K6
Phone: (705) 360-5800
Fax: (705) 360-5656

South Temiskaming Community
Futures Development Corp
P.O. Box 339
Haileybury, ON P0J 1K0
Phone: (705) 672-3021
Fax: (705) 672-5959

Further Information on FedNor

Web site: http://www.ic.gc.ca/eic/site/fednor-fednor.nsf/eng/home
Phone toll-free: 1-(877) 333-6673

FedNor 6th Floor
2 Queen Street East
Sault Ste. Marie, ON P6A 1Y3
Fax: (705) 941-2085

FedNor
100 Park Street, Suite 107
General Delivery
Kenora, ON P9N 3W9
Fax: (807) 468-2273

FedNor
107 Shirreff Ave., Suite 202
North Bay, ON P1B 7K8
Fax: (705) 494-4227

FedNor
244 Lincoln St.
Thunder Bay, ON P7B 5L2
Fax: (807) 346-8474

FedNor
74 James St
Parry Sound, ON P2A 1T8
Fax: (705) 746-4934

FedNor
120 Cedar St. S., Suite 205
Timmins, ON P4N 2G8
Fax: (705) 267-4939

FedNor
19 Lisgar Street, Room 307
Sudbury, ON P3E 3L4
Fax: (705) 671-0717

FedNor
235 Queen Street 4th Floor
Ottawa, ON K1A 0H5
Phone: (613) 941-4553

FedDev Ontario: Federal Economic
Development Agency for Southern Ontario

Announced in the Federal Budget of 2009, the formation of a Southern Ontario Development Agency (FedDev Ontario) will be designed to help overcome plant closures and slower economic growth in that region and succeed in the knowledge-based economy. It will provide more than $1 billion over five years to support economic and community development, innovation, and economic diversification. It will make contributions to communities, businesses and non-profit organizations.

The Federal Budget of 2013 committed $920 million to renew FedDev Ontario for another five years, starting on April 1, 2014.

As stated in the Federal Government's 2013 budget papers, since its inception, the Agency's main program has supported 341 projects, playing an important role in developing and supporting a more productive, diversified and competitive economy. Notable initiatives supported by FedDev Ontario include the Canadian Manufacturers & Exporters' SMART Program (see separate entry in this publications), which helps small and medium-sized manufacturers increase their productivity and competitiveness in the global economy.

Applied Research and Commercialization Initiative

The Applied Research and Commercialization Initiative is a pilot project to encourage collaboration between small and medium-sized enterprises (SMEs) and post-secondary institutions. Its goals are to accelerate innovation and to improve productivity and competitiveness in SMEs located in southern Ontario by providing up to $15 million in funding to eligible post-secondary institutions in the region.

Investing in Business Innovation

Investing in Business Innovation provides $190 million between 2010 to 2014 to help fund start-up businesses to enable them accelerate the development of new products, processes and practices and bring them to market. Funding is also available for angel investor networks and their associations to attract new investment and support the growth of angel investment funds.

FedDev will provide one-third of eligible and supported costs with at least two-thirds in cash from an angel or venture capital investor. Costs may include labour and operating expenditures, materials and supplies, consulting and/or professional fees (limited to market rate), and minor and non-capital acquisitions. Additional eligible costs for not-for-profit angel investor networks and their associations include travel and meeting costs, and administration (to a maximum of five percent of eligible and supported costs).

Applications are being accepted on an ongoing basis but applicant businesses must have a signed draft term sheet from a recognized angel or venture capital investor.

Prosperity Initiative

The Prosperity Initiative has a $210 million allocation from 2010 to 2014 to encourage businesses, not-for-profit organizations and post-secondary institutions in southern Ontario to undertake projects that will result in a more productive, diversified and competitive economy in the region.

Projects could be those which:.

- enhance productivity;
- diversify the regional economy; and,
- build a competitive advantage for southern Ontario.

Economic Development Initiative (EDI)

FedDev Ontario will invest $4 million during the period up until March 31, 2013 to support business and economic development activities that encourage sustainable growth in Ontario's Francophone communities in two priority areas.

Community Strategic Planning: to enhance the competitiveness of Francophone communities and small and medium-sized enterprises (SMEs).

Business and Economic Development: to foster Francophone tourism, cultural, knowledge-based and manufacturing industries. It will support Youth Internships and strengthen linguistic duality.

Southern Ontario Development Program (SODP)

The Southern Ontario Development Program (SODP) provides funds for projects that can stimulate local economies and enhance the growth and competitiveness of local businesses and communities.

Approximately $100 million was allocated to the SODP in 2009-10, including the following:

- $63 million through a general intake process;
- $20 million through an intake for the food and beverage processing sector;
- $15.75 million for the Canadian Manufacturers and Exporters' (CME) SMART Program to fund an estimated 300 projects that will help small and medium-sized manufacturers increase their productivity and competitiveness in the global economy; and,

- $1.6 million for the Ontario Chamber of Commerce's Export Market Access Program to help southern Ontario businesses that would like to increase their sales internationally.

Eastern Ontario Development Program (EODP)

The Eastern Ontario Development Program (EODP) assists economic renewal in five priority areas:

- business and community development;
- skills development;
- access to capital;
- retention and attraction of youth; and,
- technological enhancements.

Funding and support of the EODP is delivered via the Community Futures Development Corporations (CFDCs) located throughout Eastern Ontario.

Community Futures (CF) Program

The Community Futures (CF) Program supports 61 Community Futures Development Corporations (CFDCs) in Ontario with FedDev Ontario in charge of 37 in rural Eastern and Southern Ontario. The remaining 24 CFDCs located in the North are served by FedNor.

The CFDCs provide:

- strategic community planning and socio-economic development;
- support for community-based projects;
- business information and planning services; and,
- access to capital for small and medium-sized businesses and social enterprises.

These community-based, not-for-profit organizations are staffed by professionals and are each governed by local volunteer boards of directors familiar with their communities' needs, concerns and future development priorities.

The CFDCs servicing southern and eastern Ontario are as follows:

Prince Edward/Lennox & Addington
Community Futures Development Corp.
280 Main Street
Picton, ON K0K 2T0
Phone: (613) 476-7901
Fax: (613) 476-7235

Community Futures Development
Corporation of Chatham/Kent
245 Marlborough Street
P.O. Box 192
Blenheim, ON N0P 1A0
Phone: (519) 676-7775
Fax: (519) 676-9732

Community Futures Development
Corporation of Middlesex County
Unit # 6 R.R. # 3
22423 Jefferies Road
Komoka, ON N0L 1R0
Phone: (519) 641-6100
Fax: (519) 641-6288

Valley Heartland Community
Futures Development Corp.
91 Cornelia Street
Smiths Falls, ON K7A 5L3
Phone: (613) 283-7002
Fax: (613) 283-7005

Grenville Community Futures
Development Corp.
P.O. Box 309
Prescott, ON K0E 1T0
Phone: (613) 925-4275
Fax: (613) 925-3758

1000 Islands Community
Development Corp.
3 Market St. W.
Brockville, ON K6V7L3
Phone: (613) 345-6216
Fax: (613) 345-2391

Renfrew County Community Futures
Development Corp.
2 International Drive
Pembroke, ON K8A 6W5
Phone: (613) 735-3951
Fax: (613) 735-7840

Tecumseh Community
Development Corp.
R.R. # 1- 311 Jubilee Rd.
Muncey, ON N0L 1V0
Phone: (519) 289-2122
Fax: (519) 289-5550

Elgin Community Futures
Development Corp.
300 South Edgeware Road
St. Thomas, ON N5P 4L1
Phone: (519) 633-7597
Fax: (519) 633-5070

Sarnia-Lambton Business
Development Corp.
109 Durand Street Unit #16
Sarnia, ON N7S 5A1
Phone: (519) 383-1371
Fax: (519) 383-8115

Norfolk District Business
Development Corp.
P.O. Box 732
Simcoe, ON N3Y 4T2
Phone: (519) 428-2323
Fax: (519) 428-0074

Wellington-Waterloo CFDC
Old Quarry Commons
294 Mill Street East, Unit 207
Elora, ON N0B 1S0
Phone: (519) 846-9839
Fax: (519) 846-2343

Saugeen Economic Development Corporation
515 Mill Street PO Box 177
Neustadt, ON N0G 2M0
Phone: (519) 799-5750
Fax: (519) 799-5752

Business Development Centre
of Greater Fort Erie
45 Jarvis Street
Fort Erie, ON L2A 2S3
Phone: (905) 871-7331
Fax: (905) 871-5284

Two Rivers Community
Developemnt Centre
P.O. Box 225
Oshweken, ON N0A 1M0
Phone: (519) 445-4567
Fax: (519) 445-2154

South Niagara Community
Futures Development Corporation
198 Welland Street, 2nd Floor
P.O. Box 519
Port Colborne, ON L3K 5X7
Phone: (905) 834-2173
Fax: (905) 834-4225

Grand Erie Business Centre Inc.
11 Argyle Street North
Suite 207
Caledonia, ON N3W 1B6
Phone: (905) 765-5005
Fax: (905) 765-5750

S.D. & G. Community Futures
Development Corp.
26 Pitt Street
Cornwall, ON K6J 3P2
Phone: (613) 932-4333
Fax: (613) 932-0596

Prescott-Russell Community
Development Corporation
519 rue Principal est
Hawkesbury, ON K6A 1B3
Phone: (613) 632-0918
Fax: (613) 632-7385

Venture Niagara
20 Pine St. N., Studio A
Thorold ON L2V 1A0
Phone: (905) 735-8085
Fax: (905) 735-7253

Huron Business
Development Corp.
138 Main Street South
Seaforth, ON N0K 1W0
Phone: (519) 527-0305
Fax: (519) 527-2245

Enterprise Brant
330 West Street, Unit 10
Brantford, ON N3R 7V5
Phone: (519) 752-4636
Fax: (519) 759-0098

Perth Community Futures
Development Corporation
150 St. Patrick Street
Stratford, ON N5A 1A9
Phone: (519) 595-7570
Fax: (519) 595-7573

Oxford Small Business
Support Centre Inc.
118 Oxford Street
Ingersoll, ON N5C 2V5
Phone: (519) 425-0401
Fax: (519) 425-0803

Essex Community Futures
Development Corporation
39 Maidstone Avenue East
Essex, ON N8M 2J3
Phone: (519) 776-4611
Fax: (519) 776-9297

Bruce Community
Futures Development Corp.
P.O. Box 208
Kincardine, ON N2Z 2Y7
Phone: (519) 396-8141
Fax: (519) 396-8346

Orillia Area Community
Development Corporation
22 Peter St. S. Box 2525
Orillia, Ontario L3V 7A3
Phone: (705) 325-4903
Fax: (705) 325-6817

South Lake Community Futures
Development Corporation
183 The Queensway
Keswick, ON L4P 2A3
Phone: (905) 476-1244
Fax: (905) 476-9978

Centre For Business
and Economic Development
450 Hume Street, Unit #2
Collingwood, ON L9Y 1W6
Phone: (705) 445-8410
Fax: (705) 444-6082

Nottawasaga Futures
PO Box 184
Alliston, ON L9R 1V5
Phone: (705) 435-1540
Fax: (705) 435-6907

North Simcoe Community Futures
Development Corp.
355 Cranston Crescent,
P.O. Box 8,
Midland, ON L4R 4K6
Phone: (705) 526-1371
Fax: (705) 526-4993

Land O'Lakes
Small Business Corporation
Box 209
Sharbot Lake, ON K0H 2P0
Phone: (613) 279-2056
Fax: (613) 279-2609

Frontenac CFDC
P.O. Box 53
Harrowsmith, ON K0H 1V0
Phone: (613) 372-1414
Fax: (613) 372-9962

Kawartha Lakes Community
Futures Development Corp.
189 Kent St W, Suite 211
Lindsay, ON K9V 5G6
Phone: (705) 328-0261
Fax: (705) 328-3684

Trenval Business
Development Corp.
284B Wallbridge Loyalist Road
Belleville, ON K8N 5B3
Phone: (613) 961-7999
Fax: (613) 961-7998

Haliburton County
Development Corp.
P.O. Box 210
Haliburton, ON K0M 1S0
Phone: (705) 457-3555
Fax: (705) 457-3398

Peterborough
Community Development Corporation
351 Charlotte Street
Peterborough, ON K9J 2W1
Phone: (705) 745-5434
Fax: (705) 745-2369

Prince Edward/Lennox
& Addington CFDC - Satelllite Office
47 Dundas St. East
Napanee, ON K7R 1H7
Phone: (613) 354-0162
Fax: (613) 354-2361

CFDC of North & Central Hastings
and South Algonquin
26 Chemaushgon Street
P.O. Box 517
Bancroft, ON K0L 1C0
Phone: (613) 332-5564
Fax: (613) 332-5628

Northumberland Community Futures
Development Corporation
600 William Street Suite 600
Cobourg, ON K9A 3A5
Phone: (905) 372-8315
Fax: (905) 372-2238

Further Information on FedDev Ontario

FedDev Ontario has its headquarters in Kitchener, with branches in Ottawa, Toronto, Peterborough and Stratford.

FedDev Ontario (Headquarters)
101 Frederick Street, 4th floor
Kitchener, ON N2H 6R2
Phone toll-free: 1-(866) 593-5505
Fax: (519) 571-5750

FedDev Ontario
155 Queen Street, 14th floor
Ottawa, ON
Phone toll-free: 1-(866) 593-5505
Fax: (613) 952-9026

FedDev Ontario
151 Yonge Street
Toronto, ON M5C 2W7
Phone toll-free: 1-(866) 593-5505

FedDev Ontario
143 Simcoe Street
Peterborough, ON K9H 0A3
Phone toll-free: 1-(866) 593-5505
Fax: 705-750-4827

CME SMART Prosperity Now Program:

The CME SMART Prosperity Now Program received another round of funding in early 2012 and the name has been changed to CME SMART Prosperity Now: New Technology Expansion Funds for Export. It is funded by the Government of Ontario and the Southern Ontario Development Program (FedDev Ontario) but is administered by Canadian Manufacturers & Exporters (CME). It is to help small and medium-sized manufacturers in

110

Ontario improve their productivity as well as for business expansion so they can compete more effectively in the global economy.

There are two components as follows.

Assessment Component: which can cover up to 50% of costs to a maximum of $5,000 per assessment to help applicants develop a vision and strategy.

Project Funding Component: will assist with lean design and lean manufacturing, quality improvement, energy efficiency, IT best practices, and environmental impact reduction can provide support of up to 33.3% funding to a maximum of $75,000.

Total funding under both components cannot exceed $100,000 and funding under other government assistance programs cannot be accepted.

The Program has been designed to support approximately 325 projects.

It should be noted that the application intake process will close on May 31, 2013.

CME SMART Prosperity Now Program
Canadian Manufacturers & Exporters (CME)
6725 Airport Road, Suite 200
Mississauga, ON L4V 1V2
Phone: (905) 672-3466 xt. 3281
Phone toll-free: 1-(877) 913-4263
Fax: (905) 672-1764
Web site: www.cme-smart.ca

Eastern Ontario Development Fund

The Eastern Ontario Development Fund was announced in 2008 as a four-year program. Which has since been extended, although funding is limited. There are two funding streams,

111

one for established businesses and a regional stream for economic development organizations including municipalities.

Under the business stream, the fund may provide up to 15% of eligible project costs to a maximum grant of $1.5 million. For project investments of over $10 million that create 50 or more jobs, funding may be available in the form of a secured repayable loan, to a maximum of $5 million in provincial support. Under the regional stream, the fund may provide up to 50% of eligible project costs to a maximum grant of $1.5 million.

In order to be eligible businesses must:

- employ at least 10 people and meet certain minimum job creation thresholds;
- be able to provide three years of financial statements;
- be part of an eligible sector;
- be located in, or plan to locate in Eastern Ontario;
- have a multi year project that involves a minimum investment of $500,000 in eligible project costs.

It should be noted that businesses with 5-10 employees may be eligible under the Small Community Pilot provided they are located in municipalities with a population of less than 20,000 or with a population density of less than 100 persons per square kilometres. Projects must be a minimum investment of $200,000 over 4 years (compared to core program of $500,000). Those companies must create 50% of current employment.

Applications are accepted on a continuous intake basis.

Eastern Ontario Development Fund
Ministry of Economic Development, Trade and Employment
366 King Street East, Suite 340
Kingston, ON K7K 6Y3
Phone: (613) 542-7266
Phone toll-free: 1-(866) 909-9951
Fax: (866) 695-9951

Canada Economic Development (CED) for Québec Regions

Canada Economic Development (CED) is a major player in Québec's economic development and a leading partner of Small and Medium-Sized Enterprises (SMEs) and their support organizations.

Create or Start a Business

This program is open to the following:

- pre-startup and startup businesses;
- non-profit organizations;
- business support organizations;
- business incubation organizations;
- entrepreneurship support and research organizations;
- technology transfer centres;
- economic development organizations; and,
- university value-added corporations.

It is not open to retail businesses.

Activities can involve:

- development of new products and services;
- technology transfer to businesses;
- spinoff;
- business incubation;
- patent or license purchase;
- certification activities;
- purchase of equipment, computer tools and technology;
- fit-up, expansion or construction upgrading of facilities;
- pre-commercialization activities;

- implementation of a marketing strategy;
- management capacity building;
- recruitment of specialized resources;
- knowledge transfer;
- strategy development;
- development of business leads and searching for funding;
- networking;
- consulting and guidance services; and,
- information services

Assistance can be offered in the form of either a repayable contribution or a non-repayable contribution of up to 50% of authorized costs for SMEs or up to 90% for non-profit organizations (NPOs).

Plan a Business Succession

Assistance for planning for a business succession is open to small and medium-sized enterprices (SMEs) and organizations operating facilities or engaged in commercial activities, non-profit organizations and organizations and institutions dedicated to the promotion and dissemination of knowledge. Assistance is not provided for retail businesses.

Projects are reviewed based on specific criteria:

- anticipated results of the project;
- viability of the business or organization;
- the technical and financial management capacity;
- partner contributions in financial resources or professional services; and,
- the level of risk.

Examples of activities that could qualify are as follows:

- management capacity building;
- recruitment of specialized resources;

- knowledge transfer;
- strategy development;
- development of business leads and searching for funding;
- networking;
- consulting and guidance services; and,
- information services.

Assistance can be in the form of a repayable contribution or a non-repayable contribution of up to 50% of authorized costs for SMEs and up to 90% of authorized costs for NPOs.

Eligible are all costs directly related to the project, deemed reasonable and essential to its completion. Restrictions may apply in certain cases.

Improve a Business's Productivity

This program is open to businesses in the manufacturing, tourism or value-added service sectors; sector-based business groups or associations and non-profit organizations. It is not open to retail businesses.

Projects are reviewed based on specific criteria as follows:

- anticipated results of the project;
- viability of the business or organization;
- the technical and financial management capacity;
- partner contributions in financial resources or professional services; and,
- the level of risk.

Activities can be funded such as:

- purchase of equipment, computer tools and technology;
- fit-up, upgrading, expansion or construction of facilities;
- improvement of processes;
- improvement of operations management;

- improvement of existing products and services;
- patent or license purchase;
- certification activities;
- management capacity building;
- recruitment of specialized resources;
- knowledge transfer;
- strategy development;
- development of business leads and searching for funding;
- networking;
- consulting and guidance services; and,
- information services.

Assistance can be in the form of repayable contributions or non-repayable contributions of up to 50% of authorized costs for SMEs and 90% for NPOs,

Authorized costs are defined as those directly related to the project, deemed reasonable and essential to its completion.

Innovate, Adopt a Technology, or Ensure Technology Transfer

This program is open to:

- businesses - SMEs and organizations operating facilities or engaged in commercial activities;
- non-profit organizations;
- business support organizations;
- technology transfer centers;
- knowledge institutions;
- university value-added corporations;
- college centres for technology transfer;
- private laboratories; and,
- business associations

It is not open to retail businesses.

Projects are reviewed based on specific criteria:

- anticipated results of the project;
- viability of the business or organization;
- the technical and financial management capacity;
- partner contributions in financial resources or professional services; and,
- the level of risk.

Eligible activities can include:

- development of new products and services;
- improvement of existing products and services;
- purchase of equipment, computer tools and technology;
- technology transfer to businesses;
- patent or license purchase;
- business-related applied research;
- management capacity building;
- recruitment of specialized resources;
- associations, alliances and partnerships;
- knowledge transfer;
- prototyping, proof of concept, demonstration, technology showcases;
- strategy development;
- development of business leads and searching for funding;
- networking;
- consulting and guidance services; and,
- information services.

Assistance can be in the form of both repayable contributions and non-repayable contributions of up to 50% of authorized costs for SMEs and up to 90% of authorized costs for NPOs.

Authorized costs are those directly related to the project, deemed reasonable and essential to its completion. Restrictions may apply in certain cases.

Market or Export

Designed to help increase market share, work within value chains or penetrate new markets.

The program is open to SMEs and organizations operating facilities or engaged in commercial activities; non-profit organizations; organizations dedicated to commercialization and exports; and, business associations. It is not open to retail businesses.

Projects are reviewed based on specific criteria:

- anticipated results of the project;
- viability of the business or organization;
- the technical and financial management capacity;
- partner contributions in financial resources or professional services; and,
- the level of risk.

Examples of activities that are acceptable include:

- development of distribution network;
- purchase of equipment, computer tools and technology;
- prototyping, proof of concept, demonstration, technology showcases;
- implementation of a commercialization strategy;
- patent or license purchase;
- certification activities;
- management capacity building
- recruitment of specialized resources;
- associations, alliances and partnerships;
- knowledge transfer;
- strategy development;
- development of business leads and searching for funding;

- networking
- consulting and guidance services; and,
- information services.

Assistance can be in the form of repayable contributions or non-repayable contributions of up to 50% of authorized costs for SMEs and 90% for NPOs..

Authorized costs are defined as all those directly related to the project, deemed reasonable and essential to its completion. Restrictions may apply in certain cases.

Structure a Network

This program is not open to for-profit businesses in the private sector.

Community Futures Program (CFP)

The Community Futures Program (CFP) is managed by CED through the Community Futures Development Corporations (CFDCs) in designated rural areas throughout the Province. In addition, there is a network of Community Economic Development Corporations (CEDCs).

Capital Loans and Loan Guarantees: are provided up to a maximum of $150,000 for business start-up, expansion, equipment acquisition or business consolidation.

Youth Strategy Initiative: provides two-year interest-free loans from $5,000 to $15,000 for youth aged 18 to 35 years to help them acquire, expand, establish and upgrade businesses in their communities.

Special Fund for Business Start-ups and Succession: can provide interest-fee loans of up to $50,000 for up to eight years to facilitate the transfer of ownership of an existing business.

List of Community Futures Development Corporations (CFDCs)

SADC Pierre-de-Saurel
50, rue du Roi, bureau 2
Sorel-Tracy QC J3P 4M7
Phone: (450) 746-5595
Fax: (450) 746-1803

SADC Bellechasse-Etchemins
494-B, rue Principale, C.P. 158
Saint-Léon-de-Standon, QC G0R 4L0
Phone: (418) 642-2844
Fax: (418) 642-5316

SADC Centre-de-la-Mauricie
812, avenue des Cèdres
Shawinigan QC G9N 1P2
Phone: (819) 537-5107
Fax: (819) 537-5109

SADC de Charlevoix
11, rue Saint-Jean-Baptiste, bureau 208
Baie Saint-Paul QC G3Z 1M1
Phone: (418) 435-4033
Fax: (418) 435-4050

SADC Chibougamau-Chapais
600, 3e Rue, bureau 1
Chibougamau QC G8P 1P1
Phone: (418) 748-6477
Fax: (418) 748-7704

SADC Côte-Nord inc.
456, av. Arnaud, bureau 205
Sept-Iles QC G4R 3B1
Phone: (418) 962-7233
Fax: (418) 968-5513

SADC des Basques
400-3, rue Jean Rioux
Trois-Pistoles QC G0L 4K0
Phone: (418) 851-3172
Fax: (418) 851-3171

Eeyou Economic Group
58 Pine Street, P.O. Box 39
Waswanipi QC J0Y 3C0
Phone: (819) 753-2560
Fax: (819) 753-2568

SADC du Fjord inc.
3031 Monseigneur-Dufour Street
La Baie, QC G7B 1E8
Phone: (418) 544-2885
Fax: (418) 544-0303

SADC de l'Amiante
1035 Notre-Dame Street E
Thetford Mines, QC   G6G 2T4
Phone: (418) 338-4531
Fax: (418) 338-9256

SADC de Gaspé
15, rue Adams, bureau 200
C.P. 5012 Gaspé QC G4X 1E5
Phone: (418) 368-2906
Fax: (418) 368-3927

SADC de Gaspé-Nord
Édifice des Monts, 1er étage
10G boulevard Sainte-Anne Ouest
Sainte-Anne-des-Monts QC G4V 1P3
Phone: (418) 763-5355
Fax: (418) 763-2933

SADC Harricana inc.
550 1st Avenue W
Amos, QC J9T 1V3
Phone: (819) 732-8311
Fax: (819) 732-2240

SADC Haute-Côte-Nord inc.
459, Route 138, bureau 200
Les Escoumins QC G0T 1K0
Phone: (418) 233-3495
Fax: (418) 233-2485

SADC du Haut-Saguenay
328, rue Gagnon
St-Ambroise QC G7P 2P9
Phone: (418) 672-6333
Fax: (418) 672-4882

SADC du Haut-Saint-François
47, rue Angus Nord
East Angus QC J0B 1R0
Phone: (819) 832-2447
Fax: (819) 832-1831

SADC du Haut-Saint-Maurice inc.
290, rue St-Joseph
La Tuque QC G9X 3Z8
Phone: (819) 523-4227
Fax: (819) 523-5722

SADC des Iles-de-la-Madeleine
735, chemin Principal
C.P. 940, Cap-aux-Meules
Îles-de-la-Madeleine QC G0B 1B0
Phone: (418) 986-4601
Fax: (418) 986-4874

SADC Kamouraska
900, 6e Ave., bur.2, La Pocatière QC G0R 1Z0
Phone: (418) 856-3482
Fax: (418) 856-5053

Des Collines service point
77 Route Principale E, P.O. Box 29
La Pêche, QC J0X 2W0
Phone: (819) 456-4440

SADC Lac-Saint-Jean Ouest inc.
915, boulevard St-Joseph, bureau 102
Roberval QC G8H 2M1
Phone: (418) 275-2531
Fax: (418) 275-5787

SADC La Mitis
1534, boulevard Jacques-Cartier, bureau 101
Mont-Joli QC G5H 2V8
Phone: (418) 775-4619
Fax: (418) 775-5504

SADC de Lotbinière
238, route 269
Saint-Patrice-de-Beaurivage, QC G0S 1B0
Phone: (418) 596-3300
Fax: (418) 596-3303

SADC Manicouagan
67, place LaSalle, bureau 301
Baie-Comeau, QC G4Z 1K1
Phone: (418) 296-6956
Fax: (418) 296-5176

SADC Maria-Chapdelaine
201 Des Pères Boulevard, Suite 200
Dolbeau-Mistassini, QC G8L 5K6
Phone: (418) 276-0405
Fax: (418) 276-0623

SADC Arthabaska-Érable inc.
975, boul. Industriel Est, bureau 101
Victoriaville   QC G6T 1T8
Phone: (819) 758-1501
Fax: (819) 758-7971

SADC Matapédia inc.
123, rue Desbiens, 4e étage, bureau 401
Amqui QC G5J 3P9
Phone: (418) 629-4474
Fax: (418) 629-5530

SADC de la MRC de Maskinongé
651, boul Saint-Laurent Est
Louiseville QC J5V 1J1
Phone: (819)228-5921
Fax: (819)228-0497

SADC Nicolet-Bécancour inc.
19205, boul. des Acadiens
Bécancour QC G9H 1M5
Phone: (819) 233-3315
Fax: (819) 233-3338

SADC Nunavik Investment Corporation
P.O. Box 789
Kuujjuaq QC J0M 1C0
Phone: (819) 964-1872
Fax: (819) 964-1497

SADC Baie-des-Chaleurs
152-A, boul. Perron Ouest, bureau 201
New Richmond QC G0C 2B0
Phone: (418) 392-5014
Fax: (418) 392-5425

SADC Pontiac CFDC
1409, route 148
C.P. 425
Campbell's Bay, QC J0X 1K0
Phone: (819) 648-2186
Fax: (819) 648-2226

SADC région d'Asbestos
309, Chassé
Asbestos QC J1T 2B4
Phone: (819)879-7147
Fax: (819) 879-5188

SADC région de Coaticook
38 Child Street, Suite 140
Coaticook, QC J1A 2B1
Phone: (819) 849-3053
Fax: (819) 849-9683

SADC de la région de Matane
235, avenue St-Jérôme, bureau 312
Matane QC G4W 3A7
Phone: (418) 562-3171
Fax: (418) 562-1259

SADC région de Mégantic
5137, rue Frontenac
Lac-Mégantic QC G6B 1H2
Phone: (819) 583-5332
Fax: (819) 583-5957

SADC du Rocher-Percé
129, boul. René-Lévesque Ouest
C.P. 186
Chandler QC G0C 1K0
Phone: (418) 689-5699
Fax: (418) 689-5556

SADC du Rouyn-Noranda régional inc.
161, av. Murdoch
Rouyn-Noranda QC J9X 1E3
Phone: (819) 797-6068
Fax: (819) 797-0096

SADC du Témiscamingue
7B, rue des Oblats Nord
Ville-Marie QC J9V 1H9
Phone: (819) 629-3355
Fax: (819) 629-2793

Service point
8 King St. Huntingdon
QC J0S 1H0
Phone: (450) 264-7060

SADC Vallée de la Batiscan
390 Goulet Street
Saint-Stanislas, QC G0X 3E0
Phone: (418) 328-4200
Fax: (418) 328-4201

SADC Suroît-Sud
50, Jacques Cartier, 2e étage
Salaberry-de-Valleyfield QC J6T 4R3
Phone: (450) 370-3332
Fax: (450) 370-4448

SADC Matagami
180, place du Commerce, C.P. 910
Matagami QC J0Y 2A0
Phone: (819) 739-2155
Fax: (819) 739-4271

SADC Abitibi-Ouest
80, 12e Avenue Est # 202
La Sarre QC J9Z 3K6
Phone: (819)333-3113
Fax: (819)333-3132

SADC Barraute-Senneterre-Quévillon inc.
674, 11e Avenue, C.P. 308
Senneterre QC J0Y 2M0
Phone: (819) 737-2211
Fax: (819) 737-8888

SADC des Laurentides
1332, boul. Sainte-Adèle, bureau 230
Sainte-Adèle QC J8B 2N5
Phone: (450) 229-3001
Fax: (450) 229-6928

SADC de Portneuf
299 1st Ave. Portneuf, QC G0A 2Y0
Phone: (418) 286-4422

SADC région d'Acton inc.
1545, rue Peerless, bureau 101
Acton Vale QC J0H 1A0
Phone: (450) 546-3239
Fax: (450) 546-3619

SADC Vallée-de-la-Gatineau
100, rue Principale Sud, bureau 210
Maniwaki QC J9E 3L4
Phone: (819) 449-1551
Fax: (819) 449-7431

SADC Vallée-de-l'Or
40, place Hammond, suite 201
Val-d'Or QC J9P 3A9
Phone: (819) 874-3676
Fax: (819) 874-3670

SADC de Papineau Inc.
565, Avenue de Buckingham
Gatineau QC J8L 2H2
Phone: (819) 986-1747
Fax: (819) 281-0303

SADC de la M.R.C. de Rivière-du-Loup
646, rue Lafontaine
Rivière-du-Loup QC G5R 3C8
Phone: (418) 867-4272
Fax: (418) 867-8060

SADC de la Neigette
671 des Pionniers Street
Rimouski, QC G5N 5P4
Phone: (418) 735-2514

SADC Lac-Saint-Jean-Est inc.
625, Bergeron Ouest
Alma QC G8B 1V3
Phone: (418) 668-3148
Fax: (418) 668-6977

SADC Matawinie inc.
1080, route 343
Saint-Alphonse-Rodriguez, QC J0K 1W0
Phone: (450) 883-0717
Fax: (450) 883-2006

SADC de D'Autray-Joliette
550 Montcalm St., Suite 500
Berthierville, QC J0K 1A0
Phone: (450) 887-0990
Fax: (450) 887-0994

SADC Achigan-Montcalm inc.
104 Saint-Jacques St.
Saint-Jacques, QC J0K 2R0
Phone: (450) 839-9218
Fax: (450) 839-7036

SADC d'Antoine-Labelle
636, rue de la Madone, bureau 4
Mont-Laurier QC J9L 1S9
Phone: (819) 623-3300
Fax: (819) 623-7300

List of Economic Development Corporations (CEDCs)

Centre-Sud/Plateau Mont-Royal CEDC
3565, rue Berri, Bureau 200
Montréal QC H2L 4G3
Phone: (514) 845-2332
Fax: (514) 845-7244
Web site: http://www.cdec-cspmr.org/
E-mail:courriel@cdec-cspmr.org

CEDC Ahuntsic-Cartierville
9200, boul. de l'Acadie, bureau 104
Montréal QC H4N 2T2
Phone: (514) 858-1018
Fax: (514) 858-1153
Web site: http://www.cdec.qc.ca/
E-mail: info@cdec.qc.ca

Centre-Nord CEDC
7000, avenue du Parc, bureau 201
Montréal QC H3N 1X1
Phone : (514) 948-6117
Fax: (514) 948-4903
Web site: http://www.cdec-centrenord.org/
E-mail: avenir@cdec-centrenord.org

RESO
1751, rue Richardson, bureau 6509
Montréal QC H3K 1G6
Phone: (514) 931-5737
Web site: http://www.resomtl.com/
E-mail: reso@resomtl.com

Côte-des-Neiges/Notre-Dame-de-Grâce CEDC
4950, chemin Queen Mary, office 101
Montréal QC H3W 1X3
Phone: (514) 342-4842
Fax: (514) 342-4712
Web site: http://www.cdeccdnndg.org/
E-mail: cdec@cdeccdnndg.org

Rosemont - Petite-Patrie CEDC
2339, rue Beaubien Est
Montréal QC H2G 1N1
Phone: (514) 723-0030
Fax: (514) 723-0032
E-mail: cdecrppreception@videotron.ca

CDEC LaSalle – Lachine
410 Lafleur Avenue, Suite 50
LaSalle, QVC H8R 3H6
Phone: (514) 367-1891

Anjou/Montréal-Nord CEDC
7701 Louis-H-Lafontaine Boulevard
Anjou, QC H1K 4B9
Phone: (514) 353-7171
Fax: (514) 353-5832
Web site: http://www.cldamn.qc.ca
E-mail: info@cldamn.qc.ca

CDEC de Québec
155, boul. Charest Est, RC-1
Québec QC G1K 3G6
Phone: (418) 525-5526
Fax: (418) 525-4965
Web site: www.cdecdequebec.qc.ca

Quebec association of CEDCs
4435, rue de Rouen
Montréal QC H1V 1H1
Phone: (514) 256-6825

Canada Economic Development for Québec Regions Business Offices

Head Office

Economic Development Agency of Canada for the Regions of Québec
Dominion Square Building
1255 Peel St., Suite 900
Montréal, Quebec H3B 2T9
Phone: (514) 283-6412
Phone toll-free: 1-(866) 385-6412
Fax: (514) 283-3302
Web site: http://www.dec-ced.gc.ca

Abitibi-Témiscamingue
906 5th Avenue, Val-d'Or, QC J9P 1B9
Phone: (819) 825-5260
Toll-free:1-(800) 567-6451
Fax: (819) 825-3245

Bas-Saint-Laurent
2 Saint-Germain Street East, Suite 310
Rimouski, QC G5L 8T7
Phone: (418) 722-3282
Toll-free phone: 1-(800) 463-9073
Fax: (418) 722-3285

Centre-du-Québec
1100 René-Lévesque Boulevard, Suite 105
Drummondville, QC J2C 5W4
Phone: (819) 478-4664
Toll-free phone: 1-(800) 567-1418
Fax: (819) 478-4666

Québec – Chaudière-Appalaches
2954 Laurier Blvd., Suite 030
Québec QC G1V 4T2
Phone: (418) 648-4826
Toll-free phone: 1-(800) 463-5204
Fax: (418) 648-7291

Côte-Nord
701 Laure Blvd, Suite 202B
P.O. Box 698, Sept-Îles, QC G4R 4K9
Phone: (418) 968-3426
Toll-free phone: 1-(800) 463-1707
Fax: (418) 968-0806

Eastern Townships
202 Wellington Street North, Suite 100
Sherbrooke, QC J1H 5C6
Phone: (819) 564-5904
Toll-free phone: 1-(800) 567-6084
Fax: (819) 564-5912

Gaspésie — Îles-de-la-Madeleine
Place Jacques-Cartier
120 de la Reine Street 3rd Floor
Gaspé QC G4X 2S1
Phone: (418) 368-5870
Toll-free phone: 1-(866) 368-0044
Fax: (418) 368-6256

Île-de-Montréal
3340 de l'Assomption Blvd.
Montréal, QC H1N 3S4
Phone: (514) 283-2500
Fax: (514) 496-8310

Laval, Laurentides, Lanaudière
2990 Pierre-Péladeau Avenue, Suite 410
Laval QC H7T 3B3
Phone: (450) 973-6844
Toll-free phone: 1-(800) 430-6844
Fax: (450) 973-6851

Mauricie
Immeuble Bourg du Fleuve
25 des Forges Street, Suite 413
Trois-Rivières, QC G9A 2G4
Phone: (819) 371-5182
Toll-free phone: 1-(800) 567-8637
Fax: (819) 371-5186

Montérégie
101 Roland-Therrien Blvd., Suite 400
Longueuil QC J4H 4B9
Phone: (450) 928-4088
Toll-free phone: 1-(800) 284-0335
Fax: (450) 928-4097

Nord-du-Québec
1255 Peel Street, Suite 900
Montréal QC H3B 2T9
Phone: (514) 283-8131
Toll-free phone: 1-(800) 561-0633
Fax: (514) 283-3637

Outaouais
259 Saint-Joseph Blvd, Suite 202
Gatineau, QC J8Y 6T1
Phone: (819) 994-7442
Toll-free phone: 1-(800) 561-4353
Fax: (819) 994-7846

Saguenay--Lac-Saint-Jean
100 Saint-Joseph Street South, Suite 203
Alma QC G8B 7A6
Phone: (418) 668-3084
Toll-free phone: 1-(800) 463-9808
Fax: (418) 668-7584

Québec City
Place Iberville IV
2954 Laurier Blvd., Suite 030
Québec, QC G1V 4T2
Phone: (418) 648-4826
Phone toll-free:1-(800) 463-5204
Fax: (418) 648-7291

Centres d'Aide aux Entreprises (CAE)

The Centres d'Aide aux Entreprises (CAE) are not-for-profit corporations which were originally supported by the Government of Canada. They are designed to promote and develop their local region's economy by providing financial aid and counsel to encourage the creation and maintenance of employment.

Their board of directors are made up of representatives from business and the professions in the communities which they serve.

Their addresses are as follows:

Centre d'aide aux entreprises Haute-Montérégie (CAE)
Parc industriel E.L. Farrar
700 Lucien-Beaudin
Saint-Jean-sur-Richelieu QC J2X 5M3
Phone: (450) 357-9800
Montréal: (514) 990-0737
Fax: (450) 357-9583
E-mail address: info@caehm.com
Web site: www.caehm.com

Centre d'aide aux entreprises Haute-Yamaska et Région (CAE)
166, rue Boivin, Granby QC J2G 2J7
Phone: (450) 378-2294
Fax: 450 378-7370
E-mail: info@caehyr.com
Web site: www.caehyr.com

Centre d'aide aux entreprises de la Rive-Sud (CAE)
230, rue Brébeuf, bureau 203
Beloeil QC J3G 5P3
Phone: (450) 446-3650
Fax: (450) 446-3806
E-mail: caers@videotron.ca
Web site: www.caers.ca

Société d'aide au développement de la collectivité de la région d'Acton (SADC)
1545, rue Peerless, bureau 101
Acton Vale QC J0H 1A0
Phone: (450) 546-3239
Fax: (450) 546-3619
E-mail sadcacton@cooptel.qc.ca
Web site: www.sadcacton.qc.ca

Société d'aide au développement des collectivités du Bas-Richelieu (SADC)
67, rue George, bureau 101
Sorel-Tracy (Québec) J3P 1C2
Phone: (450) 746-5595
Fax (450) 746-1803
E-mail: sadc@bellnet.ca
Web site: www.soreltracyregion.net

Atlantic Canada Opportunities Agency (ACOA)

ACOA was established in 1987 as a federal government agency to assist in the economic development of Atlantic Canada. ACOA offers assistance in a number of areas.

Business Development Program (BDP)

The ACOA Business Development Program (BDP) provides assistance to small and medium-sized businesses in Atlantic Canada to start-up, expand, modernize and become more competitive. Non-profit organizations providing support to the business community may also qualify.

Most business sectors are eligible except retail, wholesale, real estate, government services and services of a personal or social nature.

Applications can be made by both commercial enterprises as well as not-for-profit organizations. In the for-profit area, eligible activities include the following:

- business start-up, expansion or modernization;
- developing business ideas, innovation, research and development;
- public tender bid preparation activities;
- training, productivity or quality improvements and development of environmental management systems;
- trade development and marketing; and,
- consulting advice.

For non-profits assistance can cover:

- training skills development, planning business counselling and advice;
- research and development, testing technical or innovation services;
- business networking and market development; and/or,
- construction, renovation or expansion of a facility that houses these services.

Assistance under the Program is in the form of unsecured, interest free contributions towards eligible costs of a new establishment, expansion or modernization. It also applies to a project which improves the competitiveness of the business which is applying.

The contribution is repayable on a time schedule, tailored on a case-by-case basis, depending on the circumstances.

Costs eligible for up to 50% financing include:

- the construction or acquisition of a building;
- machinery and equipment needed for the project;
- working capital requirements related to an establishment or expansion project;
- site improvements such as, land clearing and paving required for the project;
- leasehold improvements required by the project;
- leased equipment and conditional sales contracts;
- infrastructure, such as sewer and water needed for a project;
- self-built assets;
- intangible assets such as patents, trademarks and licenses; and,
- start-up costs such as insurance and interest capitalized during construction.

Costs eligible for 75% financing include the following.

Marketing: includes the development of a marketing plan; the hiring of marketing expertise to implement the plan, and related activities such as labelling, packaging, promotional materials, advertising, product demonstrations and participation at trade shows.

Training: includes the development of a training program; the hiring of training expertise to implement the plan and related activities such as training materials, seminar fees and wages during the time that employees receive off-the-job training.

Productivity/Quality Improvement: includes the development of a productivity or quality improvement plan; the hiring of expertise to implement the plan, and related activities such as: obtaining a recognized quality certification (e.g., ISO), and the cost of any technical equipment that is required.

Innovations: includes the costs related to researching and developing new or improved products, services and processes such as: the labour costs of expertise, materials, special equipment, testing and patents.

Consultant Advice: includes the costs of hiring a qualified consultant to prepare a business plan; feasibility study; investigate licensing opportunities; conduct a venture capital search; technology transfer search or provide advice to improve business skills.

Contract Bidding: in which ACOA helps identify opportunities for contracting or sub-contracting government business as well as providing financial assistance to cover 75% of eligible costs up to a maximum of $500,000. Eligible costs can include:

- bid preparation
- pre-positioning
- testing services
- patent costs
- technology transfer
- licensing
- packaging
- product literature
- specialized training
- quality assurance
- quality control
- capital costs.

An emphasis is placed on new products or services that generate employment or economic benefits; rather than providing support for products or services that already exist.

Business Proposal Development: includes the cost of turning an idea into a viable business proposal, such as the completion of a feasibility study, prototype development and gathering information on markets and raw material suppliers. The maximum contribution for this activity is $10,000.

Business Support: provides assistance for not-for-profit organizations for activities that support the business community, entrepreneurship or economic development.

Women in Business Initiative (WBI)

The Women in Business Initiative (WBI) is designed to improve the growth and competitiveness of women-owned businesses and give them greater representation in Atlantic Canada's emerging growth sectors. Financial support is only available to not-for-profit organizations.

There are several components to WBI Initiative, as follows:

- to provide access to the right business advice, information and support;
- to improve skills and offer business networking;
- to improve access to financing;
- to offer expert advice; and,
- to identify ways to enhance innovation or export capacity.

Further information can be obtained from the following:

New Brunswick Association of
Community Business Development Corporations
100 Main St., Suite 6 Bathurst, NB E2A 1A4
Phone: (506) 548-2406
Web site: www.cbdc.ca/index.php?rid=2

Enterprise Cape Breton Corporation
32 Paint Street, Unit 1, Port Hawkesbury
Light Industrial Park, N.S. B9A 3J8
Phone: (902) 625-3111
Fax: (902) 625-3266

Newfoundland and Labrador Organization
of Women Entrepreneurs (NLOWE)
2nd. Floor, regatta Plaza II
84-86 Elizabeth Avenue
St. John's, NL A1A 1W7
Phone: (709).754-5555
Fax: (709)754-0079
Phone toll-free: 1-(888) 656-9311
E-mail: info@nlowe.org
Web site: www.nlowe.org

Centre for Women in Business
166 Bedford Highway
Halifax, NS B3M 2J6
Phone: (902) 457-6449
Phone toll-free: 1-(888) 776-9022
E-mail: cwb@msvu.ca
Web site: www.msvu.ca

Enterprise Cape Breton Corporation
Silicon Island, 70 Crescent Street
Sydney, N.S. B1S 2Z7
Phone toll-free: 1-(800) 705-3926
Phone: (902) 564-3600
Fax: (902) 564-3825
E-mail: ecbcinfo@ecbc-secb.gc.ca
Web site: www.ecbc.ca

Prince Edward Island
Business Women's Association
161 St. Peter's Road, Charlottetown, PE
Canada   C1A 5P7
Phone toll-free: 1-(866) 892-6040
Phone: (902) 892-6040
Fax: (902) 892-6050
E-mail: office@peibwa.org
Web site: www.peibwa.org

Atlantic Association of Community Business
Development Corporations
Web site: www.cbdc.ca

Canada/Atlantic Provinces Agreement
on International Business Development (IBDA)

The Canada/Atlantic Provinces Agreement on International Business Development (IBDA) funds projects to help small and medium-sized companies explore, enter and succeed in international markets. It provides assistance with:

- export training and awareness;
- market information and intelligence;
- international business development activities; and,
- planning and research.

For-profit companies are **not** eligible for assistance, however, business networks, associations and not-for-profit corporations are among those which are eligible.

Young Entrepreneur Development Initiative (YEDI)

The Young Entrepreneur Development Initiative (YEDI) is designed to provide business skills for 15-34 year olds who want to pursue entrepreneurship as a career option and develop the attitudes and skills to recognize and seize business opportunities. It helps existing entrepreneurs develop business survival and growth skills. This initiative is designed to ensure that support for young entrepreneurs is factored into economic development planning and activities at the local community level.

YEDI gives support to mentorship programs, business skills workshops and learning conferences that bring young entrepreneurs together.

Further information can be obtained from ACOA's offices which are listed later in this section.

Government of Canada's Atlantic Shipbuilding Action Plan

The Government of Canada's Atlantic Shipbuilding Action Plan involves a $35 billion investment for the renewal of Canada's naval and Coast Guard fleets. While the Plan does not offer any direct financial assistance to small and medium-sized businesses located within Atlantic Canada, it does offer them the opportunity to become suppliers and sub-contractors for work performed under the initiative.

Community Business Development Corporations (CBDCs)

The Community Business Development Corporations (CBDCs) are non-profit organizations which provide assistance to rural communities to help them with specific local investment opportunities and provide counselling, mentoring and financial assistance to small business and start-up entrepreneurs.

The CBDCs are run by local boards of volunteer directors which tailor service delivery according to local needs. They work with local small and medium-sized businesses to assist in creating jobs.

The following types of loans are offered:

CBDC Youth Loan: is open to young entrepreneurs ages 18-34 interested in starting a first-time business, for modernizing it or for the first time purchase of a business. Loans can be for up to $20,000. Further details are provided in the next section, below.

CBDC General Business Loan: is designed to assist entrepreneurs to obtain financing for their business, when traditional avenues of financing are not available. It can be used for key events in the business life cycle such as business creation, purchase, and business succession planning. Loans can be for up to $150,000.

CBDC First-Time Entrepreneur Loan: provides targeted financing for those first-time entrepreneurs starting or purchasing their very first business. Loans can be for up to $150,000.

CBDC Innovation Loan: are designed to assist in the development of the knowledge-based economy by helping the adoption and commercialization of technology by rural businesses. Loans can be for up to $150,000

CBDC Social Enterprise Loan: provides tailored financing designed to assist social enterprises in rural based communities in Atlantic Canada.

CBDC Youth Loan

The purpose of the CBDC Youth Loan is to provide financing to youth from ages 18 to 34. Capital will normally be provided as an unsecured repayable loan for business startup, modernization and expansion. The maximum loan amount is $20,000 with a minimum interest rate of prime plus 2%, up to a maximum interest rate of prime plus 5%. Training is also available.

This loan can:

(a) Provide up to $20,000 per eligible Borrower in the form of a repayable, personal loan with a flexible interest rate and flexible repayment terms.

(b) Loans will normally be unsecured; however, security can be taken, where deemed appropriate by the CBDC.

(c) Financing can be in the form of a personal loan or a loan guarantee.

(d) Interest rates shall be a minimum of prime plus 2%, up to a maximum of prime plus 5%.

The objectives of the CBDC Youth Loan are to:

(a) Improve access to capital opportunities and financial leveraging abilities for business start-up, expansion, or modernization for youth ages 18 - 34.

(b) Create and maintain jobs in Atlantic Canada.

(c) Assist young entrepreneurs with the overall success of a new or existing business venture by offering training, counselling and/or financial support.

Atlantic Association of CBDCs
54 Loggie St., P.O. Box 40
Mulgrave, NS B0E 2G0
Phone: (902) 747-2232
Phone toll-free: 1-(888) 303-2232
Fax: (902) 747-2019

List of Community Business Development Corporations

New Brunswick

CBDC Restigouche
41 Water Street
P.O. Box 1089
Campbellton NB E3N 1A6
Phone: (506) 753-3344
Fax: (506) 753-7131

CBDC Chaleur
275 Main Street, Suite 212-J
Harbourview Place
Bathurst NB E2A 1A9
Phone: (506) 548-5951
Fax: (506) 548-5008

CBDC Péninsule acadienne
439 du Moulin Street, P.O. Box 3666
Station Main, Tracadie-Sheila
NB E1X 1G5
Phone: (506) 395-9700
Fax: (506) 395-5672

CBDC Madawaska
24 St.Francois St
Edmundston NB E3V 1E3
Phone: (506) 737-8925
Fax: (506) 737-8922

CBDC Victoria/Madawaska-South
551 Main St., Suite 300
P.O. Box 7295
Grand Falls NB E3Z 2W4
Phone: (506) 473-6446
Fax: (506) 473-1280

CBDC Northumberland
1773 Water St.
Miramichi NB E1N 1B2
Phone: (506) 778-2121
Fax: (506) 778-2224

CBDC Kent
190 Irving Blvd., P.O. Box 668
Bouctouche NB E0A 1G0
Phone: (506) 743-2422
Fax: (506) 743-1033

CBDC Westmorland Albert
337 MainStreet
Shediac NB E4P 2B1
Phone: (506) 532-8312
Fax: (506) 532-1373

CBDC Southwest
1910 Route 3, Suite 112
Harvey Station NB E6K 2P4
Phone: (506) 366-3022
Fax: (506) 366-3444

CBDC Charlotte/Kings-St. Stephen Office
123 Milltown Blvd.
P.O. Box 455
St. Stephen NB E3L 2X3
Phone: (506) 466-5055
Fax: (506) 466-4859

Newfoundland and Labrador

CBDC Labrador
2 Hillcrest Rd.
P.O. Box 1089, Station B
Goose Bay NL A0P 1E0
Phone: (709) 896-5814
Fax: (709) 896-4333

NORTIP CBDC
P.O. Box 140
Plum Point NL A0K 4A0
Phone: (709) 247-2040
Fax: (709) 247-2630

CBDC Emerald
P.O. Box 508
Baie Verte NL A0K 1B0
Phone: (709) 532-4690
Fax: (709) 532-4669

CBDC Central
10 Pineset Dr.
Grand Falls-Windsor
NL A2A 2R6
Phone: (709) 489-4496
Fax: (709) 489-5897

Humber CBDC
19 Union Street, Suite 4
P.O. Box 657
Corner Brook NL A2H 6G1
Phone: (709) 639-7755
Fax: (709) 639-1040

CBDC Gander
10 Roe Avenue, P.O. Box 471
Gander NL A1V 1W8
Phone: (709) 651-4738
Fax: (709) 651-3295

CBDC Eastern Initiatives
76 A Manitoba Drive
Clarenville, NL A5K 1K6
Phone: (709) 466-1170
Fax: (709) 466-1450

CBDC Trinity
21 Industrial Crescent, Suite 101
Carbonear NL A1Y 1A5
Phone: (709) 596-3849
Fax: (709) 596-7721

Avalon West CBDC
P.O. Box 419,
Placentia NL A0B 2Y0
Phone: (709) 227-2147
Fax: (709) 227-3670

CBDC Celtic
P.O. Box 134
Ferryland NL A0A 2H0
Phone: (709) 432-2662

CBDC Burin Peninsula
P.O. Bag 470 Marystown
NL A0E 2M0
Phone: (709) 279-4540
Fax: (709) 279-4545

CBDC South Coast
Box 37   St. Alban's NL A0H 2E0
Phone: (709) 538-3630
Fax: (709) 538-3439

Gateway CBDC
82 Main Street, P.O. Box 430
Port aux Basques NL A0M 1C0
Phone: (709) 695-7406
Fax: (709) 695-9726

Long Range CBDC
35 Carolina Avenue
Stephenville NL A2N 3P8
Phone: (709) 643-5606
Fax: (709) 643-6004

Prince Edward Island

CBDC West Prince Ventures
455 Main St., P.O. Box 368
Alberton PE C0B 1B0
Phone: (902) 853-3636
Fax: (902) 853-3839

CBDC Central PEI.
11 Water Street
Summerside PE C1N 1A2
Phone: (902) 888-3793
Fax: (902) 888-2399

CDBC PEI East
540 Main St., P.O. Box 758
Montague PE C0A 1R0
Phone: (902) 838-4030
Fax: (902) 838-4031

Nova Scotia

Coastal Busines CBDC
292 Charlotte St., Suite 100
Sydney Mines NS B1P 1C7
Phone: (902) 539-4322
Fax: (902) 562-1016

CBDC Northside Victoria
P.O. Box 99
1 Fraser Ave., Suite 7
Sydney Mines NS B1V 2V4
Phone: (902) 736-6211
Fax: (902) 736-6212

CBDC Guysborough County
P.O. Box 199
46 Main Street
Guysborough NS
B0H 1N0
Phone: (902) 533-2770
Fax: (902) 533-2016

CBDC Blue Water
24 Rowlings Drive
P.O. Box 39
Musquodoboit Harbour
NS B0J 2L0
Phone: (902) 889-9040
Fax: (902) 889-9101

South Shore Opportunities CBDC
7 Henry Hensey Drive
P.O. Box 1204
Liverpool NS B0T 1K0
Phone: (902) 354-2616
Fax: (902) 354-7355

CBDC Shelburne
157 Water Street, P.O. Box 189
Enterprise Square
Shelburne NS B0T 1W0
Phone: (902) 875-1133
Fax: (902) 875-4199

CBDC Yarmouth
103 Water Street (Pier 1 Complex)
P.O. Box 607
Yarmouth NS B5A 4B6
Phone: (902) 742-5364
Fax: (902) 742-1027

Digby-Clare CBDC
68 Water Street, P.O. Box 160
Digby NS B0V 1A0
Phone: (902) 245-6166
Fax: (902) 245-5011

Annapolis Ventures CBDC
P.O. Box 478, 26 Bay Rd.
Bridgetown NS B0S 1C0
Phone: (902) 665-2635
Fax: (902) 665-2769

CBDC Hants-Kings
80 Water Street, P.O. Box 2788
Windsor NS B0N 2T0
Phone: (902) 798-5717
Fax: (902) 798-0464

InRich CBDC
P.O. Box 600
15991 Central Ave.
Inverness NS B0E 1N0
Phone: (902) 258-3698
Fax (902) 258-3689

CBDC NOBL
4852 Plymouth Road, P.O. Box 817
New Glasgow NS B2H 5K7
Phone: (902) 752-7402
Fax: (902) 752-8856

CBDC Cumberland
P.O. Box 487
35 Church St.
Amherst NS B4H 4A1
Phone: (902) 667-5700
Fax: (902) 667-1452

Further Information on ACOA

Head Office

ACOA Head Office, 644 Main St.
Box 6051, Moncton, NB E1C 9J8
Phone: (506) 851-2271
Fax: (506) 851-7403
Toll-free: 1-(800) 561-7862
Web site: http://www.acoa.gc.ca

New Brunswick

ACOA New Brunswick Regional Office
570 Queen St., 3rd. Fl. P.O. Box 578
Fredericton, NB E3B 5A6
Phone: (506) 452-3184
Toll Free: 1-(800) 561-4030
Fax: (506) 452-3285

ACOA Edmundston Office
121 Church Street, Suite 407
PO Box 490, Edmundston, NB E3V 1J9
Phone: (506) 735-4236
Fax: (506) 739-7486

ACOA Miramichi Office
120 Newcastle Blvd. Suite 2
Miramichi, NB E1N 2L7
Phone: (506) 778-1909
Fax: (506) 622-2160

ACOA Northwest Office
551 Main Street, Suite 100
PO Box 7303
Grand Falls, NB E3Z 2W4
Phone: (506) 473-5556
Fax: (506) 473-6134

ACOA Southwest Office
570 Queen Street, Ground Floor
Box 578 Fredericton, NB E3B 5A6
Phone: (506) 452-3135
Fax: (506) 444-4649

ACOA Campbellton Office
97 Roseberry Street
Campbellton, NB E3N 2G6
Phone: (506) 789-4735
Fax: (506) 789-4933

ACOA Fundy Region Office
Business Resource Centre
Main Floor, 40 King Street
Saint John, NB E2L 1G3
Phone: (506) 636-4485
Fax: (506) 636-4126

ACOA Northeast Office
Harbourview Place, Suite 212-B
275 Main Street
Bathurst, NB E2A 1A9
Phone: (506) 548-7420
Fax: (506) 548-7722

ACOA Southeast Office
644 Main Street, Ground Floor
PO Box 6051 Moncton
NB E1C 9J8
Phone: (506) 851-6432
Fax: (506) 851-3961

ACOA Tracadie-Sheila Office
439 Moulin Street, PO Box 3666
Tracadie-Sheila, NB E1X 1G5
Phone: (506) 395-1025
Fax: (506) 395-5672

Canada Business - New Brunswick
570 Queen Street, P.O. Box 578
Fredericton, NB E3B 6Z6
Phone: (506) 444-6140
Toll-free phone: 1-(888) 576-4444
Fax: (506) 444-6172

Newfoundland and Labrador

ACOA Newfoundland Regional Office
10 Barter's Hill, 11th Floor
P.O. Box 1060, Station C
St. John's, NL A1C 5M5
Phone: (709) 772-2751
Fax: (709) 772-2712
Toll Free: 1-(800) 668-1010

Chapter 5 - Loans by the Federal Government or
its agencies & private sector partners

ACOA Clarenville Office
58-D Manitoba Drive
Clarenville, NL A5A 1K5
Phone: (709) 466-5980
Fax: (709) 466-5982

ACOA Gander Office
109 Trans Canada Highway
Gander, NL A1V 1P6
Phone: (709) 651-4457
Fax: (709) 256-4080

ACOA Grand Falls-Windsor Office
4 Bayley St. Grand Falls-Windsor
NL A2A 2T5
Phone: (709) 489-6600
Fax: (709) 489-8711

Canada Business -
Newfoundland and Labrador
90 O'Leary Avenue, PO Box 8687
St. John's, NL A1B 3T1
Phone: (709) 772-6022
Fax: (709) 772-6090
Toll Free: 1-(800) 668-1010

ACOA Corner Brook Office
1 Regent Square, Corner Brook
NL A2H 7K6
Phone: (709) 637-4477
Fax: (709) 637-4483

ACOA Grand Bank Office
2 Church Street, PO Box 490
Grand Bank NL AOE 1W0
Phone: (709) 832-2517
Fax: (709) 832-2309

ACOA Labrador Office
2 Hillcrest Road, PO Box 430 STN C
Happy Valley-Goose Bay, NL A0P 1C0
Phone: (709) 896-2648
Fax: (709) 896-2900

Nova Scotia

Hants / Halifax East Office
139 Park Road, unit A
Elmsdale NS B2S 2L3
Phone: (902) 259-3604
Fax: (902) 883-7054

Shelburne / Queens Office
218 Water St., Lloyalist Plaza #5
P.O. Box 1267
Shelburne NS B0T 1W0
Phone: (902) 875-7384
Fax: (902) 875-7327

ACOA Nova Scotia - Regional Office
1801 Hollis St., Suite 600
P.O. Box 2284, Station M
Halifax, NS B3J 3C8
Phone: (902) 426-6743
Fax: (902) 426-2054
Toll Free: 1-(800) 565-1228

ACOA Antigonish Office
188 Main St., Suite B-1
Antigonish, NS B2G 2B9
Phone: (902) 867-6075
Fax: (902) 863-4095

ACOA Church Point Office
1649 Highway 1
Church Point NS B0w 1M0
Phone: (902) 260-3590
Fax: (902) 260-3591

ACOA Pictou County Office
980 East River Road
New Glasgow, NS B2H 3S8
Phone: (902) 755-3746
Fax: (902) 755-2722

Yarmouth Office
103 Water Street Pier One Complex
Box 607 Yarmouth, NS B5A 4B6
Phone: (902) 742-0809
Fax: (902) 742-1027

Canada Business - Nova Scotia
1575 Brunswick Street
Halifax, NS B3J 2G1
Phone: (902) 426-8604
Toll Free: 1-(800) 668-1010
Fax: (902) 426-6530

ACOA Bridgewater Office
373 King Street
Bridgewater, NS B4V 1B1
Phone: (902) 541-5543
Fax: (902) 543-1156

ACOA Kentville Office
Economic Development Centre
35 Weber St., Suite 103
Kentville, NS B4N 1H4
Phone: (902) 679-5356
Fax: (902) 678-2324

ACOA Truro Office
35 Commercial Street
Truro, NS B2N 3H9
Phone: (902) 895-2743
Fax: (902) 897-1157

Cape Breton Island

Enterprise Cape Breton Corporation
70 Crescent St.
Sydney, NS B1S 2Z7
Phone: (902) 564-3600
Toll Free Phone: 1- (800) 705-3926
Fax: (902) 564-3825
E-mail address: ecbcinfo@ecbc.ca

Enterprise Cape Breton Corporation
32 Paint Street, Unit 1
Port Hawkesbury
Light Industrial Park
N.S. B9A 3J8
Phone: (902) 625-3111
Fax: (902) 625-3266

Prince Edward Island

ACOA Prince Edward Island Regional Office
100 Sydney St., 3rd. Floor
P.O. Box 40
Charlottetown, PE C1A 7K2
Phone: (902) 566-7492
Fax: (902) 566-7098
Toll Free: 1-(800) 871-2596

ACOA Summerside District Office
268 Water Street
Summerside, PE C1A 7K2
Phone: (902) 888-4145
Fax: (902) 888-4147

Canada Business
/ Prince Edward Island
100 Sydney Street. 3rd. Fl.
P.O. Box 40
Charlottetown, PE C1A 7K2
Phone: (902) 368-0771
Fax: (902) 566-7377
Toll Free: 1-(888) 576-4444

Ottawa

ACOA Ottawa Office
60 Queen Street, 4th Floor
PO Box 1667 STN B
Ottawa, ON K1P 5R5
Phone: (613) 954-2422
Fax: (613) 954-0429

Canadian Northern Economic Development Agency (CanNor)

CanNor is responsible for coordinating and delivering federal economic development activities in the territories, and for policy, research and advocacy. It is designed to help promote social and economic development in the North as part of the Government of Canada's integrated Northern strategy. Initially, CanNor will focus on delivering a number of existing programs which were formerly administered by Indian and Northern Affairs Canada (INAC). The programs which relate to small business include the following.

Strategic Investments in Northern Economic Development (SINED)

Strategic Investments in Northern Economic Development (SINED) provides support for the Targeted Investment Program (TIP) and for the Innovation and Knowledge Fund (I&K), both of which are featured in the following text. In addition, SINED provides funding of $100,000 per territory per annum to increase dialogue on economic development issues and to improve the capacity to deliver programs to the North. Also included in SINED is a Pan-Territorial Fund which provides $5 million over five years to support projects spanning multiple territories or including one or more provinces.

145

Innovation and Knowledge Fund: offers $2.5 million to each of the three territories (over the course of five years) to fund businesses and organizations pursuing activities involved in the support of innovation, knowledge, and the knowledge-based economy. The emphasis of I&K Fund is placed on investment areas or projects not covered by the Targeted Investment Program. It can provide up to $95,000 per project to assist with:

- financing
- primary research
- pre-commercialization
- commercialization
- product development.

Targeted Investment Program (TIP): provided $22.26 million per territory to assist with four thematic areas:

- building the knowledge base to improve mapping, make assessments of fish resources, collect socio-economic data, etc.,
- enhancing the economic infrastructure base such as feasibility studies, investments in telecommunications, tourism and innovations, etc.,
- capacity development to help small and medium-sized businesses with training, certification and expert advice on economic development; and,
- economic diversification with an emphasis on helping small and medium-sized businesses to bring new products and services to market and to help create technology clusters.

Aboriginal Economic Development

Aboriginal Economic Development comprises several programs delivered by CanNor in close collaboration with Aboriginal Affairs and Northern Development Canada (AANDC). They are as follows.

Aboriginal Business Development Program (ABDP): provides business development support to Aboriginal (Status or Non-status Indian, Métis or Inuit) entrepreneurs and organizations. It provides support of up to $100,000 for business planning, start-up, expansion and/or marketing. In the case of community owner businesses, assistance can be of up to $1 million.

As stated by CanNor, funding is available to assist a wide range of activities such as:

- business planning;
- capital costs, including associated operating costs;
- business acquisitions and expansions;
- marketing initiatives that are local, domestic or export oriented;
- new product or process development;
- adding technology to improve operations or competitiveness; or,
- financial services, business support, business related training and mentoring services.

Community Economic Development Program (CEDP): provides core financial support intended for community economic development planning and capacity development initiatives. The Program is open to organizations such as First Nations Councils, self-governing First Nations and Inuit communities but it is **not** open to businesses in the private sector.

Community Economic Opportunities Program (CEOP): provides project-based support to First Nation and Inuit communities that have opportunities for public services in economic development. The Program is open to organizations such as First Nations Councils, self-governing First Nations and Inuit communities but it is **not** open to businesses in the private sector.

Community Support Services Program (CSSP): provides funding for the implementation of national and regional plans to deliver support services to First Nation and Inuit community economic development organizations. The focus is on increasing their capacity to carry out one-time projects and ongoing activities related to economic development. The Program is open to organizations such as First Nations Councils, self-governing First Nations and Inuit communities but it is **not** open to businesses in the private sector.

Further Information

CanNor, Yukon Region
345-300 Main Street
Whitehorse, YT Y1A 2B5
Phone: (867) 667-3888
Phone toll-free: 1-(800) 661-0451

CanNor, Nunavut Region
2nd Floor, Inuksugait Plaza, Building 1104B
P.O. Box 40, Iqaluit, NU X0A 0H0
Phone: (867) 975-3734
Fax: (867) 975-3740

CanNor, Northwest Territories Region
P.O. Box 1500
Yellowknife, NT X1A 2R3
Phone: (867) 669-2627
Phone toll-free:1-(866) 669-2620
Fax: (867) 669-2406
E-mail: EcDevNWT@cannor.gc.ca

NWT Community Futures Program

The Community Futures Program supports small communities in economic difficulty to assess economic problems and opportunities and to achieve long term employment stability, growth, and adjustment.

Individual communities or groups or communities that make up a labour market area are eligible under this program.

The Department of Economic Development & Transportation provides funding to Community Futures Development Corporations (CFDCs) through this program. Funding to

CFDCs allows communities in need to be the innovators, leaders, and directors in solving their long-term employment problems.

Each CFDC is incorporated and a non-profit body run by an independent board of directors.

CFDCs performs major roles as follows:

- provides development and expansion capital through loans and loan guarantees up to a maximum of $150,000 for viable businesses that are unsuccessful in getting adequate financing elsewhere;
- provides wage subsidies for those who are unemployed and who want to start a business;
- provides technical advice and counseling to new or existing small businesses within the community; and,
- provides access to a wide range of business information and Canada Business Internet sites.

The board of directors of the CFDC is responsible for assessing, approving, or rejecting applications for investment funds and for all the overall direction or the technical advisory service operated by the CFDC.

The CFDCs which serve the Northwest Territories are as follows:

Common Web site: http://www.nwtcfa.ca/

Deh Cho Business Development Center
P.O. Box 238
Fort Simpson, NT X0E 0N0
Phone: (867) 695-2441
Phone toll-free: 1-(877) 695-2441
Fax: (867) 695-2052
E-mail address: tnoseworthy@northwestel.net

Western Arctic Business Development Services (WABDS)
2nd Floor Mack Travel Building
P.O. Box 2360 Inuvik, NT X0E 0T0
Phone: (867) 777-2836
Phone toll-free: 1-(800) 244-1203
Fax: (867) 777-3470
E-mail address: generalmanager@northwestel.net

Southwest Territorial Business Development Corporation
Suite #7 - 6 Courtoreille Street
Hay River, NT   XOE 1G2
Phone: (867) 874-2510
Fax: (867) 874-3255
E-mail address: swtbdc@northwestel.net

Sahtu Business Development Centre
P.O. Box 307, Norman Wells, NT   X0E 0V0
Phone: (867) 587-2016
Fax: (867) 587-2407
E-mail address: exec.dir.sbdc@theedgenw.ca

Thebacha Business Development Services (TBDS)
68 Portage Avenue, Box 25
Fort Smith, NT   X0E 0P0
Phone: (867) 872-2795
Fax: (867) 872-2824
E-mail address: westly.steed@thebacha.ca
Web site: www.thebacha.ca

Dogrib Area Community Futures
P.O. Box 92, Wha Ti, NT   X0E 1P0
Phone: (867) 573-3140
Fax: (867) 573-3142
E-mail address: donnamoore@tlicho.com

Akaitcho Business Development Centre
P.O. Box 427, Yellowknife, NT X1A 2N9
Phone: (867) 920-2502
Fax: (867) 920-0363
E-mail address: rstarnaud@akaitchobdc.com

Business Development Centres of Nunavut

The Community Futures Program supports small communities in economic difficulty to assess economic problems and opportunities and to achieve long term employment stability, growth, and adjustment. Individual communities or groups or communities that make up a labour market area are eligible under this program.

The Department of Economic Development & Transportation provides funding to Business Development Centres (BDCs) through this program. Funding to BDCs allows communities in need to be the innovators, leaders, and directors in solving their long-term employment problems.

Each BDC is incorporated, non-profit body run by an independent board of directors.

BDCs perform three major roles:

1. provide development and expansion capital through loans, equity financing or loan guarantees to viable businesses that are unsuccessful in getting adequate financing elsewhere;
2. provide technical advice and counseling to new or existing small businesses within the community; and,
3. provide assistance with a range of other community development initiatives such as community based economic planning, training, etc.

The Board of Directors of the BDC is responsible for assessing, approving, or rejecting applications for investment funds and for all the overall direction or the technical advisory service operated by the BDC.

The BDCs can provide small business loans of between $5,000 and $150,000. They also offer training, business counselling and assistance in preparing business plans.

The BDCs which are supported under the Community Futures Program and which serve Nunavut are as follows:

Baffin Business Development Centre
P.O. Box 1480
Iqaluit, NU X0A 0H0
Phone: (867) 979-1303
Fax: (867) 979-1508
E-mail address: val.kosmenko@baffinbusinessdevelopment.com

Keewatin Business Development Centre
P.O. Box 328, Rankin Inlet, NU X0C 0G0
Phone: (867) 645-2126
Fax: (867) 645-2567
E-mail address: kbdcgm@qiniq.com

Kitikmeot Business Development Centre (KBDC)
P.O. Box 1331, Cambridge Bay, NU X0B 0C0
Phone: (867) 983-7383
Fax: (867) 983-7380
E-mail address: mepp@kcfi.ca
Web site: www.kcfi.ca

Baffin Business Development Corporation (BBDC)

The Baffin Business Development Corporation (BBDC) is a Community Futures organization which serves 13 communities throughout the Qikiqtaaluk region. It is a business service, lending and counselling agency whose goal is to provide support to develop and foster self-reliant, viable businesses. It recognizes the importance of both traditional and non-traditional economies and the value of community involvement in improving the quality of life for Baffin residents.

BBDC operates a revolving loan fund and has received funding of $1.25 million from CanNor and an additional $410,000 from the Strategic Investments in Northern Economic Development (SINED) program. This revolving loan fund provides financing to encourage the development of small to medium-sized businesses in the Qikiqtaaluk region and has provided over 600 loans totalling $27 million since its inception.

Baffin Business Development Corporation (BBDC)
P.O. Box 1480 Inuqsugait Plaza
Iqaluit, NU X0A 0H0
Phone: (867) 979-1303
Fax: (867) 979-1508

Aboriginal Financial Institutions

There are 54 Aboriginal Financial Institutions across Canada and they also act as external delivery offices for the programs mentioned above, under Aboriginal Business Canada. Included in this number are the Aboriginal Capital Corporations (ACCs) which have revolving loan capital of about $5 million and offer secured term loans to Aboriginal businesses.

The primary focus of ACCs is to provide loans to start-up and early stage enterprises which are not yet able to borrow from traditional financial institutions such as banks. Some ACCs also offer training and advocacy services.

The addresses of the Aboriginal Financial Institutions are as follows:

Baffin Business Development Corporation
P.O Box 1480
Iqaluit, NU X0A 0H0
1104 B. Inuksugait Plaza
Iqaluit, NU X0A 0H0
Phone: (867) 979-1303
Fax: (867) 979-1508

Kivalliq Business Development Centre
P.O. Box 709
Rankin Inlet, NU X0C 0G0
Phone: (867) 645-2118
Fax: (867) 645-2170

Akaitcho Business Development Corporation
P.O Box 1287
Yellowknife, NT X1A 2N9
Phone: (867) 920-2502
Fax: (867) 920-0363

Arctic Cooperative Development Fund (ACDF)
321C Old Airport Road
Yellowknife NT X1A 3T3
Phone: (867) 873-3481
Fax: (867) 920-4052

Kitikmeot Economic Development Commission
Box 1330, Cambridge Bay NT X0E 0C0
Phone: (867) 983-2095
Fax: (867) 983-2075

Deh Cho Business Development Centre
P.O Box 238, Fort Simpson, NT X0E 0N0
Phone: (867) 695-2441
Fax: (867) 695-2052

N.W.T. Metis-Dene Development Fund Ltd.
Floor 2, 5125 50 Street
P.O. Box 1805
Yellowknife NT X1A 2P4
Phone: (867) 873-9341
Fax: (867) 873-3492

Sahtu Business Development Centre
P.O. Box 174
Norman Wells, NT X0E 0V0
Phone: (867) 587-2016
Fax: (867) 587-2407

Dogrib Area Community Futures
Rae-Edzo Office
P.O. Box 312
Rae NT X0E 0Y0
Phone: (867) 392-6875
Fax: (867) 392-6322

Däna Näye Ventures
409 Black Street
Whitehorse, Yukon Y1A 2N2
Phone: (867) 668-6925
Fax: (867) 668-3127

Bella Bella Community Development Centre
P.O Box 880
Waglisa, BC V0T 1Z0
Phone: (250) 957-2556
Fax: (250) 957-2544

Sto:lo Development Corporation
6014 Vedder Road
Chilliwack, BC V2R 5M4
Phone: (604) 858-0009
Fax: (604) 858-3829

CFDC of Central Interior First Nations
#215, 345 Yellowhead Highway
Kamloops, BC V2H 1H1
Phone: (250) 828-9833
Fax: (250) 828-9972

First Nations Agricultural Lending Association
408 Paul Lake Rd.
Kamloops BC V2H 1J8
Phone: (250) 314-6804
Fax: (250) 314-6809

All Nations Trust Company (ANTCO)
Suite 208, 345 Yellowhead Highway
Kamloops BC V2H 1H1
Phone: (250) 828-9770
Fax: (250) 372-2585

Haida Gwaii
P.O. Box 40, Massett, BC V0T 1M0
Phone: (250) 626-5594
Fax: (250) 626-5693

Tribal Resources Investment
Corporation (TRICORP)
344 Second Avenue West
Prince Rupert BC V8J 1G6
Phone: (250) 624-3535
Fax: (250) 624-3883

Nuu-chah-nulth Economic
Development Corporation (NEDC)
7563 Pacific Rim Highway
P.O. Box 1384
Port Alberni BC V9Y 7M2
Phone: (250) 724-3131
Fax: (250) 724-9967

Native Fishing Association
710, 100 Park Royal South
West Vancouver, BC V7T 1A2
Phone: (604) 913-2997
Fax: (604) 913-2995

Prince George Aboriginal
Business Development
3845 – 15 Avenue
Prince George, BC V2N 1A4
Phone: (250) 562-6325
Fax: (250) 562-6326

Tale' Awtxw Aboriginal Capital Corporation
508, 100 Park Royal South
West Vancouver, BC V7T 1A2
Phone: (604) 926-5626
Fax: (604) 926-5627

Alberta Indian Investment Corporation
Box 180 Enoch Development Building
Enoch, AB T7X 3Y3
Phone: (780) 470-3600
Fax: (780) 470-3605

Apeetogosan (Metis) Development Inc.
302, 12308 - 111 Avenue
Edmonton, AB T5M 2N4
Phone: (780) 452-7951
Fax: (780) 454-5997

Indian Business Corporation
Unit 56, 2333 18th Ave. NE
Calgary, AB T2E 8T6
Phone: (403) 291-5825
Fax: (403) 291-0953

Settlement Investment Corporation
Suite 104, 10335-172 Street, Centurion Building
Edmonton, AB T5S 1K9
Phone: (780) 488-5656
Fax: (780) 488-5811

Treaty Seven Economic Development Corp
300, 6011 – 1A St. SW
Calgary, AB   T2H 0G5
Phone: (403) 251-9242
Fax: (403) 251-9750

Beaver River Community Futures
Development Corp.
P.O Box 2678
Meadow Lake, SK S9X 1P8
Phone: (306) 236-4422
Fax: (306) 236-5818

Saskatchewan Indian Loan Company
224B – Fourth Avenue South
Saskatoon SK S7K 5M5
Phone: (306) 955-8699
Fax: (306) 373-4969

Clarence Campeau Development Fund
254 Robin Crescent
Saskatoon SK S7L 7C2
Phone: (306) 657-4870
Fax: (306) 657-4890

Saskatchewan Indian Equity Foundation Inc.
224B Fourth Avenue South
Saskatoon SK S7K 5M5
Phone: (306) 955-4550
Fax: (306) 373-4969

SaskMetis Economic Development Corporation
#108 – 219 Robin Crescent
Saskatoon, SK S7L 6M8
Phone: (306) 477-4350
Fax: (306) 477-4352
Direct Line: (306) 373-2512

Northwest Community Futures
Development Corp
103 – 1202 101 Street
North Battleford SK S9A 0Z8
Phone: (306) 446-3200
Fax: (306) 445-8076

Visions North
P.O. Box 810
LaRonge SK S0J 1L0
Phone: (306) 425-2612
Fax: (306) 425-2205

Anishinabe Mazaska Capital Corporation
#811-294 Portage Avenue
Winnipeg, MB R3C-0B9
Phone: (204) 940-5000
Fax: (204) 940-5003

Cedar Lake CFDC
P.O. Box 569, #1 St. Godard Street
The Pas, MB R9A 1K6
Phone: (204) 627-5450
Fax: (204) 627-5460

Dakota Ojibway
4820 Portage Avenue
Headingley, MB R4H 1C8
Phone: (204) 988-5373
Fax: (204) 988-5365

Louis Riel Capital Corporation
340 – 150 Henry Avenue
Winnipeg, MB R3B 0J7
Phone: (204) 589-0772
Fax: (204) 589-0791

Kitayan CFDC
#345 – 260 ST. Mary Avenue
Winnipeg, MB R3C 0M6
Phone: (204) 982-2170
Fax: (204) 943-3412

North Central CFDC Manitoba
P.O Box 1208, Station Road
Thompson, MB R8N 1P1
Phone: (204) 677-1490
Fax: (204) 778-5672

Northwest Manitoba Community
Futures Development Corp.
Box 188, 499 Sherritt Avenue
Lynn Lake, MB R0B 0W0
Phone: (204) 356-2489
Fax: (204) 356-2785

Southeast CFDC
200 – 208 Edmonton Street
Winnipeg MB R3C 1R7
Phone: (204) 943-1656
Fax: (204) 943-1735

Tribal Wi-chi-way-win Capital Corporation
203 - 400 St. Mary Avenue
Winnipeg MB R3C 4K5
Phone: (204) 943-0888
Fax: (204) 946-5318

Indian Agricultural Program of Ontario
220 North Street
P.O. Box 100
Stirling ON K0K 3E0
Phone: (613) 395-5505
Fax: (613) 395-5510

Waubetek Business Development Corporation
General Delivery
Whitefish River Community Centre
Birch Island ON P0P 1A0
Phone: (705) 285-4275
Fax: (705) 285-4584

Nishnawbe Aski Development Fund
2nd FL, 106 Centennial Square
Thunder Bay, ON P7E 1H3
Phone: (807) 623-5397
Fax: (807) 622-8271

Ohwistha Capital Corporation
P.O Box 1394
Cornwall, ON K6H-5V4
Phone: (613) 933-6500
Fax: (613) 933-7808

Tecumseh Development Corporation
R.R. #1, 311 Jubilee Road
Muncey, ON N0L 1Y0
Phone: (519) 289-2122
Fax: (519) 289-5550

Two Rivers Community Development Centre
P.O Box 225, 16 Sunrise Court
Ohsweken, ON N0A 1M0
Phone: (519) 445-4567
Fax: (519) 445-2154

Wakenagun Community Futures Dev. Corp.
P.O Box 308
Moose Factory, ON P0L 1W0
Phone: (705) 658-4428
Fax: (705) 658-4672

OMAA Development Corporation (ODC)
Floor 2 Walrus Building #1
452 Albert Street East
Sault Ste. Marie ON P6A 2J8
Phone: (705) 949-8220
Fax: (705) 949-5691

Corporation Développement
Économique Montagnaise
1005 Boul Laure, Suite 110
Sept-Îles, QC G4R 4S6
Phone: (418) 968-1246
Phone toll-free: 1-(800) 463-2216
Fax: (418) 962-2449

EEYOU Economic Group/CFDC Inc.
58 Pine Street, Wasanipi, PQ J0Y 3C0
Phone: (819) 753-2560
Fax: (819) 753-2568

Tewatohnhi'saktha Business Loan Fund Ltd.
P.O. Box 1110, Kahnawake QC J0L 1B0
Phone: (450) 638-4280
Fax: (450) 638-3276

Nunavik Investment Corporation
P.O. Box 239
Kuujjuaq, Quebec J0M 1C0
Phone: (819) 964-2035
Fax: (819) 964-1497

SOCCA (Native Commerical
Credit Corporation)
265-201 Place Chef Michel-Laveau
Wendake, QC G0A 4V0
Phone: (418) 842-0972
Fax: (418) 842-8925

Ulnooweg Development Group Inc.
P.O. Box 1259
Truro, NS B2N 5N2
Phone: (902) 893-7379
Fax: (902) 893-0353

Canada Mortgage and Housing Corporation (CMHC)

Canada Mortgage and Housing Corporation (CMHC) is the Government of Canada's national housing agency with a mandate to help Canadians gain access to a wide choice of quality affordable homes. CMHC has been in operation for over 56 years and concentrates on four areas of housing activities: housing finance, assisted housing, research and information transfer and export promotion.

Seed Funding for Projects in Canada

CMHC offers Seed Funding of up to $20,000 per housing project and is available for early stage projects that are:

- affordable;
- innovative;
- community-based; or,
- any combination of the above characteristics.

Up to $10,000 of the funding can be in the form of a grant, with no repayment required, to cover the costs of the following:

- analysis of need and/or demand for the proposed housing project;
- definition of objectives; or,
- development of a business plan.

A further amount of up to $10,000 may be obtained as a repayable interest-free loan for the following types of activities:

- incorporation of a not-for-profit organization (where applicable);
- preliminary design of the housing project (new construction, renovation or conversion); or,
- preliminary financial viability analysis.

159

The following are eligible to apply under this program:

- a not-for-profit organization;
- a non-profit housing cooperative;
- a non-profit co-operative;
- a Faith-based organization
- a municipality;
- a First Nation;
- a private entrepreneur; or,
- a group of individuals who may or may not intend to become incorporated.

Recipients will be selected through an open proposal call process which will take place at least once per year.

CMHC Renovation Programs for Projects in Canada

These programs are targeted to low-income households and comprise the following elements.

Residential Rehabilitation Assistance Program (RRAP) - Homeowners: CMHC provides financial assistance in the form of fully forgivable loans to owners of affordable housing which are substandard, to cover 100% of the cost to rehabilitate the property to a minimum level of health and safety and also address the needs of adults with disabilities. Assistance can be for up to $16,000 per unit ($19,000 in Northern areas and $24,000 in Far North areas).

Rental Residential Rehabilitation Assistance Program (RRAP-C) - Conversion: CMHC provides financial assistance in the form of fully forgivable loans for landlords to convert non-residential properties into affordable self-contained rental housing units and/or bed units. Assistance can be for up to $24,000 ($28,000 in Northern areas and $36,000 in Far North areas).

Residential Rehabilitation Assistance Program (RRAP) - Rooming House: CMHC provides financial assistance in the form of fully forgivable loans to owners of rooming houses which are substandard, to cover 100% of the cost of mandatary repairs to rehabilitate the property to a minimum level of health and safety and also address the needs of adults with disabilities. Assistance can be for up to $16,000 per bed unit ($19,000 in northern areas and $24,000 in far north areas).

Residential Rehabilitation Assistance Program (RRAP) for Persons with Disabilities: CMHC provides financial assistance in the form of fully forgivable loans allowing homeowners and landlords to modify their dwellings so that they are more accessible to persons with disabilities. Assistance can cover 100% of the cost for up to $16,000 ($19,000 in Northern areas and $24,000 in Far North areas) for each self-contained rental unit created or $24,000 ($28,000 in Northern areas and $36,000 in Far North areas) for each bed unit.

Residential Rehabilitation Assistance Program (RRAP) -Secondary/Garden Suite: CMHC provides financial assistance in the form of fully forgivable loans to allow low-income seniors and adults with disabilities to modify their dwellings so that they can create a secondary self-contained unit. Assistance can cover 100% of the cost for up to $24,000 ($28,000 in Northern areas and $36,000 in Far North areas) for each self-contained rental unit created.

Emergency Repair Program (ERP): can provide assistance for occupants in rural areas to undertake emergency repairs. The level of assistance can be for up to $6,000 per unit in southern areas of Canada, $9,000 per unit in northern areas and $11,000 per unit in far northern areas.

Shelter Enhancement Program (SEP): CMHC provides funding to organizations (non-profits and charities) that provide housing services to victims of family violence. Funding of up to $24,000 per unit under SEP may be used to repair or rehabilitate existing shelters or transitional housing, or it may be used to create new shelters or transitional housing, provided a source of operating funding is available. For new shelters CMHC may contribute up to 100% of capital costs. Higher levels of assistance of up to $28,000 for northern areas and $36,000 for remote communities in The Northwest Territories, The Yukon, Labrador and Northern Québec.

Home Adaptations for Seniors' Independence (HASI): provides financial assistance to homeowners and landlords for home adaptations to extend the time that low-income seniors, aged 65 and older, can live in their own home independently. The assistance is in the form of a forgivable loan, up to $3,500, to cover the cost of minor home adaptations.

Proposal Development Funding (PDF) for Projects in Canada

Under its Proposal Development Funding (PDF), CMHC provides repayable interest-free loans of up to $100,000 to facilitate the development of affordable housing. The program is open to all private entrepreneurs, housing cooperatives, First Nations or other housing proponents who can demonstrate their ability to produce a viable affordable housing project which meets CMHC's criteria.

Eligible expenses include such items as soil load-bearing tests, environmental site assessments, project drawings and specifications, professional fees, cost estimates, management plan, option to purchase, development permits, contract documents and application fees.

Further Information

Canada Mortgage and Housing Corporation
700 Montreal Road, Ottawa, ON K1A 0P7
Phone: (613) 748-2000 Fax: (613) 748-2098
Web site: www.cmhc-schl.gc.ca

CMHC Atlantic Business Centre
1894 Barrington St. Barrington Tower, 9th Fl.
Halifax, NS B3J 2A8
Phone: (902) 426-3530
Fax: (902) 426-9991

CMHC Charlottetown Branch Office
Royal Trust Building,
Suite 300, 3rd Floor
119 Kent Street,
Charlottetown, PE C1A 1N3
Phone: (902) 566-7336
Fax: (902) 556-7350

CMHC St. John's Branch Office
P.O. Box 9400
St. John's, NL A1A 3V6
Phone: (709) 772-4400
Fax: (709) 726-1166

CMHC-Moncton
774 Main Street
Suite 300
Moncton, NB E1C 9Y3
Phone: (506) 851-7424
Fax: (506) 851-6188

CMHC Québec Business Centre
1100 René-Lévesque West,1st Floor
Montréal, QC H3B 5J7
Phone: (514) 283-2222
Fax: (514) 283-7835

CMHC Québec City Office
2590 boulevard Laurier
Place de la Cité – Tour Belle cour
9th floor, suite 900
Québec, QC G1V 4M6
Phone: (418) 649-8080
Fax: (418) 649-8099

CMHC Saguenay Office
100 Lafontaine Street
Saguenay, QC G7H 6X2
Phone toll-free: 1-(888) 772-0772
Fax: (418) 698-5519

CMHC Gatineau Office
259 boulevard St Joseph, Suite 202,
Gatineau, QC J8Y 6T1
Phone toll-free: 1-(888) 772-0772

CMHC Ontario Business Centre
100 Sheppard Ave. E, Suite 300,
Toronto, ON, M2N 6Z1
Phone: (416) 221-2642
Fax: (416) 250-3310

CMHC
Prairie, Nunavut and Northwest
Territories Business Centre
Suite 200, 1000 - 7th Avenue S.W.
Calgary, AB T2P 5L5
Phone: (403) 515-3000
Fax: (403) 515-2930

CMHC Edmonton Office
210, 10405 Jasper Ave.
Edmonton, AB T5J 3N4
Phone: (780) 423-8700
Fax: (780) 423-8702

CMHC Calgary Office
Suite 200, 1000 – 7th Avenue, S.W.
Calgary, AB T2P 5L5
Phone: (403) 515-3000
Fax: (403) 515-2930

CMHC Regina Office
Suite 120, 1870 Albert Street
Regina, SK S4P 4B7
Phone: (306) 841-4975
Fax: (306) 780-6645

CMHC Saskatoon Office
P.O. Box 1107
Saskatoon, SK S7K 3N2
Phone: (306) 975-4900
Fax: (306) 975-6066

CMHC Winnipeg Office
600-175 Hargrave Street,
Winnipeg, MB R3C 3R8
Phone: (204) 983-5600
Fax: (204) 983-8046

CMHC NWT Office
Suite 402, 3106 – 3rd Avenue
Whitehorse, YT Y1A 5G1
Phone toll-free: 1-(877) 499-7245
Fax: (867) 873-3922

Nunavut - CMHC Northern Housing
Building 626 (Tumiit Plaza), Suite 200
Iqaluit, NU X0A 0H0
Phone toll-free: 1-(877) 499-7245

CMHC
Northern Housing —
CMHC Activity in Yukon, NWT and Nunavut
Suite 200, Northern Housing
000–7th Ave, S.W.
Calgary, AB T2P 5L5
Phone: (403) 515-3000
Phone toll-free: 1-(877) 499-7245
Fax: (403) 515-2930

6

Loans & Loan Guarantees by Provincial/Territorial Governments or their Agencies

Provincial Lending Institutions

Many provinces have their provincial equivalents of the Federal Business Development Bank. These include:

- Investissement Québec
- Nova Scotia Business Inc.
- Innovation PEI
- Alberta - Agriculture Financial Services Corporation (AFCS)
- N.W.T. Business Development & Investment Corporation (BDIC)
- Nunavut Business Credit Corporation (NBCC)

The activities of these operations are covered in detail in the following pages together with several other provincially funded lending initiatives.

Investissement Québec (IQ)

Established in mid-1998, Investissement Québec (IQ) has a mandate to assist innovative, new economy businesses.

Eco-Financing

Eco-Financing provides loans or loan guarantees. To be eligible, businesses should operate in one of the following sectors:

- manufacturing;
- new economy (biotechnology, pharmaceuticals, information and computer technologies, aeronautics, aerospace, materials engineering and instrumentation);
- research laboratories;
- tourism;
- recycling;
- environmental restoration;
- waste recovery and processing;
- call centres; or,
- aquaculture, sea farming, marine biotechnology and horticultural specialties.

According to Investissement Québec. The following projects are eligible:

- acquisition of capital assets for greenhouse gas (GHG) reduction;
- working capital expenditures, including R&D for GHG reduction;
- expenditures for the qualification, quantification and certification of offset credits (carbon credits); and,
- acquisition of offset credits to comply with business sector standards.

The minimum amount of the loan or loan guarantee provided by Investissement Québec is $50,000 and the maximum duration of the financial assistance is 10 years. A loan guarantee can cover up to 70% of the net loss, or 75% in outlying regions (Abitibi-Témiscamingue, Bas-Saint-Laurent, Côte-Nord, Gaspésie—Îles-de-la-Madeleine, Mauricie, Nord-du-Québec, Outaouais (excluding the municipality of Gatineau) and Saguenay—Lac-Saint-Jean).

The maximum amount provided by the financial institution can be up to 100% of project-related expenses, depending on the nature of the project.

For loans granted directly by Investissement Québec, the amount provided can be up to 75% of the total project cost. Repayment of capital can be deferred for a maximum of two years. Security is required and is based on the financing granted.

UNIQ Financing

UNIQ Financing allows businesses to benefit from financing at all stages of their development, from start-up to growth to the transfer to new owners. It provides loans, loan guarantees or quasi-equity financing. It has two components, depending on the nature of the project.

Working Capital: is open to Québec businesses in all economic sectors except for agriculture. Businesses that are not eligible for finance and insurance; real estate; services to individuals; retail sales and related or comparable activities; and, other sectors in which the client base is made up mainly of individuals, except for the tourism sector. On the other hand, Financière agricole du Québec programs can benefit from UNIQ Financing.

Eligible projects could include:

- acquisition of intangible assets (trademarks, patents, etc.);
- product or market development;
- financing of a short-term financial commitment (line of credit, letter of guarantee);
- working capital (due to growth of the business);
- refinement and marketing of new or improved products or services; and,
- refinancing.

To qualify, businesses must have a sound financial structure, adequate management, qualified staff and a solid organization.

Loan guarantee can be provided to repay the net loss incurred by the financial institution that grants a loan, line of credit, letter of credit or other short-term financial commitment. Quasi-equity financing may be offered in the form of debentures or subordinated debt.

The minimum amount of financing from Investissement Québec is $50,000. It may cover up to 100% of the project costs.

The loan guarantees may cover up to 85% of the net loss.

The maximum duration of the financial assistance is 10 years.

Repayment of the capital amount may be deferred up to 12 months.

Capital Assets: is open to Québec businesses in all economic sectors except agriculture; businesses that are not eligible; are finance and insurance; real estate; services to individuals; retail sales and related or comparable activities and other sectors in which the client base is made up mainly of individuals, except for the tourism sector.

Financière agricole du Québec programs can benefit from UNIQ Financing.

Most projects are eligible such as:

- purchase of machinery, office equipment or transportation equipment;
- expansion, construction or modernization of a building;
- business start-up;
- entering a new market;
- refinancing; or,
- succession or business transfer via share acquisition.

Businesses must have a sound financial structure, adequate management, qualified staff and a solid organization.

Investissement Québec can provide you with a loan, a loan guarantee or quasi-equity financing. Term loans are offered at competitive market rates and loan guarantees will repay the net loss incurred by the financial institution that grants a loan, line of credit, letter of credit or other short-term financial commitment. Quasi-equity financing may be offered in the form of debentures or subordinated debt.

The minimum amount of financing from Investissement Québec is $50,000. Financing may cover up to 100% of the project costs. Loan guarantees may cover up to 85% of the net loss. The maximum duration of the financial assistance is 20 years and repayment of the capital amount may be deferred up to 24 months.

IMPLIQ Financing

IMPLIQ Financing is open to cooperative undertakings such as a cooperative constituted under the Québec Cooperatives Act or the Canada Cooperatives Act; federation or confederation of cooperatives; subsidiary or subsidiary of another subsidiary under the majority control of one or more cooperatives; a non-profit organization (NPO), including a subsidiary of a NPO or a non-profit legal entity that was constituted under Part III of the Québec Companies Act or Canada Not-for-Profit Corporations Act.

IMPLIQ Financing is designed to meet financing needs of start-ups and growth businesses.

Most projects are eligible such as:

- working capital;
- financing for financial commitments;
- acquisition of intangible assets (trademarks, patents, etc.);
- product or market development;
- fine-tuning and marketing of products or services;
- financing for new or existing worker-shareholder cooperatives;
- capital asset acquisitions; or,
- acquisition of cooperatives shares.

Businesses must have adequate management, qualified personnel and a sound organization. They must also be financially viable and have a social aim. Moreover, they must have solid community roots that help ensure the success of its undertakings.

Loan guarantees may be available to repay the net loss on a loan, line of credit, letter of credit or any other form of financing provided by a financial institution.

169

The minimum financing provided by Investissement Québec is $25,000. Financing can cover up to 100% of project costs. A loan guarantee can cover up to 85% of the net loss.

The maximum duration of the financial assistance is 10 years for projects involving an increase in working capital and 20 years for projects involving the acquisition of capital assets.

Depending on the project, it may be possible to defer repayment of the capital.

Financing of Refundable Tax Credits

The minimum amount of the loan guarantee provided by Investissement Québec is $50,000 for the SRED tax credits and $20,000 for the other tax credits. The loan guarantee can cover up to 80% of the net loss. The amount provided may cover up to 75% of refundable tax credits for one fiscal year (two years in some exceptional cases).

The maximum duration for financial assistance is 18 months. Repayment of the capital amount comes directly from the tax credits to be paid.

Financing of R&D for Exporting Businesses

For companies engaged in exporting, scientific research and experimental development (SRED) activities giving rise to refundable tax credits under the tax laws of Québec and Canada. If revenues from international exports are at least $5 million or account for at least 15% of its total revenues.

Investissement Québec can provide a loan guarantee, i.e., a repayment guarantee on the net loss of a loan granted by a financial institution. The minimum amount of the loan guarantee provided by Investissement Québec to exporting businesses is $50,000 to finance scientific research and experimental development (SRED) activities. The loan guarantee covers 85% of the net loss and the maximum duration of the financial assistance is two years. The maximum loan amount, $500,000 provided by the financial institution can cover up to 75% of the cost of the project.

Interest rates are set by the financial institution and interest is payable to the financial institution from the first loan disbursement.

Capitalization of Social Economy Companies

IQ can offer loans or, in some cases, purchase preferred shares in a cooperative, federation or confederation of cooperatives governed by the Québec Cooperatives Act or a non-profit which produces goods or services for its members or the community.

Such entities should derives most of their revenue from commercial activities carried out with private or public-sector consumers. It can provide between $25,000 and $500,000 to cover:

- business start-up;
- development or expansion project; or,
- consolidation.

If there is a need for equity capital, a second equity partner is generally recommended, however, it is required when the equity need exceeds $100,000. The financial assistance may not exceed 35% of the project costs and the maximum duration of financing is 10 years, with a possible five-year extension. Repayments of the capital amount will be deferred for at least two years (maximum five years) after the first disbursement.

ESSOR: Support for Investment Projects

This program is administered jointly by Investissement Québec and the Ministère du Développement économique, de l'Innovation et de l'Exportation. It can provide a loan, an interest-free loan or a loan guarantee.

The program targets for-profit companies, cooperatives and social economy companies with activities similar to those of private for-profit companies in the following sectors:

- manufacturing;
- software publishing;
- private research centres;
- environmental services; and,
- tourism, subject to certain restrictions.

Eligible projects with expenditures of $250,000 and over, including:

- investment projects aiming to create a new business or expand (or modernize) an existing business;
- projects involving the implementation of a process to provide a service or the establishment of a manufacturing facility leveraging a proven green technology developed in Québec;
- projects to construct, adapt, expand or acquire a building in order to create new research and development (R&D) facilities for active research businesses that do not own research facilities and for those that carry out research in Québec in facilities that they own.

Projects that do not involve capital asset expenditures but for which the cumulative increase in payroll over the first three years following the project start date is $2 million or more.

Business projects with eligible expenditures of less than $250,000 may be considered in the Nord-du-Québec region and part of the Côte-Nord region including the municipalities and Aboriginal reserves located in Caniapiscau Regional County Municipality and the Basse-Côte-Nord territory.

Projects must be completed within three years and must not have a negative impact on existing businesses and must contribute to maintaining or creating jobs. Also, assistance must complement private financing sources and other regular government programs.

Financing is in the form of a loan or loan guarantee to cover up to 70% of the net loss. The maximum term of the financial assistance is 10 years.

Financial assistance may not exceed 50% of the total project cost. However, it may amount to 55% in the case of projects carried out in the Bas-Saint-Laurent region and 60% in the case of projects carried out in remote regions (Abitibi-Témiscamingue, Côte-Nord, Nord-du-Québec and Gaspésie-Îles-de-la-Madeleine). Repayment of the principal may be deferred in some conditions.

The ESSOR program also has a component focusing on the feasibility of an investment project and covers feasibility studies, market studies, process evaluations, etc.

Further information can be obtained from the ministère des Finances et de l'Économie toll-free at 1- (866) 463-6642.

Further Information

Investissement Québec - Head Office
413, Saint-Jacques, office 500
Montréal, QC H2Y 1N9
Phone: (514) 873-4375
Fax: (514) 873-5786
Web site: www.investquebec.com

Branch Offices

Investissement Québec
4805, boul. Lapinière, bureau 4100
Brossard QC J4Z 0G2
Phone: (450) 676-2123

Investissement Québec
500, ave. Daigneault
Case postale 1360, suite 10 A
Chandler, QC G0C 1K0
Phone: (418) 689-2549

Investissement Québec
230, boul. Saint-Joseph
Gatineau QC J8Y 3X4
Phone: 819 772-3211

Investissement Québec
3300, boulevard de la Côte-Vertu, bureau 210
Montréal QC H4R 2B7
Phone: (514) 873-1401

Investissement Québec
Montréal (East)
7100 Jean-Talon Street East, suite 1250
Montréal, QC H1M 3S3
Phone: (514) 873-9292

Investissement Québec
Région ouest de Montréal
413, rue Saint-Jacques, bureau 500
Montréal QC H2Y 1N9
Phone: (514) 873-4375

Investissement Québec
1200, route de l'Église, bureau 500
Québec QC G1V 5A3
Phone: (418) 643-5172

Investissement Québec
70 St-Germain Street East
3rd floor, suite 100
Rimouski, QC G5L 8B3
Phone: (418) 727-3582

Investissement Québec
454, ave. Arnaud
Sept-îles, QC G4R 3A9
Phone: (418) 964-8160

Investissement Québec
3950, boulevard Harvey, 2e étage
Saguenay QC G7X 8L6
Phone: (418) 695-7865

Investissement Québec
100 Laviolette Street, 3rd floor
Trois-Rivières, QC G9A 5S9
Phone: (819) 371-6012

Investissement Québec
1100, boul. René-Lévesque, bureau 102
Drummondville QC J2C 5W4
Phone: (819) 478-9675

Investissement Québec
3030 Le Carrefour Boulevard, suite 902
Laval, QC H7T 2P5
Phone: (450) 680-6161

Investissement Québec
170, Principale, suite 202
Rouyn-Noranda, QC J9X 4P7
Phone: (819) 763-3300

Investissement Québec
11535 First Avenue, suite 303
Saint-Georges, QC G5Y 7H5
Phone: (418) 222-5768

Investissement Québec
200 Belvédère Street North
3rd floor, suite 3.10
Sherbrooke, QC J1H 4A9
Phone: (819) 820-3224

Youth Promoters Program (Jeunes Promoteurs)

The Société de développment économique Ville-Marie's (SDEVM's) mission is to offer front-line services to businesses in the Borough of Ville-Marie.

The Youth Promoters Program entitled "jeunes promoteurs" caters to young entrepreneurs who are resident in Québec; in the age bracket 18-35; who are prepared to work full-time in starting a business in a field in which they already have some knowledge.

Two sub-programs are devoted to pre-start-up and start-up businesses in downtown Montreal, offering non-refundable grants.

Entrepreneurs should have experience or training in their business project's field, and should work full-time for their company.

Young Promoters - Start-up

The SDEVM (CLD) may grant from $6,000 up to $10,000 per entrepreneur and a maximum of $20,000 per project.

The grant should be devoted to one of the following:

The creation of a first or second business by the entrepreneur: covers capital expenditures (long-term assets, equipment, etc.); technology acquisitions (patents, software, etc.); or, working capital needs forecasted for the first year of operation.

The acquisition of a company: for training, the SDEVM (CLD) may grant $1,000 per entrepreneur to pay for training to an entrepreneur who benefits from a Young Promoters grant. Training should be relevant to the business project. Assistance can cover registration costs; educational materials; and other justified expenses. Applicants must personally invest from $6,000 to $10,000 and be based in the SDEVM's (CLD) territory for at least 2 years.

It should be noted that businesses located on the SDEVM territory, Young Promoters program could also be offered through SAJE Montreal-Metro.

The Société de développment économique Ville-Marie
615 René-Lévesque Blvd. West, Suite 720
Montreal, QC
H3B 1P5
Phone: (514) 879-0555
Fax: (514) 879-0444

Nova Scotia Department of Economic and Rural Development and Tourism

The Department of Economic and Rural Development and Tourism focuses on public policy, especially as it relates to promoting the best environment for businesses to start and expand in the new economy. Many programs to assist business are now offered by a Crown corporation called Nova Scotia Business Inc.

Nova Scotia Business Development Program

The Nova Scotia Business Development Program is designed to help small business get started and existing businesses expand. It provides help through qualified consultants for business operators to review and assess their practices and develop new approaches to ensure success. This includes activities such as:

- staff training and recruitment;
- market research and business plan development;
- advertising and promotional plans;
- visual merchandising techniques; and,
- fiscal management tools.

Assistance can cover 50% of total costs, to a maximum of $10,000. In the case of groups participating in the same activity, assistance can cover 75% of total costs, up to a maximum of $12,000. per applicant, and will be made available to groups participating in the same activity.

Capital Investment Incentive

The Capital Investment Incentive (CII) can contribute 20% up to a maximum of $1 million toward the cost of technologically-advanced machinery, clean technology, equipment, software and hardware with preference given to exporters in:

- advanced manufacturing and processing;
- development of non-traditional sources of energy;
- life-sciences;
- aerospace and defence;
- information and communication technology (ICT);
- ocean technology;
- professional, scientific and technical services excluding legal services; accounting, tax preparation, bookkeeping and payroll services; advertising and related services; photographic services; veterinary services; translation and interpretation services.

Under certain circumstances, strategic gateway and trade related activities may be eligible under the CII. Acquisitions less than $25,000 will not be considered.

Economic and Rural Development and Tourism
Capital Investment Incentive
1660 Hollis St., Suite 600
Halifax, NS B3J 1V7
Phone: (902) 424-8822

Workplace Innovation and Productivity Skills Incentive (WIPSI)

The Workplace Innovation and Productivity Skills Incentive (WIPSI) is designed to encourage businesses to invest in employee and management skills development, and improve productivity. It offers workforce training incentives of $5,000 to $10,000 to:

- improve productivity;
- increase innovation and long-term competitiveness;
- support the introduction of new technology, machinery and equipment, or work processes;
- provide employees with transferable skills;
- upgrade skills;
- enhance international competitiveness; and,
- foster workplace diversity.

The program is open to businesses, industry associations and private-sector unions with the exception of businesses primarily involved in wholesale, retail, accommodation, and food service.

Assistance can cover:

- the purchase of training from a formal training institution or qualified external or internal training provider;
- registration, tuition or course fees;
- international training;
- management skills development;
- skills development training leading to certification;
- training that supports workplace diversity; and,
- other skills development and training based on a valid business case.

Mail:
Department of Economic, Rural Development and Tourism
P.O. Box 2311
Halifax, NS B3J 3C8

Department of Economic, Rural Development and Tourism
Workplace Innovation and Productivity Skills Incentive
Centennial Building, 1660 Hollis St., Suite 600
Halifax, NS B3J 1V7
Phone: (902) 424-5294
Fax: (902) 424-0500
E-mail: comm@gov.ns.ca
Web site: www.gov.ns.ca/econ/

Credit Union Small Business Loan Guarantee Program

The Credit Union Small Business Loan Guarantee Program enables credit unions to deliver financial assistance to establish new business, grow existing business and empower entrepreneurs with the support they need to create employment for themselves and others.

Credit Union Immigrant Small Business Loan Financing Program

Credit Union Immigrant Small Business Loan Financing aims to help immigrants who are interested in starting, expanding or buying a small business.

Nova Scotia Jobs Fund

The Nova Scotia Jobs Fund supports industry sectors, offers regional support, assists small businesses programs, and invests in infrastructure and large industrial ventures.

Aerospace and Defence Loan (ADL) program

The Aerospace and Defence Loan (ADL) program provides repayable loans for non-recurring costs associated with attracting new contracts.

Nova Scotia Strategic Opportunities Fund Inc. (SOFI)

The Nova Scotia Strategic Opportunities Fund Inc. (SOFI) can provide loans of at least $1 million for projects in certain strategic areas. If qualified foreign investors make an investment of $400,000 in return for the ability to immigrate, the Federal Government loans the money to the province for investment, then the province returns the $400,000 to the Federal Government in five years. They in turn, return it to the immigrant investor.

Nova Scotia Strategic Opportunities Fund Inc.

The Nova Scotia Strategic Opportunities Fund Inc is one in which the provincial government can provide loans of at least $1 million for a project that:

- contributes to economic development and job creation;
- promotes export development;
- promotes the development and/or application of Information Technology;
- promotes research and development and/or technology transfer; or,
- promotes the development and/or application of environmentally sustainable technologies and infrastructure, manufacturing and production, and other business practices.

Nova Scotia companies and organizations can submit proposals in areas such as job creation, export development, information technology, environmentally sustainable infrastructure, manufacturing and production.

The Board of Directors of the Nova Scotia Strategic Opportunities Fund Incorporated ensure loans are secure and projects meet loan criteria. The Board also oversees the portfolio to mitigate risk and ensure liquidity of the funds.

Economic and Rural Development and Tourism
Centennial Building
1660 Hollis St., Suite 600
Halifax, NS B3J 1V7

P.O. Box 2311
Halifax, Nova Scotia
B3J 3C8

Phone: (902) 424-6721
Fax: (902) 424-1263
Web site: www.ci.gc.ca/english/immigrate/business/investors/index.asp

Nova Scotia Business Inc.

Nova Scotia Business Inc. is a Crown corporation which offers the following assistance to business in the Province.

Debt Financing

Nova Scotia Business Inc. offers loans, loan guarantees, payroll rebates and equity financing. Funds are to be used to assist companies to expand and to attract outside investors. Financing will not be offered to companies that will unfairly impact another similar business in the Province. Loans can be for amounts up to a maximum of $15 million dollars with repayment periods designed to meet the lenders needs.

Loans can be used for purposes such as the following:

- purchases of land and improvements to land;
- purchases or the construction of buildings and other structures, expansions or renovations to existing buildings and other structures where these structures are used for business;
- construction or purchase, of equipment, furnishings, and other fixed assets; and,
- provision of working capital based on financing in certain limited and well-defined circumstances.

Guarantees

NBSI also offers loan guarantees. Further information is available from an NSBI Business Financing Account Manager.

Further Information

Nova Scotia Business Inc.
1800 Argyle Street, Suite 701
PO Box 2374
Halifax, NS B3J 2R7
Phone: (902) 424-6650
Toll-free within Nova Scotia: 1-(877) 360-2124
Fax: (902) 424-5739
E-Mail address: info@nasbi.ca
Web site: http://www.novascotiabusiness.com

Enterprise Cape Breton Corporation (ECBC)

Enterprise Cape Breton Corporation (ECBC) is a federal Crown corporation which has been legislated to promote and assist the financing and development of industry in Cape Breton Island and the Mulgrave area. ECBC is also the local delivery agent for ACOA's programs for the region.

ECBC may provide assistance of between 25% and 75% of eligible costs for developing or upgrading a website with e-commerce capabilities and for capital assistance and export assistance.

Capital Assistance: provides loans to businesses to cover a portion of the capital costs for the construction, expansion or modernization.

Export Assistance: is provided by ECBD to help businesses become export ready.

E-commerce: provides assistance to both commercial and non-commercial enterprises to help defray the costs of incorporating e-commerce capabilities in web sites.

Enterprise Cape Breton Corporation operates from its head office in Sydney with a satellite office in Port Hawkesbury.

Enterprise Cape Breton Corporation
70 Crescent Street
P.O. Box 1750 . Sydney, NS B1P 6T7
Phone: (902) 564-3600
Phone toll-free: 1-(800) 705-3926
Fax: (902) 564-3825
E-mail: information@ecbc-secb.gc.ca,
Web site: www.ecbc.ca

Enterprise Cape Breton Corporation
32 Paint Street, Unit 1
Port Hawkesbury
Light Industrial Park
NS B9A 3J8
Phone: (902) 625-3311
Fax: (902) 625-3266

New Brunswick: Economic Development

Economic Development is a government department with a mandate to generate "economic prosperity by partnering with our stakeholders to develop opportunities for growth, innovation and globalization". It offers a number of business assistance programs.

Export Development Program

The Export Development Program is designed to support New Brunswick companies which are exporting outside the Maritime provinces. It is open to companies which process, manufacture or produce an exportable product, service, technology or intellectual property of a business to business nature.

Assistance can cover up to 50% of eligible expenses to a maximum of $5,000 per Canadian project and $10,000 per international project. Over the course of the Government's fiscal year, April 1 - March 31, the maximum assistance per company is $20,000.

Companies can make up to three applications within the same market area and similar activity.

It should be noted that any professional services must be arms' length and that in-house expertise is not eligible.

Assistance will cover:

- market reconnaissance;
- trade shows;
- business conferences;
- outbound missions;
- market planning;
- export marketing;
- matchmaking and lead generation;
- international business training;
- product and service adaptations to meet international requirements; and,
- business development visits.

Eligible costs include economy airfare or mileage; and provide per diems for two persons attending trade shows and training. They can also cover conference and exhibit costs such as space rental, booth furnishings, shipment of materials, registration fees.

In the case of incoming business partners, the program can cover return travel to New Brunswick as well as per diems.

The Program can also cover product or service adaptation costs to meet international requirements. As well as pre-production costs for activity-specific promotional and sales materials.

Marketing plans and campaigns for specific exporting activities are covered as well as the costs for professional translation of promotional materials, packaging and labelling for international markets plus professional interpretation services, for international interactions, matchmaking and lead generation. It can also cover export training costs to attend conferences, courses and seminars.

INNOV8 Program

The "INNOV8" Program is designed to reduce the risk of researching, developing, acquiring and implementing new intellectual property, innovative technologies, skills and processes. It does this by attempting to make it easier for entrepreneurs and start-up companies to access to mentorship, incubation and venture capital.

Funding is available to firms in the following sectors:

- ICT;
- biosciences;
- industrial fabrication;
- aerospace and defence;
- value-added wood; and,
- value-added food.

Assistance is designed to help with:

- improved processes,
- increased productivity,

- technological advancement,
- increased commercialization,
- export; or,
- innovation.

Funding can be for 50% to a maximum of $50,000 for companies:

- developing intellectual property;
- specialized software;
- hardware;
- equipment;
- performing research and development;
- prototyping;
- seeking access to capital;
- to cover training costs directly associated with technological advancement or enhancement in the manufacturing or production process;
- to cover in-house or third-party software development costs associated with new products, processes or projects deemed to be necessary for technological advancement;
- patent filing costs;
- travel costs to technical shows, conferences, plant visits, etc. for the acquisition of specialized knowledge, or information on competitive technologies, processes and products;
- in-house support of or travel to participate in technical training programs provided by an accredited third party for the acquisition of new skills or processes;
- product and service testing to validate new product market readiness;
- costs for advanced, innovative or "disruptive" internet or telecommunications projects;
- to seed funding from ACOA, Industry Canada or Venture Capital agent with funding to accelerate the commercialization of a new product or process;
- to implement Six-Sigma, lean initiatives, productivity and quality assurance programs and first-time qualification or certification to meet recognized standards or codes.; and,
- for assistance in the acquisition of strategic technology assets and/or services resulting in increased competitiveness.

It should be noted that up to three applications can be made by each company per year but that the maximum funding to any one company per fiscal year is $100,000. On the other hand, the minimum funding per project is $1,000.

Digital Media Development Program

The purpose of the Digital Media Development Program is to encourage growth in New Brunswick's video game sector to develop intellectual property by providing an annual payroll rebate for eligible full-time positions.

To be eligible for the program, the applicant company must:

- develop game engines or games with either entertainment or serious gaming applications;
- operate on a full-time year-round basis;
- own the Intellectual Property being supported by this program;
- be legally incorporated in the province of New Brunswick, with its head office and principal place of business in New Brunswick and its employees developing an eligible product in New Brunswick;
- have neither annual gross revenues in excess of $20 million nor total assets in excess of $10 million during the preceding taxation year on an associated corporation basis; and,
- demonstrate that it is not in a research stage, but is at an advanced stage of development and has demonstrated the potential for commercial application.

Eligible products include:

- game engines;
- games with entertainment or serious gaming applications.

The assistance is in the form of a non-repayable annual payroll rebate. The Digital Media Development Program will provide a 30% salary rebate up to a maximum of $15,000 per full-time employee per year. The rebate will be provided for production employees who are, for tax purposes, New Brunswick residents. This rebate will be limited to a maximum of $500,000 per company per year.

Any recipient of Digital Media Development Program funding is not eligible for financial assistance from any other provincial program. Eligible payroll rebates will be reduced by any amount of government assistance received or receivable.

Financial Assistance to Industry Program (FAIP)

Financial Assistance to Industry Program (FAIP) provides direct loans and loan guarantees to fund capital expenditures and provide working capital to enable the establishment, expansion, or maintenance of companies in the following categories:

- manufacturing;
- processing;
- selected tourism;
- selected commercial service sector (business to business with focus on export activity or import displacement); and,
- information technology sectors.

New Brunswick Growth Program

The New Brunswick Growth Program provides financial assistance to businesses involved in the following sectors:

- manufacturing and processing;
- information technology and related industries;
- tourism activities or service operations;
- business-to-business services involved in export or import replacement; or,
- cultural enterprises.

For Establishment of New Businesses: the New Brunswick Growth Program can provide non-repayable contributions of 50% of eligible costs to a maximum of $500,000 (equivalent to a maximum of $15,000 per new job created) to establish a "year-round" business. In the case of seasonal tourism businesses, non-repayable contributions can be for up to 50% of eligible costs to a maximum of $50,000.

For Expansion, Diversification or Productivity Improvements: the New Brunswick Growth Program can provide non-repayable contributions of 30% of eligible costs to a maximum of $60,000 for the expansion, diversification or productivity improvement of a "year-round" business. In the case of seasonal tourism businesses, non-repayable contributions can be for up to 30% of eligible costs to a maximum of $30,000.

Further Information

Economic Development
670 King Street
P.O. Box 6000
Fredericton, NB E3B 5H1
Phone: (506) 453-2727
Fax: (506) 444-4182
Web site: www.newbrunswick.ca

Innovation PEI

Innovation PEI is the lead development agency for the Province. The corporation solicits and supports investment, creating jobs and wealth for the Island; actively supports small business; encourages entrepreneurship and investment risk sharing; and actively promotes PEI as a competitive place to do business.

Entrepreneur Loan Program

The Entrepreneur Loan Program will provide up to $50,000 for qualified entrepreneurs to invest in new or expanding businesses. Loans are arranged through participating financial institutions and are guaranteed by Prince Edward Island Business Development for the life of the loan; to a maximum of five years.

Interest is charged at prime plus 2% and those with loans in good standing at the end of the first year will receive a rebate of the interest paid during that first year.

Applicants should be residents of PEI and should be the owner/operator of the business. In the case of partnerships, each partner should be a co-applicant and in the case of incorporated companies, each shareholder must be a co-applicant. All applicants and co-applicants should be over 18 years of age. Also, a cash equity of 30% of the amount of the loan is required and if this is borrowed, the assets of the business cannot be pledged as security for the loan.

Proceeds of loans cannot be used to purchase an existing business; finance transactions between related businesses and individuals or to pay existing debts.

A business plan has to be submitted in the case of businesses that are applying under the expansion component of the program. It must demonstrate an incremental increase in sales volume and/or the number of people employed by the business. Support may also be provided if the objective is to maintain the level of employment through the diversification of products or services.

Applicants can apply only once for a loan unless they have applied for and successfully paid off a previous loan. Also, the applicant and/or family members cannot own any similar business for which the new business may be considered a natural extension.

Students who operate a summer business can receive a $3,000 loan guarantee. Repayment is required by October 31 of the year in which the loan was granted. Students should be enrolled in a high school, college or university and intend to return to school in the Fall.

They should be resident of PEI. Students who have successfully paid off a previous loan may re-apply. A cash equity of 20% is required but this may be in cash or kind.

Eligible businesses for both entrepreneurs and students are those involved with manufacturing, processing, services, wholesale, retail, franchise and resource-based industries that operate at least 6 months out of the year. Specifically excluded are the following:

- professional services;
- bed and breakfast;
- desktop publishing;
- real estate;
- schools;
- the growing, extraction and harvest of any traditional resource based products;
- food and beverage services*;
- grocery/convenience stores*;
- personal services*;
- rentals*; and,
- trades, construction, contractors*.

(*where sufficient capacity exists)

It should be noted that the eligibility of approved sectors may change from time to time especially if growth in a sector became detrimental to other businesses in that sector.

Businesses must commence withing four weeks of receipt of funds. The applicants are responsible for obtaining all insurance, licenses and permits required to operate the business. They should open an account with the lending institution. In the event that the business is subsequently sold, any outstanding amount of the loan should be immediately repaid.

Winter Production Financing Program

The Winter Production Financing Program offers repayable loans of 75% (up to $10,000) on the cost of production (including materials and labour) of crafts and giftware during the winter months and which are intended for sale during peak selling periods.

Further Information

Innovation PEI
94 Euston St., P.O. Box 910
Charlottetown, PE C1A 7L9
Phone: (902) 368-6300
Fax: (902) 368-6301
Toll-free phone: 1-(800) 563-3734
E-mail: business@gov.pe.ca
Web site: http://www.peibusinessdevelopment.com

Communities Economic Development Fund (CEDF)

The Communities Economic Development Fund (CEDF) is a Manitoba Crown Corporation. It offers financial assistance as well as consulting services.

Business Loan Program

Business Loan Program offers loans and loan guarantees to support small business development or expansion in northern Manitoba, as well as loans to Aboriginal peoples in conjunction with Aboriginal economic programs within Manitoba, outside the City of Winnipeg.

CEDF Business Line: provides working capital loans backed by asset security. The loans are offered at Prime plus 2.25% for a 5 year term and are renewable. During the first 36 months clients can opt to repay only interest. The loan limit is $75,000.

CEDF Equipment Line: for equipment purchases and refurbishment in all industry sectors. Loans can be for up to $1 million. And have up to a 10 year term and bear fixed interest at CEDF rates.

CEDF Builder Line: of up to $2 million to finance property; including business acquisition where property is involved Loans are conventional mortgages with an option of floating rates or fixed rates with amortizations up to 15 years and 5 year terms.

It should be noted that CEDF requires a minimum down payment on its equipment and property loans and that a higher deposit may be required where determined by risk. The maximum limit under all programs is $2 million to any client or group of companies controlled by common shareholders.

In addition, CEDF can provide a variety of short term financing options for businesses such as bid bonding (asset backed), bridge financing for contract or funding agreements, and many other financing needs.

Fisheries Loan Program

The Fund assumed responsibility for the Fisheries Loan Program, as of April 1, 1992. This provides funding for licensed commercial fishing operators.

EDF Harvester Loans: of up to $50,000 (subject to earnings levels) for the purchase or repair of equipment used in a viable fishing operation as well as to assist in the purchase of quota entitlement. Loans are offered at floating rates based on prime or CEDF cost of funds. CEDF levies a premium for life insurance (currently 3/4% per annum) for fishers under the age of 65. CEDF currently offers a 2% Young Fisherman's discount to new fishers.

It should be noted that fish loans may not be used to repair equipment owned by a third party unless the fishers are partners and loans for quota entitlement are restricted to $1.25 per pound of quota purchase.

Further Information

The main office of the fund is located in Thompson with branches in Swan River, Gimli, The Pas and Winnipeg.

Head Office:
Communities Economic Development Fund (CEDF)
15 Moak Crescent, Thompson, MB R8N 2B8
Phone: (204) 778-4138
Toll-free phone: 1-(800) 561-4315
Fax: (204) 778-4313
Web site: www.cedf.mb.ca

Business Loans:
3 - 1000 Main St, Swan River, MB R0L 1Z0
Phone: (204) 734-5025
Fax: (204) 734-5261

Fisheries Loans:
Box 1277, Hwy 9 & 4th Street S., Gimli, MB R0C 1B0
Box 10548, Otineka Mall, Opaskwayak, MB R9A 1K5
Unit 8 - 1680 Ellice Avenue, Winnipeg, MB R3H 0Z2
Phone toll-free: 1-(888) FISH-678

Manitoba Industrial Opportunities Program (MIOP)

Manitoba Industrial Opportunities Program (MIOP) provides financial incentives, in the form of repayable loans or loan guarantees, to assist companies to locate or expand in

Manitoba. The term is 60 months. Minimum loan size is $500,000 and the maximum is $5 million. Typically loans are in excess of $500,000. All loans must be fully secured.

Projects should involve:

- major capital investment in manufacturing, processing or production of other value added tangible items and the proposed capital investment should be in excess of applicant's historical level of annual capital expenditures and significant in terms of the asset base of the company;
- high tech industries as well as financial services along with head office operations of the retailing, wholesaling and distribution sectors; and/or,
- creation of significant numbers of long term jobs and their types will be a prime consideration.

Minimum equity required is 20%. Total assistance from all levels of government cannot exceed 50% of eligible project costs. Projects are considered on a case-by-case basis, but must result in significant long-term job creation. Support packages are tailored to meet the requirements of each project and take into consideration:

- the amount of capital investment;
- the stability, salary and skill levels of the jobs created and their impact on the diversification of the technological/industrial base of the Province;
- the amount of regional development (will be given high priority); and,
- the increase exports or replace imports (which are viewed favourably).

Projects are subject to a cost-benefit analysis and risk appraisal.

An application fee may be required prior to instructions from the client to proceed with developing a Formal Agreement/Letter of Offer. In addition, a legal and administrative fee is payable on acceptance of any final offer. Any additional fees and expenses can be deducted from the first advance.

Manitoba's Industrial Opportunities Program (MIOP)
Manitoba Entrepreneurship, Training and Trade
1040 – 259 Portage Avenue Winnipeg, MB R3B 3P4
Phone: (204) 945-1015
Phone toll-free: 1-(800) 282-8069
Fax: (204) 945-1193

Saskatchewan Ministry of the Economy

The Ministry of the Economy is charged with establishing partnerships involving all levels of government, industry, labour, Aboriginal people, post secondary institutions, and other stakeholders dedicated to achieving economic growth in the Province. Its Board of Directors comprises a broad cross-section of stakeholders and leaders and it will establish industry-led Strategic Issues Councils to advise the Province on ways to enhance its competitive advantage.

Small Business Loans Associations (SBLA) Program

The Small Business Loans Associations (SBLA) are designed to provide business development opportunities to the non-traditional entrepreneur by making loans to smaller businesses. They are also designed to enhance the economic status of individuals by offering access to resources not otherwise available, in order to facilitate business ownership.

In order to form a Small Business Loans Association, four or more community-based groups (individuals, partnerships, co-operatives or corporations) should incorporate under the Business Corporations Act or the Co-operatives Act, as either "profit" or "non-profit". Rural Development Corporations and Regional Economic Development Authorities (REDAs) may qualify as SBLAs because of their broad membership base.

Once approved, SBLAs can apply to Saskatchewan Industry and resources for a revolving line of credit of up to $200,000. Using this line of credit, a SBLA can then make loans of up to $20,000 to new and existing businesses that are experiencing difficulty in obtaining financing through traditional means. Interest on the loans can vary according to the association but cannot exceed 10% per annum. Also, the maximum term on the loans is five years. Principal repayments are returned by the SBLA to Saskatchewan Industry and resources but the SBLA retains the loan interest to cover its administrative expenses.

Preference is given to businesses that can create jobs and add services to the communities. Also considered is the ability of a business to lever the loan to obtain bank or credit union financing, and in this way help entrepreneurs who might not otherwise get started.

Businesses that are not eligible to receive assistance include those that are engaged in direct farming, exploration, residential real estate or multi-level marketing schemes. Charitable organizations are also excluded.

Businesses can use SBLA loans to purchase assets, such as equipment, but they cannot be used for operating expenses or for the repayment of existing debt.

Businesses which wish to borrow from a SBLA should contact their local association for program information and an application form. A business plan has to be submitted with the application, together with a $30 administration fee. A general security agreement and signed promissory note will also be required.

Small Business Loans Association Program
Ministry of the Economy
200 - 3085 Albert Street
Regina SK S4S 0B1
Phone: (306) 787-4707
Fax: (306) 798-0796
E-mail: SBLA@enterprisesask.ca

SaskPower Northern Enterprise Fund (SPNEF)

The SaskPower Northern Enterprise Fund supports the development of businesses and provides training for professional and technical jobs in the North. Money for the Fund is contributed by the sale of electricity from three of SaskPower's northern hydro stations. Prior to June 1998, these contributions amounted to about $900,000 per year.

The Fund is administered by seven Directors and applications must receive a majority vote to be accepted. It is open to northern residents within the historic Administration District.

Preference is shown to submissions which help to diversify or expand existing businesses. New enterprises are also approved, especially when they contribute to the economic development of the community.

Generally, any commercially viable project may be considered including:

- the acquisition of fixed assets;
- refinancing of existing borrowings;
- the purchase of an existing business; and,
- establishing a new business.

Applicants must invest at least 10% of their own assets in the project and the equity must be relevant to the proposed business. It is possible to access other program monies and use these in addition to the assistance offered by the Fund.

Support is in the form of loans or loan guarantees, to a maximum of $100,000. Projects requiring larger investments may be syndicated with other financial institutions.

Those who wish to apply should complete an application form and submit a copy of their business plan. The latter should clearly state how much money is required and what it will be used for. In addition, financial statements, marketing information and sales contracts must clearly demonstrate the viability of the business. Applications are reviewed at the Board meeting held once a month.

Applications are judged on the following criteria:

- project viability
- debt serviceability

- management ability and related experience
- credit history
- equity contribution
- security.

SaskPower Northern Enterprise Fund
P.O. Box 220, Beauval, SK S0M 0G0
Phone: (306) 288-2258   Fax: (306) 288-4667
Toll-free phone: 1-(800) 864-3022
Web site: http://www.nefi.ca

Northern Development Fund

In February 1995, the Saskatchewan Government provided further details of the Northern Development Fund. This initiative is designed to stimulate economic development in Northern Saskatchewan.

Youth Entrepreneurship Grant Program: encourages the development of entrepreneurial and business skills in Northern Saskatchewan to residents under the age of 30. Assistance will cover up to 70% of eligible costs to a maximum of $10,000 per project.

Marketing Promotion Research and Development Grant Program: provides targeted financial and technical assistance for new business development, diversification and business expansion. Assistance will cover up to 70% of eligible costs to a maximum of $10,000 per project and up to $25,000 in overall grant money.

Business Skill and Organizational Development Grant Program: provides targeted financial and technical assistance to help improve the business skills of northern entrepreneurs as well as community development organizations. Assistance will cover up to 70% of eligible costs to a maximum of $2,500.

Primary Production Loan Program: provides support for individuals engaged in traditional northern production activities such as for the purchase of capital equipment for wild rice production, trapping and commercial fishing.

Saskatchewan First Nations and Métis Relations
Mistasinihk Place, Box 5000
La Ronge, SK S0J 1L0
Phone: (306) 425-4200
Toll-free phone: 1-(866) 663-4065
Fax: (306) 425-4267
Web site: www.economy.gov.sk.ca/NDF

Alberta - Agriculture Financial Services Corporation (AFSC)

Agriculture Financial Services Corporation (AFSC) is a provincial Crown corporation which has merged with the Alberta Opportunity Company (AOC). AFSC reports directly to the Alberta Minister of Agriculture, Food and Rural Development. It is partly funded by the government but also has many alliances with private sector companies.

Commercial Loan Program

The Commercial Loan Program can be used to start, expand, purchase, or upgrade facilities, equipment, or other capital assets needed for a commercial enterprise. Loans can be for up to $5 million and it is possible to re-borrow up to the maximum limit as loans are paid down or paid out.

Web site: www.afsc.ca
Phone toll-free: 1-(877) 899-2372
AFCS maintains business loan offices throughout Alberta:

The First Citizens' Fund (FCF)

The First Citizens' Fund is a $25 million fund established by the Government of British Columbia in 1969. Interest earned on the fund is dedicated to enhancing social, educational, and economic development opportunities for North American Aboriginals (status, non-status, Métis and Inuit) who normally reside in British Columbia.

Specifically the fund supports:

- business loans;
- business support officers;
- business advisory centres in Prince George, Cranbrook and Fort St. John;
- elders transportation;
- student bursaries;
- friendship centres (program directors); and,
- heritage, language and culture.

Business Loan Program

The objective of the Business Loan Program is to support Aboriginal economic development through:

- assisting with the expansion of existing Aboriginal businesses;
- supporting the establishment of successful new businesses that are owned and operated by Aboriginal people;
- supporting Aboriginal people to acquire existing businesses;
- supporting the development of Aboriginal business management abilities; and,
- creating employment opportunities for Aboriginal people.

The lifetime maximum program loan amount is $76,125.00 (inclusive of borrower's fee of $1,125.00) of which 40% can be forgiven. The forgiven contribution is applied by installments on a pro-rata basis over the term of the loan.

Loans can be used for the creation, expansion, upgrading or purchase of Aboriginal businesses.

The program is open to all types of businesses but will not provide financing for revolving lines of credit or for refinancing of existing businesses.

The eligibility criteria are as follows:

- applicants must be North American Aboriginal ancestry (status, non-status, Métis and Inuit) who live in British Columbia;
- the applicant business must be at least 51% owned and operated by North American Aboriginal people living in British Columbia;
- the business must be a proprietorship, partnership, cooperative, or an incorporated company;
- the applicant business may include Aboriginal non-profit societies that intend to organize and run a separate business;
- a detailed, workable business plan must be submitted that fully explains the business proposal;
- the business plan must show that the proposed business can lead to permanent employment opportunities;
- the business head office and main business operation must be in British Columbia;
- the applicant business must meet the equity and security requirements as defined by the Aboriginal Capital Corporation to which application is being made;
- applicants must not already have received their "Lifetime Maximum Amount" of $76,125 which is the total maximum amount in Program Loans that a borrower is eligible to receive under the Loan Program.

In general, 15% equity contributions are required by the applicant and security must be provided in the form of promissary notes, charge on assets, corporate and personal guarantees. Terms and repayment schedules will be established on a case-by-case basis and interest rates are set by the Aboriginal Capital Corporation that is administering the loan.

All loan participants are assigned a Business Services Officer who is responsible for providing assistance with planning, financing, counselling, business training workshops, aftercare and mentoring.

Further Information

All Nations Trust Company
208 - 345 Yellowhead Highway
Kamloops, BC V2H 1H1
Phone: (250) 828-9770
Fax: (250) 372-2585
Toll Free: 1-(800) 663-2959
E-mail address: antco@antco.bc.ca
Web site: www.antco.bc.ca

Tribal Resources Investment Corporation
344 West 2nd. Avenue
Prince Rupert, BC V8J 1G6
Phone: (250) 624-3535
Fax: (250) 624-3883
Toll Free: 1-(800) 665-3201
E-mail address: tricorp@citytel.net
Web site: www.tricorp.ca

Tale'awtxw Aboriginal Capital Corporation
Suite 508 - 100 Park Royal
West Vancouver, BC V7T 1A2
Phone: (604) 926-5626
Fax: (604) 926-5627
Toll-free phone: 1-(800) 779-7199
E-mail address: info@tacc.ca
Web site: www.tacc.ca

First Nations Agricultural Lending Association
7410 Dallas Dr.
Kamloops BC
Phone: (250) 314-6804
Toll-free phone: 1-(866) 314-6804
Fax: (250) 314-6809
E-mail address: info@fnala.com
Web site: www.fnala.com

Nuu-chah-nulth Economic
Development Corporation
7563 Pacific Rim Hwy, PO Box 1384
Port Alberni, BC V9Y 7M2
Phone: (250) 724-3131
Toll-free phone: 1-(866) 444-6332
Fax: (250) 724-9967
E-mail address: nedc@island.net
Web site: www.nedc.info

Yukon: Venture Loan Guarantee Program

The Venture Loan Guarantee Program is open to new business start-ups or expansions of existing businesses registered in the Yukon, which have less than 100 employees and under $5 million in gross revenues.

The business program is an initiative between the Government of Yukon and:

- Bank of Montreal;
- Bank of Nova Scotia;
- Business Development Bank of Canada;
- Canadian Imperial Bank of Commerce;
- Däna Näye Ventures;
- Royal Bank of Canada; and,
- Toronto Dominion Bank.

Assistance is in the form of guarantees for 65% on loans, for which there is little or no security. The minimum loan that will be considered is $10,000 and the maximum is $100,000. Terms can be for up to a maximum of six years and interest-only payments are required in the first year. A one-time fee of 1.5% is payable at the time of the issue of the guarantee.

To be eligible, businesses should be start-ups or expansions with under $5 million in gross revenues and fewer than 100 employees. They should be involved in one of the following activities:

- development and distribution of new products or services;
- the export of goods or services;
- export substitution;
- high technology;
- information services; or,
- tourism attractions that need upgrading.

Business activities which are not eligible include:

- retail operations;
- tourism accommodations;
- refinancing of existing debt;
- speculative real estate transactions;
- changes in ownership; and,
- transactions involving withdrawal of shareholder loans.

Venture loans represent those portions of loans for which there is inadequate or no security and are established as a separate loan. The bank will take all reasonable security to support the loan, such as personal guarantees and general security agreements, as deemed appropriate.

Equity requirements are determined by the bank, based on the nature of the project and the risk involved.

Applications should be made at private sector banks or financial institutions, which in turn will evaluate the projects and either approve or reject them. These banks or financial institutions will be responsible for loaning the money and collecting interest and repayments of principal.

Business Development, Business and Industry Branch
Department of Economic Development
PO Box 2703 (F-2) Whitehorse, YT Y1A 2C6
Phone: (867) 393-7014
Phone toll-free: 1-(800) 661-0408 ext. 7014
Fax: (867) 393-6944

Däna Näye Ventures (DNV)

Däna Näye Ventures (DNV) is a Yukon-based and Aboriginal owned and controlled institution with a mission to assist Yukon people and communities to become more self-reliant. It will provide finance for development, as well as advisory services, to entrepreneurs and Yukon businesses. At the same time it undertakes to preserve the Yukon environment, respect for social and cultural values of the Yukon people and place a strong emphasis on developing people as the key resource for building successful businesses.

It offers assistance to business in the following areas.

Yukon Micro Loan Fund

The Yukon Government provided $258,000 to fund a three year pilot project designed to improve access to capital for budding entrepreneurs.

The Yukon Micro Loan Fund is modelled after similar programs across Canada. These programs differ from conventional lending arrangements in that they have more flexible requirements for collateral, personal credit history and employment status.

The Fund is a pool of loan capital generated to support micro-entrepreneurs in their activities. The federal Department of Indian Affairs and Northern Development and Däna Näye Ventures have also contributed to the program.

Administered by Däna Näye Ventures, this program will also provide successful applicants with training and support. It also involves training local volunteer facilitators to manage peer lending groups so the program can be offered throughout the Yukon.

Borrowers can receive initial loans of up to $2,000. As loan recipients develop a successful track record, the loan ceiling could be raised to $8,000; in $2,000 increments. Terms are for 3 months to 3 years.

Loans can be used for any business purpose such as:

• to buy or lease equipment, tools, computers, leasehold improvements, craft materials and supplies, etc.,
• pay for first and last months business rent, advertising or purchase inventory.

DNV holds information sessions several times a year which provides applicants with the opportunity to meet other potential peer lending circle members.

Aboriginal Business Development Program (ABDP)

DNV is a delivery agent of the Aboriginal Business Development Program (ABDP) for the Yukon and the northern British Columbia communities of Atlin, Good Hope Lake and Lower Post. Funding is available for activities such as:

*   developing business, marketing or feasibility plans;
*   establishing a business or acquiring information technology;
*   expanding/acquiring a profitable business or developing new products, services or production processes;
*   project-related management; or,
*   accounting and professional business advice after starting a business.

Further Information

Däna Näye Ventures, 409 Black Street
Whitehorse, YT Y1A 2N2
Phone: (867) 668-6925 Fax: (867) 668-3127
Toll-free phone: 1-(800) 661-0448
E-mail address: dnv@dananaye.com
Web site: www.dananaye.yk.net

N.W.T. Business Development & Investment Corporation (BDIC)

The N.W.T. Business Credit Corporation (BCC) and the Northwest Territories Development Corporation have been merged to form a new entity known as the N.W.T. Business Development & Investment Corporation (BDIC).

At the time of writing the activities of the former Business Credit Corporation and the Development Corporation continue to be offered under the BDIC.

BDIC continues the mandate of the former Northwest Territories Development Corporation to create jobs and income opportunities in less developed communities in the Northwest Territories. In order to accomplish this mandate, it may create and operate businesses or invest as a minority partner in new or expanding businesses.

Term Loans

Term Loans are available for up to $2 million. Repayment terms are for a maximum of five years with amortization over 25 years. In certain circumstances, interest may be deferred for up to three years.

Standby Letters of Credit (SLC)

Standby Letters of Credit (SLC) can be used in cases where a business makes a bid and contract security is required. Alternatively, SLCs can be used in cases where suppliers require security of payment. The maximum term is usually one year.

Standby Letter of Credit Facility

The SLC Facility usually has terms of 5 years and features an aggregate dollar limit. Commission of between 2% and 4% is charged, depending on the risk.

BDIC Working Capital Guarantee

BDIC Working Capital Guarantee helps businesses obtain working capital financing (i.e. operating lines of credit or overdraft) by guaranteeing a working capital arrangement with the lender's bank in the form of an Irrevocable Standby Letter of Credit.

Contributions

BDIC can make contributions of up to $10,000 in Level I Communities (including Hay River, Fort Smith and Inuvik) and $20,000 in Level II Communities. These are the maximum contributions over a five-year period and applicants must have annual sales of under $500,000. In addition artists, crafts-people and renewable resource harvesters are eligible.

Funds can be used for start-up expenses, expansion, the acquisition of assets, marketing, feasibility assessments, business plans and research projects. Applicants should be able to demonstrate that new employment will be created.

BDIC and SBDC sign MOA

In March 2010, BDIC and the Sahtu Business Development Centre (SBDC) signed a Memorandum of Agreement to offer a range of credit and venture capital financing options to Sahtu's clients. The Agreement is to provide for joint client transactions in order to enhance the financing options offered to clients. This will also enable the SBDC to entertain loan applications for amounts exceeding its lending limit.

Further Information

N.W.T. Business Development & Investment Corporation (BDIC)
Suite 701, 5201 - 50th Ave. Yellowknife, NT X1A 3S9
Phone: (867) 920-6452
Fax: (867) 765-0652
Web site: http://www.bdic.ca

Nunavut Business Credit Corporation (NBCC)

The Nunavut Business Credit Corporation (NBCC) is a Territorial Crown Corporation, with a Board of Directors of up to 12 persons. NBCC provides financing up to $1 million to both Inuit and non-Inuit businesses based in Nunavut. Terms can be for up to 25 years and loans are at competitive interest rates. NBCC accepts applications for new and established businesses looking to expand or better establish themselves in their market.

Loans can be used for:

- the purchase of fixed assets;
- leasehold improvements;
- consolidation of debt;
- bid bond security for contractors;
- providing working capital for inventory acquisition; and,
- interim or bridge financing.

Nunavut Business Credit Corporation
Box 2548
Suite 100, Parnavak Building
Iqaluit, NU X0A 0H0
Phone: (867) 975-7891
Phone tol-free: 1-(888) 758-0038
Fax: (867) 975-7897
E-mail address: credit@nbcc.nu.ca
Web site: http://www.nbcc.nu.ca

7

Other Non-Conventional Loans

Ulnooweg Development Group Inc. (UDG)

The Ulnooweg Development Group Inc. is a non-profit, Aboriginal Capital Corporation which operates in the Atlantic Provinces. It offers two types of loans to peoples of Aboriginal origin.

Ulnooweg Business Loan

The Ulnooweg Loan is open to Aboriginal business owners in Atlantic Canada and can be used for any business need, including expansion, acquisition and refinancing. The maximum loan size is $250,000 and the interest is 12.75% with flexible loan repayment plans.

Ulnooweg Youth Business Loan

The Ulnooweg Youth Business Loan is available to Aboriginal business owners in Atlantic Canada who are aged 35 or younger. Loans can be used for anything except refinancing. The maximum loan size is $15,000 with loan interest generally set at 8.5% and a maximum 5-year payback schedule. There is potential for forgiveness of up to 25% of the value of the loan.

Small Loan Program for the Cottage Craft Industry

The Small Loan Program for the Cottage Craft Industry provides loans of up to $1,000 with fixed interest rate at 8% and a pay-back term of one year. Loans can be used for purchasing inventory, raw materials, tools and for marketing purposes.

Further Information

Ulnooweg Development Group Inc.
P.O. Box 1259, 835 Willow St.
Truro, NS B2N 5N2
Phone: (902) 893-7379
Fax: (902) 893-0353
Web site: www.ulnooweg.ca

Ulnooweg Development Group Inc.
Kchikhusis Commercial Center
150 Cliffe Street, Box R14
Fredericton, NB E3A 2TI
Phone: (506) 455-9334
Fax: (506) 444-7582

Ulnooweg Development Group Inc.
P.O. Box 20007, Town Centre Post Office
90 Main St. Stephenville, NL A2N 3R8
Phone: (709) 643-5005 Fax: (709) 643-5006

Saint John Community Loan Fund

The Saint John Community Loan Fund can provide micro business loans of up to $7,500 for local entrepreneurs who have difficulty obtaining credit through conventional sources. Each loan carries a 10% fee and an interest rate of the current prime rate plus 3%. Loan decisions are made by a committee.

Saint John Community Loan Fund
133 Prince Edward St. Saint John, NB E2L 3S3
Phone: (506) 652-5626 Fax: (506) 652-5603
E mail address: loansw@loanfund.ca
Web site: http://www.loanfund.ca

Financial Assistance Program for Young Entrepreneurs
Société d'Investissement Jeunesse

Candidates for this program must be between 18 and 35 years old. Candidates must be Canadian citizens or landed immigrants who have lived in the Province of Québec for at least the last two years.

Projects must involve implementing a business plan such as starting, acquiring or investing in a business (Partnership).

The business must be profit-oriented, have its head office in Québec, and be incorporated at the time the Bureau de la société d'investissement jeunesse (S.I.J.) funding is provided. The firm may be involved in any type of business except for real estate speculation, brokerage of real estate securities, or the practice of a profession such as lawyer, doctor, dentist, accountant or notary.

Candidates must personally invest a cash sum equal to at least 10% of the total financial requirements of the business. In projects involving more than one entrepreneur, their total investment must also be equal to at least 10%.

Entrepreneurs must work full-time in the proposed business.

The Société d'Investissement Jeunesse guarantees 100% of personal loans extended by any of the following financial institutions, which recognize the merits of its program:

- BMO Group financier
- TD Canada Trust
- Caisses Desjardins
- Canadian Imperial Bank of Commerce
- Laurentian Bank of Canada
- RBC Royal Bank of Canada
- Scotia Bank
- National Bank.

The ceiling on personal loan guarantees is $75,000 per eligible entrepreneur, depending on the financial structure of the project. In the case of three or more eligible entrepreneurs, the total guarantee may not exceed $225,000.

An annual management fee amounting to 2% of the loan guarantee is charged. Other fees may be payable depending on the nature of the project. For example a royalty on sales of up to 3%; stock purchase options on up to 10% of company shares.

The interest rate should not exceed the lender's prime plus 1%. Principal is repaid progressively on a term of five years. No principal repayment is necessary in the first year. Repayment of the principal begins in the 13th month and takes the form of equal monthly payments according to the following schedule:

Year	Principal Payable
1	0%
2	10%
3	20%
4	30%
5	40%
	100%

The interest is paid monthly starting the first month following disbursement of the loan, and there are no penalties for loan prepayment.

Procedure for obtaining an S.I.J. Loan Guarantee involves preparing a complete business plan for the company which determines its financial requirements and then finding the necessary sources of financing. Among other things, this includes arranging a long-term and personal loan from a financial institution as required by the program.

All business proposals submitted to the S.I.J. are assigned to a financial analyst who normally contacts the entrepreneur within 10 working days after receipt of the application to inform him or her of its eligibility for the program.

The time required for analysis depends on the quality of the documents submitted. If the business plan is complete and the Application for Financial Assistance is properly filled out, it normally takes an average of 5 to 6 weeks to reach a final decision.

The decision to provide a loan guarantee involves signing an agreement under which the entrepreneur and the company undertake to:

- hand over to the S.I.J. the entrepreneur's share certificates as a pledge of commitment;
- adhere to the shareholders' agreement submitted to the S.I.J. in the case of more than one shareholder;
- maintain the ownership structure of the business in the same form as when the S.I.J. loan guarantee was extended;
- not withdraw the personal investment(s);
- not declare or pay any shareholder dividends; and,
- not extend any advances of loans to the shareholders, owners or related companies.

Centre de transfert d'enterprises Capitale-Nationale
76, rue Saint-Paul, Bureau 100
Québec, QC G1K 3V9
Phone: (418) 529-8475 xt 263
Fax: (418) 529-6750
E-mail address: francis.nadeau@ctecn.qc.ca
Web site: www.ctecn.qc.ca

Youth Employment Services (YES)

Youth Employment Services (YES) offers a series of workshops covering business topics and a workshop series for self-employed artists. YES provides individual counselling, coordinates networking/support groups for novice entrepreneurs, hosts an annual youth employment conference, and provides access to a resource library and computers.

Grants

Entrepreneurship Contest: offers an award of $1,000 for a business start-up. At the time of writing, the contest had been closed.

Business Loans

New business loans are available for up to $45,000 through Youth Employment Services in partnership with the Canadian Youth Business Foundation (CYBF).

The eligibility criteria for applicants are as follows:

- be between 18 and 34 years of age and be eligible to work in Canada;
- demonstrate relevant knowledge and/or experience within the industry;
- work in the business on a full-time basis;
- present a business plan demonstrating the viability of the proposed business; and,
- be in business for less than 12 months (from the time of the first sale).

Further Information

Youth Employment Services (YES)
666 Sherbrooke St. W., 7th Fl.,
Montreal, QC H3A 1E7
Phone: (514) 878-9788
Fax: (514) 878-9950
E-mail: info@yesmtl.org
Web site: http://www.yesmtl.org

Fondation du maire: le Montréal Inc.

The Fondation du maire: le Montréal Inc. helps young Montrealers who aspire to launch their own business by providing them start-up grants to cover a maximum of 25 % of a project's start-up costs from $5,000 to a maximum of $30,000. Entrepreneurs that wish to obtain a grant must attend an information session and meet with a coordinator at least one week prior to the deadline dates. They must also submit a comprehensive file before the deadline dates and present their project in front of an evaluation committee.

To be eligible, they must be between 18 and 35 years of age and be a Canadian citizen or permanent resident. They should have an annual personal revenue of less than or equal to $35,000 or be the beneficiary of government assistance (employment insurance, income security or Self-Employment Program). They should have a personal balance sheet equal to or less than $25,000. They must have resided within the agglomeration of Montreal for at least three consecutive months and have been in business for less than twelve months. They should own over 50% of the company's shares or jointly hold them with other eligible entrepreneurs; as the case may be.

The Fondation du maire: le Montréal Inc.
1550 Metcalfe, suite 603
Montréal QC H3A 3P1
Phone: (514) 872-8401
Fax: (514) 872-2957
Web site: http://www.montrealinc.ca

Réseau Québec Community Credit (RQCC) Network

The RQCC Network provides access to credit to people excluded from traditional financial networks and funding for the creation of enterprises and the economic reintegration.

The first level of support is the niche community credit in Québec, including business angels and love money, which comes to the phases of pre-startup and startup for smaller funds.

Community credit allows some informal investors to be grouped. It offers them the opportunity of an ethical investment, but also a place of business support, support / consulting, consultants or simply involvement in corporate structures organizations community credit (loan committee, council Administration and support committees).

Credit supply members RQCC rarely exceeds $20,000 per project. In the case of "bridge loans" higher amounts may be given for a short period for community organizations, social enterprises or companies developing awaiting payment funding .

Across the RQCC, its members provide an average loan of $2,650 for Circles loan for a period of 12 to 36 months and $ 7,200 for the Community Loan Fund which has a duration of 2.5 years. The support is for the duration of the loan.

In 2011-2012, $ 1.3 million had been loaned by RQCC members in Québec.

In 12 years, 1,700 loans totalling $10 million were granted by member organizations and an estimated 4,210 jobs were created. The average rate of refund obtained by each organization is 91%.

The Québec Community Credit Network (RQCC) comprises twenty-three (23) members operating in twelve (12) administrative regions of the province. The diversity of practices reflects the specific needs of each region.

Québec Community Credit Network
3333, rue du Carrefour, room A-291
Quebec QC G1C 5R9
Phone: (418) 529-7928
Phone toll-free: 1-(877) 810-7722
Fax: (418) 266-0139
E-mail:info@rqcc.qc.ca

Member Organizations

Microcredit KRTB
2456 Commercial south
Témiscouata-sur-le-Lac QC G0L 1X0
Phone: (418) 899-6858
Fax: (418) 899-2212

Credit-Access Network
76 St Germain Street West, Suite 105
Rimouski QC G5L 4B5
Phone: (418) 734-0012
Fax: (418) 734-8753
Web site: www.reseauaccescredit.com

Community support fund inc.
Circles borrowing Saguenay Lac-St-Jean
240, rue Bossé, Chicoutimi QC G7J 1L9
Phone: (418) 698-1176 xt 245
F ax: (418) 543-9912
Web site: www.lefec.org

Credit Fund Community Ilnu Mashteuiatsh
1516 Ouiatchouan Street
Mashteuiatsh QC G0W 2H0
Phone: (418) 275-5757
Web site: www.sdei.ca

Lending circles Charlevoix
6, rue Saint-Jean-Baptiste, Suite 102
Baie St-Paul QC G3Z 1L7
Phone: (418) 435-3673 xt 245
Fax: (418) 435-0126
Web site:
www.cerclesdempruntdecharlevoix.org

Fonds d'emprunt Québec
155, boul. Charest Est, Suite 120
Québec QC G1K 3G6
Phone: (418) 525-0139
Fax: (418) 525-6960
Web site: www.fonds-emprunt.qc.ca

Community Loan Fund of the Mauricie
Fonds communautaire d'emprunt de la Mauricie
743, boulevard St-Maurice
Trois-Rivières QC G9A 3P5
Phone: (819) 371-9050
F ax: (819) 371-7968
Web site: www.fcem.qc.ca

Lending circles Pro-Gestion Estrie
93, Wellington North
Sherbrooke QC J1H 5B6
Phone: (819) 822-6163
Fax: (819) 822-6045
Web site: www.progestion.qc.ca

Community Loan Association
of Montreal (ACEM)
Circles borrowing Island Montreal
3680 Jeanne-Mance, Suite 319
Montreal QC H2X 2K5
Phone: (514) 843-7296
Fax: (514) 843-6832
Web site: www.acemcreditcommunautaire.qc.ca

Company F / Aurora
1274 , rue Jean-Talon East, Suite 204
Montreal QC H2S 2L9
Phone: (514) 381-7333 xt 204
Fax: (514) 381-6481
Web site: http://www.compagnie-f.org/

Circles borrowing Development
Corporation Eastern (CDEST)
2030, boul. Pius IX, Suite 201
Montreal QC H1V 2C8
Phone: (514) 256-6825 xt 246
Fax: (514) 256-0669
Web site: www.cdest.qc.ca

Lending circles of women use Option
365 Greber Boulevard, Suite 203
Gatineau QC J8T 5R3
Phone: (819) 246-1725 xt 227
Fax: (819) 246-5310
Web site: www.optionfemmesemploi.qc.ca

Access micro-credit Gaspésie
183, Grand Pre, Bonaventure QC G0C 1E0
Phone: (418) 534-3834
Fax: (418) 534-4995
Web site: www.creditcommunautaire.org

Micro-credit Lotbinière
153 Boul.Laurier
Laurier Station QC G0S 1N0
Phone: (418) 728-3330
Fax; (418) 596-3303
Web site: www.microcreditlotbiniere.org

Société Communautaire
Lavalloise d'Emprunt (SOCLE)
512, boulevard des Laurentides, Suite 202
Laval QC H7G 2V4
Phone: (450) 668-1200
Web site: www.socle.org

Fonds communautaire d'Accès au micro-crédit
96 Turgeon Street, Suite 200
Sainte-Thérèse QC J7E 3H9
Phone: (450) 818-4830 xt 22
Fax (450) 818-4832
Web site: www.fondsmicrocredit.qc.ca

Fonds d'Emprunt des Laurentides
Laurentian Community Projects
(borrowing circles)
508, rue Principale
Lachute QC J8H 1Y3
Phone: (450) 562-3553
Fax: (450) 562-1601
Web site: www.felaurentides.org

Community Loan Association
of the South Shore (ACERS)
2010-B, chemin de Chambly
Longueuil QC J4J 3Y2
Phone: (450) 679-5822
Fax: (450) 748-1677
Web site: www.acers.qc.ca

Service clubs of the South Shore
230 Brébeuf Street, Suite 201
Longueuil QC J3G 5P3
Phone: (450) 446-8279
Fax: (450) 446-3806
Web site: www.cercles-entraide.ca

Compagnie F Entrepreneurship for Women

Compagnie F is a member of the RQCC Network. It operates a light lunch café and provides self-employment training and coaching for women entrepreneurs. Marketing and promotion training will also provide the tools to improve skills through practical exercises, workshops, mentoring and networking activities.

Aurora - Loan Circle & Business Training Program

Aurora is a micro-credit and entrepreneurship training program offered in English. It is available to low income women who live in Greater Montreal.

It features the following:

- entrepreneurship training course to develop one's business plan and create a network;
- up to $5,000 in micro-credit for business start-up (through a structure called a loan circle);
- Harvard case study method each week;
- support groups and individual business coaching;
- references to other resources and useful programs in Montreal; and,
- 12 week training (one and a half days per week).

Free information sessions are offered to explain the program.

Compagnie F, Entrepreneurship for Women
1274 Jean-Talon East, Office 204
Montréal, QC H2R 1W3
Phone: (514) 381-7333
Fax: (514) 381- 6481
Web site: http://www.compagnie-f.org

221

Fonds d'Emprunt des Laurentides

The Fonds d'Emprunt des Laurentides is a member of the RQCC Network. It offers several forms of financial assistance.

Loan Circles for Women: are group sessions oriented on the start up of a business. These group sessions are for women with a clear idea for a business, but have no business plan. The women entering this program learn the stages of starting a business, basic notions in administrations used in everyday life and in their company and how to make a business plan step by step with a dynamic group.

Loan funds: is a program of individual coaching offered to everyone. It includes help to improve the business plan, business coaching according to the specific needs of the promoters, preparing for the loan application with the Fond d'Emprunt des Laurentides or any other financial institutions. It is designed for men and women who already began their process of starting a business. These persons have a complete business plan or completed up to 50%, and have specific needs.

Microcredit: is to grant loans to business owners excluded from traditional networks of financing to make their business prosper and reach financial autonomy. It is for men and women who want to get a loan to start a business or to consolidate their project. They must go through the "Fonds d'Emprunt" in order to have access to microcredit.
.

Fonds d'Emprunt des Laurentides
508, rue Principale
Lachute QC J8H 1Y3
Phone: (450) 562-3553
Phone toll-free: 1-(888) 782-3553
Fax: (450) 562-1601
E-mail address: info@felaurentides.org
Web site: http://www.felaurentides.org

Cercles d'Emprunt de Montréal

The Cercles d'Emprunt de Montréal operates a micro loan fund for the Montreal area. It offers micro-credit loans of $1,000, $2,000 and $5,000. Financing is restricted to members of the credit circle.

Cercles d'Emprunt de Montréal
366, rue Victoria, bureau 7
Westmount QC H3Z 2N4
Phone: (514) 849-3271

Drummondville Economic Development Authority

The mission of the Drummondville Economic Development Society (CLD Drummond) is to promote commerce, industry, and tourism and by way of this create favourable conditions for economic development in the MRC.

Young Business Developers Funds

The Young Business Developers Funds was created to financially help young entrepreneurs with a subsidy in their first business project. Assistance will cover 15% to a maximum of $6,000 of the total cost. The level of assistance will not exceed the total amount invested by the young developer.

Applicants must be between 18 and 35 years in age and starting a business in the MRC of Drummond and will create at least 2 jobs over the first two years of operation, including the entrepreneur's job.

Business must be in the following sectors: manufacturing, distributing or wholesaling, or a business that brings a new product and/or service to the region.

Local Investment Funds (FLI)

The Local Investment Funds (FLI) is an investment fund for the creation and preservation of jobs through financial help in the form of a loan to start or expand a small to medium sized business in the MRC of Drummond.

Assistance is fixed at 25% of admissible expenses with a minimum of $5,000 and a maximum of $100,000.

This fund is for businesses with 100 or fewer employees, in start up or expansion, and that are in manufacturing, distributing or wholesaling, or recreation-tourism.

Further Information

Drummondville Economic Development Authority
1400, rue Michaud
Drummondville QC J2C 7V3
Phone: (819) 477-5511
Fax: (819) 477-5512
Web site: http://www.sded-drummond.qc.ca

Aboriginal Loan Guarantee Program

The Aboriginal Loan Guarantee Program was announced in the 2009 Budget and provides $250 million in support of Aboriginal participation in new renewable green energy infrastructure like wind, solar and hydroelectric. By participating in renewable energy projects, First Nation and Métis communities can benefit from jobs and training as projects are developed and from dividends

Sandy Roberts
Director of the Strategic Project Finance Branch
Ontario Financing Authority
Phone: (416) 325-1557
E-mail address: algp@ofina.on.ca

Community Micro Finance Program

The Community Micro Finance Program is offered by Alterna Savings to those who are self-employed or planning to start a small business. It offers the following:

- access to small business loans at competitive interest rates;
- financing for a legitimate business which operates seasonally, full or part-time; and,
- a full service financial institution to facilitate small business financial needs.

The Calmeadow Metro Fund was originally launched in 1994 to provide business credit to self-employed individuals who were unqualified for credit from traditional lenders in the Greater Toronto Area. It later became the Metro Credit Union Community Micro Loan Program and more recently, the Alterna Community Finance Loan Program.

The program works on the premise that larger financial institutions find it hard to fit small businesses into their lending criteria due to a variety of factors. As a credit union, Metro Credit Union understands the needs of small business and recognizes that small business is the driving force of the economy. It assists in providing and encouraging, and supportive environment for self-employment.

The qualification guidelines are as follows:

- all applicants must be a graduate from a recognized business training program;
- all applicants must have legal residency in Canada;
- all applicants must be a minimum of 19 years of age;
- operate a legal, seasonal, full or part-time business;
- have a low income due to self-employment;

- conduct financial business activities at Alterna Savings once the loan is approved; and,
- have an interview with a credit officer.

Prospective Community Micro Loan Program borrowers will:

- need collateral or a co-signer as required for all loans;
- be entitled to loans amounting from $1,000-$15,000;
- have a loan interest rate of variable prime + 6%; and,
- be required to pay a 6% administration fee which is based on the total value of the loan.

It should be noted that administration fees and interest are subject to change without further notice.

Documents required are as follows:

- a well documented business plan
- loan application
- 12 month projected cash flow
- at least two business and personal references
- photo identification.

Further information can be obtained from:

Toronto and Area:
Susan Henry, Manager
Community Economic Development Specialist
165 Attwell Drive
Toronto, ON M9W 5Y5
Phone: (416) 252-5625 ext. 3404
E-mail: Susan.Henry@alterna.ca
Web site: https://www.alterna.ca

Ottawa & Area:
Community Micro Loan Coordinator
400 Albert Street
Ottawa, ON K1R 5B2
Phone: (613) 560-0100

Ottawa Community Loan Fund (OCLF)

Ottawa Community Loan Fund (OCLF) is a not-for-profit social finance organization, which provides funding to aspiring entrepreneurs, social enterprises and internationally trained talent who would not otherwise qualify for or have access to credit from traditional financial institutions in the Ottawa region. It works in partnership with the Canadian Youth Business Foundation (see separate entry under Federal assistance) and can offer loans of up to $45,000 for entrepreneurs aged 18 to 39.

Ottawa Community Loan Fund
First Floor, 80 Aberdeen Street
Ottawa, ON K1S 5R5
Phone: (613) 266-2159
Fax: (613) 686-3172
Web site: http://oclf.org

ACCESS Community Capital Fund (ACCF)

The ACCESS Community Capital Fund (ACCF) is a registered Canadian charity based in Toronto and has partnered with Alterna Savings to provide individuals without collateral or credit history access to micro-loans on the basis of the quality of their abilities, skills, and commitment, as well as the strength of their business plan.

ACCF operates microloan programs through local chapters in the GTA covering specific areas as follows:

*   Black Creek (covered in more detail below)
*   Thorncliffe Park
*   East Scarborough
*   Regent Park
*   Lawrence West
*   Southwest Scarborough.

The ACCESS Central Office provides microloans in the remaining areas of the GTA not covered by the above community chapters.

At the time of writing, loans totaling $400,000 had been issued.

Generally, the maximum loan amount is $5,000. In addition to the loan amount, there is a 5% admin fee which can be paid at the time of the loan and can be added to the loan amount. For example, for a $5,000 loan, applicants should enter $5250 as the loan amount. Average payment terms for a $5,000 loan is 18 months, but this can be adjusted up or down depending on the situation.

Applicants must meet the following conditions:

- must be a Canadian citizen or Landed Immigrant;
- must be a resident of Ontario and the business must be located within the GTA;
- must be 18 years of age or older;
- must own 51%+ of the business (or in the case of a partnership, all partners must be willing to co-sign for loan);
- must be legally registered as a sole proprietorship, partnership or corporation; and,
- must use the loan to start or expand a business offering a product or service (cannot be used to pay off debt).

It can be helpful if the applicant has desirable assets, but this is not an absolute requirement.

Loan applicants should have completed or be currently enrolled in a relevant business training program. They are currently operating a business and are able to supply supporting documentation of business activities. They have past experience in a similar business or profession.

To apply for a micro-loan, applicants must submit an application form, a business plan and projected cash flow for the initial one year period.

Access Community Capital Fund (ACCF)
215 Spadina Ave. Suite 405
Toronto ON M5T 2C7
E-mail: info@accessccf.com
Web site: www.accessccf.com/central

ACCESS Black Creek Micro-Credit Program

The Black Creek Micro-Credit Program was established in 2007. It provides loans to get businesses in the community up and running. It is supported by the Access Community Capital Fund and Alterna Savings. It can be accessed by start-up entrepreneurs in the residential area in the watershed of Black Creek from Steeles Avenue in North Toronto to Highway 401 and from Keele Street to Highway 400.

The Micro-Credit Program supports local community members who have sound business ideas but are unable to get credit from mainstream banks. They can obtain up to $5,000 for self-employment activities for a business start-up. Loans are repayable in 12-18 months and are administered by Alterna Savings.

Upon successful repayment of the initial loan, borrowers are eligible to apply for larger loans to support an expansion of their business operations.

Support is also offered under the Provincial Summer Company program for high school, college and university students who want to start and run a business over the summer. They are eligible to receive a $3,000 grant from the province plus free workshops and mentoring support.

Black Creek Micro-Credit Program
107 - 36 Marsh Grass Way
Toronto, ON   M3N 2X4
Phone: (416) 747-5616
E-mail address: microlending@blackcreekcapacity.ca
Web site: www.accessccf.com/black_creek

Toronto Community Foundation:
Youth Micro Loan Initiative

The Toronto Community Foundation has established the Youth Micro-Loan Initiative which is an intensive social enterprise/business training program that will enable marginalized youth to foster a business idea into a realistic business plan to guide their business operation. It is focussed on Toronto's priority neighbourhoods with a specific focus on the city's west end:

Participants will have access to a defined set of resources and tools, mentors, business development professional and community-based partners. At the end of training, and on completion of a business pitch, where they will present their business plans to a panel, participants will have the opportunity to access up to $5,000 seed funding for a small business start-up.

UrbanArts
Community Arts Council
Phone: (416) 241-5124
E-mail: info@urbanartstoronto.org.

PARO Centre for Women's Enterprise

PARO's Peer Circles are designed to help women to increase their capacity for economic self-reliance. Peer Circles are self-selected groups of 4 to 7 women whose members share and network amongst themselves for mutual business benefit. Circle members share their experiences, advise each other, support each other and help each other expand their contact networks.

Peer Circle members also provide lending support by being collectively accountable and providing references for each other, allowing PARO to use different lending criteria than those of traditional banking institutions. Peer lending has helped many Circle members to grow their businesses and set new goals for the future.

PARO Centre for Women's Enterprise
105 May Street North, Suite 110
Thunder Bay, ON P7C 3N9
Phone (807) 625-0328
Phone toll-free: 1-(800) 584-0252
Fax (807) 625-0317
E-mail: info@paro.ca
Web site: www.paro.ca

Louis Riel Capital Corporation (L.R.C.C.)

Louis Riel Capital Corporation (L.R.C.C.) is a Manitoba, Métis-owned lending institution and resource centre which was established under the Canadian Aboriginal Economic Development Strategy (CAEDS). It has a mandate to offer loans for start-ups, acquisitions or expansion of commercial businesses owned and controlled by Métis individuals throughout Manitoba.

Business Loan Program

The L.R.C.C. Business Loan Program provides small business loans for start-up, acquisition or expansion. Loans can be for the acquisition of capital assets or to provide bridge financing for other external financing that has been committed but not yet disbursed.

The general terms and conditions which apply are as follows:

- the project must be Metis or Non-Status Indian ancenstry (MNSI) owned and controlled;
- all eligible applicants will be required to provide an appropriate amount of equity in their proposed operation or expansion;
- the project is viable in that it has the potential to produce income that will cover operating costs, a reasonable income for the owner, loan repayment and has long-term potential for profitability;
- appropriate skills that should allow the applicant to successfully carry on the business;

- training, education, and experience may be conditional prior to approving funding;
- applicants must reside in Manitoba and the applicants' business shall be based in Manitoba; and,
- all loans must be adequately secured.

Application forms can be obtained at the address below and applicants should indicate the number of jobs that will be created and include a project description, marketing plan, financial plan together with projections. In addition, three years of historical financial information should be provided.

Bridge Financing

LRCC can offer Bridge Financing which consists of short term loans to bridge external financing that is committed but pending disbursement.

Further Information

Louis Riel Capital Corporation
340 -150 Henry Ave.
Winnipeg, MB R3B 0J7
Phone: (204) 589-0772
Fax: (204)589-0791
E-mail: info@lrcc.mb.ca
Web site: http://www.lrcc.mb.ca/

Assiniboine Credit Union (ACU)
Business and Community Financial Centre (BCFC)

BCFC offers traditional business lending and also the Community Economic Development Program. Together, the Business and Community divisions of BCFC serve businesses of all sizes from very large to micro-enterprises, co-operatives and not-for-profit organizations.

Assiniboine Credit Union (ACU)
Business and Community Financial Centre
2nd. Floor, 200 Main Street
Box 2, Station Main
Winnipeg MB R3C 2G1
Phone toll-free: 1-(877) 958-8588
Fax toll-free: 1-(877) 958-7348
Web site: www.assiniboine.mb.ca

Tribal Wi-Chi-Way-Win Capital Corporation (TWCC)

Commercial Lending Program

Tribal Wi-Chi-Way-Win Capital Corporation (TWCC) offers loans of up to $175,000 for business start-up or the acquisition and expansion of on and off-reserve businesses for members of their communities as follows:

- Island Lake Tribal Council
- Keewatin Tribal Council
- West Region Tribal Council
- Interlake Reserves Tribal Council
- Swampy Cree Tribal Council
- Norway House First Nation
- Nelson House First Nation
- Cross Lake First Nation
- Fisher River First Nation
- Sagkeeng/Fort Alexander First Nation
- Jackhead First Nation
- Waywayseecappo First Nation.

Loans can be used for:

- acquiring fixed assets;
- working capital;
- bridge financing while awaiting permanent financing that has been approved or to provide advances against completed construction work pending the receipt of payment;
- franchise or dealer fees.

Loans cannot be used for:

- consumer purchases such as automobiles, home improvements, debt consolidation;
- to finance leasehold improvements;
- to finance goodwill;
- to finance accounts receivable or inventory; or,
- to support agriculture, trapping, fishing, arts or crafts.

Collateral security for loans is required of at least 25% of the amount of any loan.

The following loans are eligible for consideration by Tribal Wi Chi Way Win.

Direct Term Loan: will be provided for the purpose of acquiring fixed assets to be used for business purposes. These loans are generally amortized over a two to ten year period.

Working Capital Loans: will be provided for the purpose of improving the working capital position of a business where there is securable equity in the fixed assets of the business. Working Capital Loans are normally amortized over a one to two year period.

Bridging Loans: may be made available to provide bridge financing while the borrower is awaiting payment or funding from a third party. Some examples include interim financing, pending receipt of the proceeds of grants or other funding, where approval has been received and all the conditions have been satisfied. In the case of construction, to provide advances against completed work on construction projects where there is repayment from mortgage loans or other secure financing. To make loans available for franchise or dealer fees subject to the viability of the proposed venture.

Franchise or Dealer Fees: can be provided subject to the viability of the project.

First Nations Farm Credit Program

This program provides funding of up to $175,000 for start-up, acquisition and expansion of viable farming operations for all First Nations people in Manitoba. Terms and conditions are very similar to those under the Commercial Lending Program (above).

Further Information

Head Office:
Tribal Wi Chi Way Win Capital Corporation
Peguis First Nation
Peguis, MB R0C 1N0

Sub-Office:
Tribal Wi-Chi-Way-Win Capital Corporation (TWCC)
419 Notre Dame Avenue
Winnipeg, MB R3B 1R3
Phone: (204) 943-0888
Fax: (204) 946-5318
Phone toll-free: 1-(800) 568-8488
E-mail: info@twcc.mb.ca
Web site: http://www.twcc.mb.ca

Sub-Office for farm Credit:
27-2nd Avenue
Dauphin, MB R7N 3E5
Phone: (204) 638-6132
Fax: (204) 638-2854

Saskatchewan Indian Equity Foundation (SIEF)

The Saskatchewan Indian Equity Foundation (SIEF) provides the following loans.

Agricultural Development Loans

Agricultural Development Loans are short-term operating loans for equipment and livestock purchases to qualifying Saskatchewan Indian farmers.

The following conditions apply:

- only treaty or status Indians residing in Saskatchewan are eligible;
- must be a viable farming, ranching or related agribusiness operation in Saskatchewan;
- the maximum financing for capital items is 70%;
- all loans must be secured by eligible assets;
- security may include chattel mortgage security, security under the Personal Property Security Act, conditional sales contract, assignment of crop insurance, security over crops and inventory, assignment of other payments or receipts, life insurance on the borrower, branding of livestock with SIEF's registered brand; and,
- a band council resolution is required from the Chief and Council giving SIEF access onto the reserve to inspect and realize upon security.

Applicants must include a statement of net worth, past income/expense statements, cash flow projections, cropping and/or livestock plan, and general information regarding the applicant's management ability and character. Applications will be assessed on their individual merits and must demonstrate:

- that the operation is or can be viable;
- that the owners have a reasonable equity investment in the project;
- that there is a realizable security to adequately cover the loan;
- that cash flows will service all debt requirements;
- that management capacity is in place; and,
- that past credit history is satisfactory.

Commercial Loans

Commercial loans are commonly used for capital expenditures of heavy equipment such as graders, freight trucks, buses and taxis. These loans may also be used for the purchase of a business.

Through the commercial loan program, up to $150,000 is available for individuals, up to $350,000 for Bands and up to $500,000 for Tribal Councils.

Further Information

Saskatchewan Indian Equity Foundation (SIEF)
Asimakaniseekan Askiy Reserve
202A Joseph Okemasis Drive
Saskatoon, SK S7N 1B1
Phone: (306) 955-4550
Fax: (306) 373-4969

Saskatchewan Indian Equity Foundation (SIEF)
Room 128 - 1 First Nations Way
Regina, SK S4S 7K2
Phone: (306) 522-2811
Fax: (306) 522-2812

Agriculture Manager
Saskatchewan Indian Equity Foundation (SIEF)
1192 - 102 Street
North Battleford, SK S9A 1E9
Phone: (306) 446-7486
Fax: (306) 446-7447
Web site: http://www.sief.sk.ca/

First Nations and Métis Fund

The First Nations and Métis Fund is the first Aboriginal fund in Canada which will make investments in Saskatchewan-based First Nations and Métis businesses. The Fund will make investments between $1 million and $3 million. The mandate of the Fund is to strengthen Aboriginal participation in Saskatchewan's diverse economy and to help create economic development opportunities and jobs for First Nations and Métis people.

The Fund's stated areas of investment are as follows:

- value-added agriculture;
- advanced technology;
- energy;
- mining;
- forestry and forestry developments;
- manufacturing; or,
- Aboriginal-themed tourism.

Investments can be made at the following stages.

Start-ups: new businesses which have developed or acquired products or services and are ready to proceed to commercialization.

Early-stage investments: businesses which have been in operation for some time, but have not yet fully developed their product or service.

Expansions: businesses which require financing to expand sales, or to launch a new product or service.

Management buyouts: adding new management and capital to acquire control of a business and realize its potential for expansion.

Restructuring or turnarounds: adding investment and making changes in management, staffing, operations or marketing strategies to help the business succeed.

Investments are usually in the form of:

- debt;
- sub-debt;
- equity; and/or,
- a combination of various financial instruments.

Applicants must be able to make a minimum equity contribution to the project.

First Nations & Métis Fund
830, 410 22nd Street East
Saskatoon, SK S7K-5T6
Phone: (306) 665-0200
Fax: (306) 652-8186
Email: fnmf@sasktel.net
Web: www.fnmf.ca

SaskMetis Economic Development Corporation (SMEDCO)

The SaskMetis Economic Development Corporation (SMEDCO) offers a number of loan programs with loan interest starting at 7.5% but with a maximum lending limit of $500,000.

Direct Capital Loans

SMEDCO's Loan Program is often used to lever financial assistance from other public and private sources and is used for projects which are basically sound but where, because of risk or other factors, no other funding sources will provide loans.

The project must be Métis owned or controlled and at least 2/3 of the positions to be created must be filled by Métis people. Each project should be feasible in its proposed location (the needed infrastructure and support services are available or can be obtained at a reasonable cost) and should be viable with the potential to produce income which will cover operating costs, a reasonable income for the owner, loan repayment and will have long-term potential for profitability.

The applicant(s) must have proven ability to effectively manage a business or have the required knowledge and skills to manage a business and reside in Saskatchewan.

Shared or Syndicated Loans

For very large projects SMEDCO may "share" the loan with other lenders. The conditions are similar to those for Direct Capital Loans.

Bridge Loans

SMEDCO's Bridge Loans are short-term loans designed to bridge external financing that is committed but pending disbursement. Bridge Loans are usually used to finance Aboriginal Business Canada Contributions.

The conditions are similar to those for Direct Capital Loans.

Working Capital Loans

SMEDCO's Working Capital Loans are demand loans to finance a portion of start-up or working capital requirements such as advertising, inventory and receivables.

The conditions are similar to those for Direct Capital Loans.

Métis Youth Program

Métis Youth Program is open to those aged 18 to 35 and who are interested in owning a business.

SMEDCO's Youth Business Development Officer can provide assistance with:

- youth business loans;
- business planning;
- business start-up advice;
- information on other business programs for Métis; and,
- post lending support.

Further Information

SaskMetis Economic Development Corporation
Suite 101 - 1630 Quebec Avenue
Saskatoon, SK S7K 1V7
Phone: (306) 477-4350
Fax: (306) 373-2512
E-mail address: smedco@smedco.ca
Web site: www.smedco.ca

Clarence Campeau Development Fund (CCDF)

The Clarence Campeau Development Fund (CCDF) was established in 1998. It has several components to assist Métis entrepreneurs and business-owners.

Loan/Equity Contribution Program

Provides businesses and communities with equity contributions or loans to assist in leveraging financing from other institutions and agencies. Funds can be used for:

- purchase or start up of a new business;
- purchase of an existing business; or,
- business expansion.

241

The maximum contribution is 35% of the project costs up to a maximum of $200,000 per project. The contribution is repayable.

The applicant must contribute a minimum of 5% of the project. Higher risk projects will require larger equity injections by the applicant. The applicant's equity may be in the form of cash, machinery, equipment, real estate, or other unencumbered assets. Sweat equity may be considered.

Applicants must provide a business plan that shows that they will be able to repay the contribution.

Métis Women's Equity Program

Métis Women's Equity Program is designed to assist Saskatchewan Métis Women who wish to become entrepreneurs overcome barriers and enhance their ability to leverage financing and support services from financial institutions and business support agencies. It can provide equity assistance of up to 65% of project costs to a maximum of $10,000. It should be noted that total project costs cannot exceed $ 25,000 (excluding working capital) and applicants must contribute a minimum of 5% equity to the project.

Métis Equity Contribution Program (MERP)

The Métis Equity Contribution Program (MERP) is intended to increase the involvement of Métis entrepreneurs in the Energy and Resource sectors. It can provide financial assistance of the lesser of $500,000 or 50% of the value of fixed assets plus 35% of working capital and inventory costs identified in the program. The minimum level of funding under this program is $250,000 up to a maximum of $1,000,000.

Businesses funded under this program must generate a minimum of 60% of its revenue from the Energy and Resource sectors.

Each business must be supported by a professional business plan and demonstrate the feasibility and viability of the business. Investments are in the form of common shares, preferred shares, mortgages or other forms of debt.

Funds can be used to establish a new business; purchase an existing business or for the expansion or renovation of a business that will result in increased capacity and revenue. Applicants must be a Saskatchewan resident of Métis ancestry or a Saskatchewan Corporation or Partnership that is operating in the province of Saskatchewan.

Métis Youth Equity Program

The Métis Youth Equity Program is designed to assist Saskatchewan Métis Youth ages 18 to 35 with the desire to become entrepreneurs, overcome barriers and enhance their ability to leverage financing and support services from other financial institutions and agencies. It can provide equity assistance of up to 65% of project costs to a maximum of $10,000 It should be noted that total project costs cannot exceed $ 25,000 (excluding working capital).

Funds can be used to:

* purchase an existing business;
* start a new business; or,
* expand or renovate an existing business.

Security is required in the form of a promissory note and the repayable contribution term cannot exceed five years The contribution is interest free

Businesses funded under this program must be for-profit and demonstrate viability through a sound business plan and applicants must contribute a minimum of 5% equity to the project

Large Scale or Joint Venture Projects

Assistance of up to 50% ($201,000 minimum) is offered to Métis entrepreneurs to assist them in entering into mutually advantageous business arrangements with non-Métis businesses. Such projects should result in employment opportunities for Métis and involve projects with capital expenditures of up to $2 million. Priority is given to high end, value added projects. Funding assistance is repayable.

Development of Management and Marketing Skills Program

This component provides financing (up to 75% of eligible training costs) to assist Métis persons in upgrading their skills to successfully manage a business or to provide management counselling. The funding is provided for short courses only and degree and post-graduate studies are excluded. Assistance will cover course costs, tuition and books but not living costs. The assistance is not repayable.

Business Plan Assistance Program

CCDF can supply up to $10,000 to cover up to 75% of the costs of engaging a consultant to conduct research; prepare a business plan and attract financing. Funding assistance is not repayable.

Support for Aftercare Program

CCDF can supply up to $10,000 to cover up to 100% of the costs during the first two years of a business operation to permit the business to engage the services of a professional consultant to identify areas of the business that need special attention. Funding assistance is not repayable.

Community Business Development

This component is designed to help Métis development corporations and institutions investigate and identify economic and business development opportunities.

Further Information

Clarence Campeau Development Fund
2158 Airport Drive
Saskatoon, SK S7L 6M6
Phone: (306) 657-4870
Toll-free phone: 1-(888) 657-4870
Fax: (306) 657-4890
E-mail address: info@clarencecampeau.com
Web site: http://www.clarencecampeau.com/ccdf/

Clarence Campeau Development Fund
2380 2nd Avenue
Regina, SK S4R 1A6
Phone: (306) 790-2233
Phone toll-free: 1-(877)-359-2233
Fax: (306) 790-2220
E-mail address: regina.info@clarencecampeau.com

Le Conseil de la Coopération de la Saskatchewan

Le Conseil de la Coopération de la Saskatchewan offers microloans of up to $5,000 to new francophone entrepreneurs (with 51% of greater ownership in the business) to grow or start a business. To be eligible, they must have been unsuccessful in obtaining financing elsewhere.

The program is not open to businesses that are engaged in mining, farming, real estate or are charitable organizations.

Application for a loan is by way of submitting a business plan.

Le Conseil de la Coopération de la Saskatchewan
1440, 9th Ave., Suite 205
Regina SK S4R 8B1
Phone: (306) 566-6000
Phone toll-free: 1-(800) 670-0879
Fax: (306) 757-4322
Web site (French only): http://www.ccs-sk.ca/enterprise/financement_n37.html

Momentum

Momentum is the new name for MCC Employment Development. Momentum is a community development organization which offers loan programs which could be of interest to local entrepreneurs in the Calgary area.

Micro Business Loans

Micro Business Loans are offered to Calgary residents who are experiencing difficulty in obtaining bank financing. They rely on the character of the applicant and work in conjunction with a peer support group that can offer coaching support and assistance in preparing a business plan.

Loans can be for up to $7,500 and carry an interest rate of prime plus 1-1/2%. In addition, there is a loan administration fee of 5% of the amount of the loan.

Loans can be used for:

- licensing and registration;
- tools or equipment;
- advertising; and,
- inventory.

Applicants for loans must:

- attend a business training program;
- complete a business plan; and,
- fill out an application form.

FundAbility Loans

FundAbility Loans of up to $10,000 are available to entrepreneurs with disabilities who live in Calgary. It provides them with an opportunity to repair their credit history. Interest is charged at prime plus 2%.

Loans can be used for:

- licensing and registration;
- tools or equipment;
- advertising; and.
- inventory.

Applicants for loans must:

- attend a Momentum business training program;
- complete a business plan; and,
- fill out an application form.

Immigrant Access Fund

Loans of up to $5,000 can be obtained by Calgary residents under the Immigrant Access Fund.

Momentum, in partnership with the Immigrant Access Fund Society, provides the loans which can be used to help pay for the costs of Canadian accreditation, training or upgrading for immigrants who want to work in their professional field in Canada.

Further Information

Momentum
#16 - 2936 Radcliffe Dive S.E.
Calgary
AB T2A 6M8
Phone: (403) 272-9323
Fax: (403) 235-4646
E-mail: info@momentum.org
Web site: www.momentum.org

Apeetogosan Métis Development Inc.
Small Business Loans

Applications can be submitted for Small Business Loans of under $50,000 to assist Aboriginal businesses. They can be supported with a short-form business plan that can be used to accompany the application.

All loan requests over $50,000 will require an in-depth business plan unless the business has already been operating and wishes to expand. In this case, the last three years of financial statements are required to support the application. Should the financial statements not indicate an adequate cash flow to service the loan request, then it will be necessary to provide a business plan outlining how the loan will be repaid.

Through, Pinnacle Business Services Ltd., (a subsidiary) business consultants can provide assistance in business planning, business valuation, accounting and other business services for a fee.

Applicants should have a 10% minimum equity in the business. The loan will also require the necessary security as per policy.

Apeetogosan Métis Development Inc.
#302, 12308 – 111th Avenue
Edmonton, AB T5M 2N4
Phone: (780) 452-7951
Toll-free phone: 1-(800) 252-7963
Fax: (780) 454-5997
E-mail address: office@apeetogosan.com
Web site: http://www.apeetogosan.com/

Pinnacle Business Services Ltd.
#302, 12308 – 111th Avenue
Edmonton, AB T5M 2N4
Phone: (780) 453-1992
E-mail address: office@pinnaclebusiness.com

Trustee Loan Program

All Nations Trust Company (ANTCO) is Aboriginal owned with shareholders comprising Bands, Tribal Councils, Aboriginal Organizations, Métis Associations, Status, Non-Status and Métis individuals.

Trustee Loan Program

In addition to being a delivery agent for the First Citizen's Fund Loan Program, the ANTCO also delivers the Trustee Loan Program. This can provide business loans which are 100% repayable with financing up to $100,000.00 for first-time borrowers and up to $200,000.00 for repeat borrowers. Collateral security requirements are assessed according to each business project.

Business Equity Fund (BEF) Program

Business Equity Fund Program can provide non-repayable contributions for eligible capital and business support to start, expand or acquire a viable Aboriginal owned business as well as non-repayable contributions for business planning, marketing and other related business support services.

The BEF may contribute up to a maximum of $99,999 for individuals and incorporated businesses, and up to $250,000 for community owned businesses, based on a viable business plan and subject to other financing being in place.

Further Information

All Nations Trust Company
208 - 345 Yellowhead Highway
Kamloops, BC V2H 1H1
Phone: (250) 828-9770
Fax: (250) 372-2585
Toll Free: 1-(800) 663-2959
E-mail address: antco@antco.bc.ca
Web site: www.antco.bc.ca

Northern Development Initiative Trust

The formation of the Northern Development Initiative was announced in 2003, when the Province of British Columbia proposed to use $135 million of the proceeds realized from the lease of BC Rail assets to create a new corporation that would be dedicated to fostering economic development and job creation in central and northern regions of the Province. The Trust was formally established in 2005 and is independently governed by a board of thirteen regionally-based directors. It is an initiative of the Province of British Columbia.

Northern Development Initiative Trust is an independent regional economic development corporation focused on stimulating economic growth and job creation throughout central and northern British Columbia.

To date, $111 million in funding has been committed to 1,068 projects in communities throughout central and northern British Columbia; 5,154 jobs have been created; 1,890 partnerships with 681 organizations have attracted over $1 billion in new investment to the region.

73% of investments are in small communities with populations less than 5,000.

Community grant writers have been approved for $39.8 million in funding since 2010.

The corporation supports community economic development initiatives with funding for economic diversification infrastructure, feasibility studies, marketing, capacity building, grant writing, community halls, recreational facilities, and community foundations.

Northern Development directly invests in private business to create new jobs throughout the region via $30 million in dedicated funding to support capital investment and new job training in central and northern BC.

Funding is focused on ten primary investment areas:

- agriculture;
- economic development;
- energy;
- forestry;
- mining;
- Olympic opportunities;
- pine beetle recovery;
- small business;
- tourism; and,
- transportation.

The following programs relate to small and medium sized businesses that operate in Northern British Columbia.

Northern Industry Expansion Program

On February 20, 2013, it was announced that the Northern Development Initiative Trust has teamed up with National Bank of Canada to provide a new source of financing that will help small and medium-sized businesses in the region grow alongside the economy and create new jobs.

The program will now support supply chain financing with a 25% loan guarantee for up to 25% of the authorized National Bank loan for purchase order financing or receivables financing to a maximum of $1 million.

Supply chain financing through National Bank provides eligible companies with the front end financing to purchase materials and inventory to fulfill large contracts. Receivables financing through National Bank provides immediate cash to a company once work is completed and is secured by an invoice to an end customer. Receivables financing provides working capital to the company to alleviate short-term cash flow challenges before the invoice is paid.

The Northern Development loan guarantee is intended to leverage National Bank financing, and makes it easier for small and medium sized companies to take on major contracts and expand their businesses to create more jobs.

Businesses in manufacturing, resource processing and the supply sectors in Northern Development's service area, which includes communities from Lytton north to Fort Nelson and Valemount west to Haida Gwaii, are eligible to apply for this program. Businesses in the Northern Development service area can immediately begin to work with National Bank to determine whether their lending needs qualify for this program.

Renata King, Director, Business Development
Northern Development Initiative Trust
Phone: (250) 561-2525
E-mail: renata@northerndevelopment.bc.ca

Greg Harder, Senior Manager, Western Canada
Global Banking
National Bank of Canada
Phone: (604) 661-5520
E-mail: gregory.harder@nbc.ca

Competitiveness Consulting Rebate

The Competitiveness Consulting Rebate provides a rebate of 50% to a yearly maximum of $30,000 to cover the cost of business competitiveness consulting for small and medium sized manufacturers, resource processing companies, and their first line suppliers. Consulting should be geared towards increasing productivity, revenues, and profitability.

The rebate is designed to help central and northern BC manufacturers, processors, and their suppliers grow their businesses, implement world-class business practices and be more competitive in the global market.

The consulting is provided by regional and national consultants with a verified track record of competitiveness consulting expertise. The consultants may be provided by the Business Development Bank of Canada (BDC) or by regional consulting companies that have qualified for consideration to supplement the BDC consultant roster. There is no requirement to be a client of the BDC, however, the consulting can be financed through the BDC.

Consulting can be customized to suit unique business requirements.

Further Information

Northern Development Initiative Trust
301 – 1268 Fifth Ave. Prince George, BC V2L 3L2
Phone: (250) 561-2525
Fax: (250) 561-2563
E-mail: brodie@northerndevelopment.bc.ca
Web site: http://northerndevelopment.bc.ca

Yukon: Venture Loan Guarantee Program

The Venture Loan Guarantee Program is open to new business start-ups or expansions of existing businesses registered in the Yukon, which have less than 100 employees and under $5 million in gross revenues.

The business program is an initiative between the Government of Yukon and:

• Bank of Montreal;
• Bank of Nova Scotia;
• Business Development Bank of Canada;
• Canadian Imperial Bank of Commerce;
• Däna Näye Ventures;
• Royal Bank of Canada; and,
• Toronto Dominion Bank.

Assistance is in the form of guarantees for 65% on loans, for which there is little or no security. The minimum loan that will be considered is $10,000 and the maximum is $100,000. Terms can be for up to a maximum of six years and interest-only payments are required in the first year. A one-time fee of 1.5% is payable at the time of the issue of the guarantee.

To be eligible, businesses should be start-ups or expansions with under $5 million in gross revenues and fewer than 100 employees. They should be involved in one of the following activities:

*   development and distribution of new products or services;
*   the export of goods or services;
*   export substitution;
*   high technology;
*   information services; or,
*   tourism attractions that need upgrading.

Business activities which are not eligible include:

*   retail operations;
*   tourism accommodations;
*   refinancing of existing debt;
*   speculative real estate transactions;
*   changes in ownership; and,
*   transactions involving withdrawal of shareholder loans.

Venture loans represent those portions of loans for which there is inadequate or no security and are established as a separate loan. The bank will take all reasonable security to support the loan, such as personal guarantees and general security agreements, as deemed appropriate.

Equity requirements are determined by the bank, based on the nature of the project and the risk involved.

Applications should be made at private sector banks or financial institutions, which in turn will evaluate the projects and either approve or reject them. These banks or financial institutions will be responsible for loaning the money and collecting interest and repayments of principal.

Business Development
Business and Industry Branch
Department of Economic Development
PO Box 2703 (F-2)
Whitehorse, YT Y1A 2C6
Phone: (867) 393-7014
Phone toll-free: 1-(800) 661-0408 ext. 7014
Fax: (867) 393-6944

Northwest Territories Métis Dene Development Fund (MDDF)

The Northwest Territories Métis Déne Development Fund (MDDF) is a cooperative effort between the Northwest Territories Métis Development Corporation and the Denendeh Development Corporation. It provides financial services and business assistance service to Metis and Dene people of the Northwest Territories in order to stimulate the growth and development of aboriginal entrepreneurship.

Eligible applicants must be of Métis or Dene origin and are members of the Métis locals or Dene Bands of the Northwest Territories and are resident in the Northwest Territories. In addition, they must be of legal age of majority.

In the case of an organization or corporation, it must be owned or 51% controlled by persons of Metis or Dene origin and are members of the Métis locals or Dene bands of the Northwest Territories and are resident in the Northwest Territories. It must have its registered office in the Northwest Territories.

Loans and Loan Guarantees

Direct loans: available to eligible applicants for capital, operating or interim financing for business purposes.

Loan guarantees: to support loan applications of eligible applicants from conventional financial institutions for business purposes.

Maximum loan to any one borrower or group or related borrowers is $275,000 (with exception up to $350,00). Interest rates are variable and dependent upon an assessment of the risk associated with the project, term of the loan and loan size. Loans may be amortized up to 25 years with a maximum term of 5 years. The minimum equity of the applicants in the project must be at least 10% in the form of cash, value of land, equipment, etc.

An application fee is $100 for loans up to $5,000 and $250 for loans up to $25,000 and thereafter a 1% fee of the amount borrowed up to the loan maximum of $275,000.

Application Forms and Business Plan Forms can be obtained from the Fund's office

Further Information

Northwest Territories Métis Dene Development Fund
4908-50th Street
P.O. Box 1405
Yellowknife, NT X1A 2P1
Phone: (867) 873-9341
Fax: (867) 766-3745
E-mail: admin@nwtmddf.com
Web site: www.nwtmddf.com

Arctic Co-operative Development Fund (ACDF)

The Arctic Co-operative Development Fund (ACDF) is designed to give Arctic communities, that are looking for support and assistance in starting co-operative ventures, financial services for their member owners so that they can help each other achieve and maintain financial stability, sound business practices and operational growth.

ACDF is a self-managed fund of pooled financial resources, owned and controlled by the co-operative businesses accessing the capital.

It provides the following assistance.

Development Financing: is available for the improvement, expansion and/or replacement of facilities and equipment. This financing can be both short term and long term and is also available to co-operatives to enter new business ventures and to assist emerging co-operatives to become established.

Long-Term Financing: is available to co-operatives to stabilize and strengthen the operations of co-operatives and provide them with an opportunity to reduce their existing long-term debt in an orderly manner.

Working Capital Financing: is available for co-operatives to purchase up to one year's supply of merchandise inventory or other material to operate their business during winter months.

Facility Development: provides facility leasing to co-operatives with an option to purchase the facility some time in the future.

Co-operative Development: assists community groups to identify business opportunities, complete feasibility analysis, develop business plans, and where appropriate, develop a community based co-operative.

Arctic Co-operative Development Fund
321 Old Airport Development
Yellowknife, NT
Phone: (867) 873-3481
Fax: (867) 920-4052
E-mail address: info@arcticco-op.com
Web site: http://www.arcticco-op.com/acdf.html

Makigiakvik and Nunavut Sivumut Small Business Financing

Nunavut Sivumut provides funding of up to $5,000 for business start-up or business expansion. The applicant must have equity of at least 10% in the business.

Eligible activities for assistance embrace the following:

* harvesting caribou;
* seal, turbot, char, and clams; and,
* carvers--tools and equipment such as sewing machines, carving tools for making crafts and the purchase of fur and fabric for making traditional clothing.

Phone: (867) 979-8953 or Phone: (867) 979-8958
Fax: (867) 979-3707
Toll free Phone: 1-(800) 561-0911

Kakivak Association

The Kakivak Association provides the following business services.

Sivummut Grants: are available to eligible Inuit owned businesses to support the establishment or expansion of their business.

These can include a combination of grant contributions and a Makigiaqvik Loan.

* Business pre-start-up: up to $5,000
* Business start-up: up to $10,000
* Business expansion: up to $10,000

The maximum level of assistance is $25,000 in total grants. In addition support is available to help applicants run their business

The Makigiaqvik Loan Fund: provides micro loans up to $50,000.00 to Inuit small businesses with terms of up to seven years. Loans are designed to create long-term employment.

Small Tool Grants: provides grants of up to $1,000 for artists or craftspeople to assist with the purchase of tools and supplies. Applications can be made again after five-years. Funding is also available for a one-time grant of up to $2,500.00 to assist in the purchase of sewing machines.

Economic Opportunity Fund (EOF): provides grants up to $10,000 to tourism operators or businesses located within the parks in the six communities: Grise Fiord, Resolute Bay, Arctic Bay, Pond Inlet, Qikiqtarjuaq and Pangnirtung.

Kakivak Association
Parnaivik Building 924
Box 1419, Iqaluit, NU X0A 0H0
Phone: (867) 979-0911
Toll free phone: 1-(800) 561-0911
Fax: (867) 979-3707
E-mail: info@kakivak.ca
Web site: www.kakivak.ca

Kitikmeot Economic Development Commission (KEDC)

Kitikmeot Business Assistance Program (KBAP)

Kitikmeot Corporation receives funding each year from Nunavut Tunngavik Inc. to promote small business development in the Kitikmeot region of Nunavut by providing loans and contributions under the Kitikmeot Business Assistance Program.

The Commission provides contributions of up to $5,000 which are non-repayable.

Interest-free loans of up to $25,000 are also available for terms of up to three years with payment based on the cash flow of the project or client. Monthly repayments may or may not be required depending on circumstances. Loans are normally secured by promissory notes, personal guarantees, chattel mortgages or the assignment of accounts receivable.

To be eligible, applicants must be registered under the Nunavut Land Claims Agreement or are Inuit-owned businesses that are owned by Kitikmeot Inuit.

Funding may also be considered for organizations sponsoring special business or community economic development projects that will provide broad-based benefits to Inuit of the community or region. For all programs, the client must generally contribute a minimum of 10% equity toward total project costs as evidence of commitment to the business or project. Acceptable forms of equity include cash, sweat equity, and assets contributed to the project by the client.

Loans can be used for:

- feasibility studies, pilot projects;
- business creation or expansion activities;
- marketing initiatives; or,
- business skills development.

Loans cannot be used to acquire boats, outboard motors, snowmobiles or ATVs.

Nunavut Sivummut Grant Program

The purpose of the program is to help provide jobs and income to Kitikmeot Inuit by providing financial assistance to establish and expand viable Inuit-owned businesses in the region. Nunavut Sivummut provides contributions of up to $2,000 per application. Support is for carvers, seamstresses, or other small businesses owned by Kitikmeot Inuit. Terms and conditions of a contribution are included in a Letter of Offer that is sent out to the client once funding has been approved. Contributions are generally non-repayable

First Nations and Inuit Youth Employment Strategy

Funding for the First Nations and Inuit Youth Employment Strategy can provide funding to businesses owned by Inuit in the Kitikmeot region for hiring summer students as well as youth who are facing barriers to employment.

Further Information

Kitikmeot Economic Development Commission
Box 18, Cambridge Bay, NU X0E 0C0
Phone: (867) 983-2458
Web site: www.kitia.ca

8

Loans for Agriculture, Agri-Foods, Aquaculture & Fisheries

Farm Credit Canada (FCC)

Farm Credit Canada (FCC) is a federal Crown corporation which provides financial and business management options for small and medium-sized Canadian producers and farm-related businesses. It supports individuals, partnerships, companies and co-operatives engaged in farming and offers a number of lending products.

Advancer Loans

Advancer Loans are pre-approved loans that enable funds to be re-advanced as operations grow. They can be used to purchase land, buildings, livestock or other personal property. They carry variable rates but can be converted in whole or in part into a term loan with a fixed repayment schedule. Security must be a real property mortgage.

AdvancerPlus Loans

AdvancerPlus Loans provide financing that revolve with operating costs. They are designed to provide the working capital needed to keep day-to-day operations running smoothly. They are revolving, pre-approved loans with variable interest rates that provide money for working capital. They can be used to purchase supplies, fuel, fertilizer, seed and feed. Repayments can be made monthly, quarterly, semi-annually or annually to match cash flow.

Construction Loans

Construction Loans are available to finance projects that will be completed within 18 months of the receipt of financing. Repayment of principal is not required until the building has been completed and once that has been achieved, the loan can be converted into another FCC fixed rate loan. Security must be a real property mortgage.

American Currency Loans

In order to protect those producers and businesses which conduct a large portion of their business in American Dollars against losses that might be sustained as a result of currency fluctuations, loans of over $1 million can be made in US currency and payments can also be made in the same currency. Security must be a real property mortgage.

First Step Loan

First Step loans are available to those who have graduated from a recognized post-secondary program within the past three years or are currently enrolled in and have successfully completed two years of a recognized post-secondary program. Loans can be for up to $75,000 to purchase agriculture-related equipment with down payments of as low as 10%.

A business plan must be submitted which outlines opportunities and risks.

Young Farmer Loan

The Young Farmer Loan is available to those under 40 years of age and can be used by those with a solid business plan to purchase agriculture-related assets of up to $500,000. Loans feature closed variable rates at prime plus 0.5% and special fixed rates also available Loans are normally secured with real property and repayments can be made on a monthly, quarterly, semi-annual or annual basis.

Flexi-Loan

Flexi-Loans are designed for those who want to expand while managing their cash flow. They permit borrowers to pause the principal portion of their payment. A pause under a Flexi-Loan can last up to 12 months, however, a minimum of one year of regular payments must be made before the first pause and pauses cannot be taken back-to-back.

Flexi-Loans help borrowers manage temporary downturns or to take advantage of opportunities while maintaining their credit rating. Security is normally secured with real or personal property. Repayment can be made by monthly, quarterly, semi-annual or annual payments. Loans can carry fixed or variable rates

Performer Loans

Performer Loans offer lower interest rates when a business achieves pre-set financial goals and ratios. They depend on goals such as a proven track record of repayments together with certain improved financial ratios. Essentially, they are rewards for achieving certain levels of performance.

Personal Property Loans

Personal Property Loans can be used to finance livestock, equipment or quota. Security for the loan is provided by the item that is financed. Such loans can be at fixed or variable rates and carry flexible repayment terms. The maximum term is 10 years.

Mortgage Loans

Mortgage Loans can be used by Canadian farmers to finance land or buildings. Amortization periods can be for 3 to 29 years with interest rates fixed for up to 20 years. Three types of loans are available.

Long-Term Mortgages can be used to purchase real estate or farm land; to finance land improvements and buildings, including homes or to refinance existing debt.

Variable Rate: carry variable interest rates and can facilitate repayment of 10% of the original principal at any time. They can also be converted into another FCC loan at any time.

Variable Open: similar to variable rate above, but with the option to repay any amount at any time.

Fixed Closed: are secured by a mortgage on the property and can be at fixed interest rate terms and can be renewable for 1,2,3,4,5,7,10, 15 or 20 years.

Fixed Rate Plus 10: are loans at a fixed interest rate for terms of five, seven, and 10 years. They permit prepayment of up to 10% of the original amount at any time with no prepayment charge.

Capacity Builder Loans

Capacity Builder Loans provide eighteen month pre-approved loans at competitive interest rates for the purchase of quota and breeding livestock. Principal payment is not required during the disbursement period. Pre-payment can be made at anytime on a monthly, quarterly, semi-annual or annual basis.

Transition Loans

Transition Loans are designed to help those who want to purchase a farm from someone who is retiring. FCC guarantees 100% of the funds to the vendor and offers three customized payment options:

*   the buyer puts down 10% for the purchase (versus 25% for most standard loans);
*   the vendor receives approximately 40-60% of sale proceeds up-front; and,
*   the remaining funds are disbursed to the vendor over the next four years.

Cash Flow Optimizer Loans

Cash Flow Optimizer Loans provide the freedom to use money that would normally go to paying principal and reinvest it in other areas of the operation. Thus, a cattle farmer who has loaned money to purchase land need only pay interest for the loan; freeing up the money that would normally go to pay down the principal. He could use this to expand his herd. This helps to improve his cash flow and enables his money to be better leveraged. Such loans can be used to purchase land, buildings, livestock or other personal property.

1-2-3 Grow Loans

The 1-2-3 Grow Loan is designed for new farmers to give them time to repay their loan after starting or expanding their livestock operation. It offers three customized payment solutions:

- an interest only payment option for up to five years for those who have some cash flow at the start of their operations and want to re-invest it;
- a tiered interest rate payment plan for those whose cash flow grows more quickly; or,
- a payment deferral feature for operations with no start-up cash flow.

Energy Loan

Energy loans are available to bring operators one step closer towards energy self-sufficiency. The Energy Loan helps make the switch to renewable energy sources like biogas, geo-thermal, wind or solar power.

There are no loan processing fees on the first $500,000 and applicants can also take advantage of provincial and federal energy grants and incentives (where available).

This loan is normally secured with real or personal property.

Loans carry fixed or variable rates. Repayment can be made monthly, quarterly, semi-annually or annually.

267

Enviro-Loan

Enviro-Loans are open to producers and value-added agricultural businesses that are making environmentally focussed improvements to their operations. Pre-approved credit can be obtained for manure storage facilities or other improvements designed to meet environmental standards. Principal payments are not required until projects are complete (i.e., for up to 18 months from the start of construction).

Start Now - Pay Later Loans

Producers of grapes, apples, tender fruits or berries who will not see financial returns on new plantings for several years can benefit from Start Now – Pay Later Loans. Repayment can be deferred for up to three years or it is possible to pay interest only for up to five years. Multiple draws can be arranged.

Forestry - Spring Break Loans

Spring Break Loans help forestry operators to purchase equipment (both new or used) or for short-term harvesting rights. Security for the loan is provided by the equipment being purchased or, in the case of harvesting rights, security is usually registered as a continuing collateral mortgage. Amortization periods can be for up to five years on used equipment and harvesting rights, and up to seven years on new equipment. The repayment schedule can be adjusted to coincide with harvesting season.

Equipment Leasing

FCC can arrange for new or used equipment leasing at select equipment dealerships It offers competitive lease rates and less up-front cost than a loan down payment. Leases have fixed payments with terms between two and five years. Payments can be made monthly, quarterly, semi-annually or annually.

Leases can be for a period of up to five years and require no security deposit or additional security. There is also flexibility in setting purchase option price for the end of lease.

FCC Ventures

FCC Ventures is the venture capital division of Farm Credit Canada. Since its formation in 2002, it has provided over $70 million in venture capital financing to small and medium sized companies in the following sectors:

* value-added food manufacturing and processing
* development and manufacturing of agricultural equipment
* commercial processing
* commercial-scale farming
* businesses that support the agricultural sector
* ag-biotech.

Further information on FCC Ventures can be obtained from Rick Hoffman by phone at: (306) 780-5708 or by e-mail at: Rick.Hoffman@fcc-fac.ca or from the Aviro Ventures Partnership which manages the fund at: (404) 215-5490.

Crop Inputs

Crop Input are loans arranged through an FCC Alliance Partner, who knows the industry. They feature customized pre-approved lending limits which can cover up to 100% of crop input purchase costs with deferred payment date which extends the marketing window for crops.They offer an option to defer payment of fall purchases to the next crop year, upon renewal of credit facilities. They have competitive variable interest rates until the due date.

It is also possible to obtain revolving credit for re-advances following pay-down and the potential to roll fall advances into the next crop year.

A loan and general security agreement and/or promissory note is required.

Feeder Cattle and Breeding Livestock

Loans to purchase feeder cattle and breeding livestock loans can be arranged through an FCC Alliance Partner who knows the industry. Loans permit a modest down payment, or pooled or non-pooled security deposit accounts, depending on the alliance partner.

Loans are structured to the applicant's needs and feature competitive variable or fixed rates and a faster realization of equity through proportionate payments. There are no prepayment penalties.

Feeder cattle can be purchased on a revolving loan with each draw repayable upon sale of the livestock, within one year of disbursement.

Breeding livestock can be purchased on a term loan that corresponds with the age of the cows and the operation's cash flow (generally one, three or five-year terms with level annual principal plus interest payments).

First charge security is on the financed cattle (offspring, as applicable), supported by a credit facility agreement and security agreement. It also requires an assignment of livestock insurance and assignment of security deposit funds, if applicable.

National Equipment Dealers Finance Program

Financing for new or used farm equipment can be arranged through FCC Alliance Partners, who know the industry. These partners are located across the country. Two steps are involved:

- the dealer calls the FCC Customer Service Centre and provides details of the purchase; and,
- the applicant supplies personal information to a qualified FCC staff member.

The one-stop financing boasts of minimal paperwork and fast turnaround times. Only low down payments are required and there are no administration fees. Loans can be for up to 10 years with variable or fixed rates. There are no prepayment penalties and security is taken on financed equipment only.

Farm Credit Canada (FCC) Energy Loan

The Farm Credit Canada (FCC) Energy Loan was announced in February 2010. It is designed to assist producers and agribusiness owners who want to make the move towards producing their own renewable energy. It is designed to help producers invest in the technologies to harness the many sources of energy all around Canadian farmyards.

A recent FCC Vision survey showed that 60% of individuals surveyed are considering new ways to find financial value by reducing their environmental impact. The survey, completed in November 2009 by 1,172 producers and agribusinesses across the country, revealed that 37% of those people looking at reducing their impact are considering the use of renewable energy sources in their operation.

The Energy Loan will help producers and agribusiness operators purchase and install on-farm energy sources like biogas, geo-thermal, wind or solar power. The Energy Loan offers an interest term of up to five years at variable or fixed rates and with monthly, quarterly, semi-annual and annual payments available.

For more information visit: www.fccvision.ca/InAction.aspx

Further Information

Farm Credit Canada-Corporate Office
1800 Hamilton Street P.O. Box 4320
Regina, SK, S4P 4L3
Phone: (306) 780-8100
Phone toll-free: 1-(888) 332-3301
Fax: (306) 780-8919
E-mail: csc@fcc-sca.ca
Web site: www.fcc-sca.ca

ACC Farmers Financial

The Agricultural Credit Corporation (ACC) is a not-for-profit farm organization founded in 1992 by a coalition of farm organizations and is now comprised of nineteen producer associations and marketing boards. Since that time, ACC have provided in excess of $3 billion dollars in operating funds to Canadian producers. ACC offers low cost operating loans to producers across Canada.

Advance Payments Program (APP)

Coverage includes eighty varieties of crops and livestock in Ontario. Producers must be enrolled in either Production Insurance or AgriStability to apply to the program. It should be noted that farm-fed crops are not eligible.

Producers can receive a cash advance on up to 50% of the expected average market price of the agricultural product or commodity. Producers can access up to $400,000 of financing with the first $100,000 interest-free and next $300,000 at bank prime.

Up to 18 months of financing available if used with advance payments program for crops in storage. Cash advances are repaid as the agricultural product is sold or when producers are entitled to a payment under a Business Risk Management (BRM) program.

Livestock Advances: are based on number of animals currently on the farm times a set dollar amount per animal or per cwt. The program covers beef, hogs and sheep.

Field crops: include barley, canola, coloured beans, corn, flue-cured tobacco, mixed grain, oats, rye, seed corn, soybeans, spelt, white beans, winter and spring wheat

Berry crops: include strawberries, raspberries, blueberries and cranberries.

Coverage is also available for:

- fresh market vegetables
- greenhouse vegetables
- greenhouse cut flowers and potted plants
- fresh market grapes and tender fruits
- processing grapes
- sugar beets
- deciduous trees and container shrubs.

Commodity Loan Program (CLP)

This Program provides operating funds for crop inputs up to $750,000. The interest rate is bank prime. Loans are available at different times throughout the year, depending on the crops included in the loan. Loans are available as early as December for winter wheat and March through June 30 for spring crops.

It is repaid by Direct Debit to account at financial institution when crops are designated for feeding on the farm. Crops must be insured through Production Insurance.

Approved loan advances are based on both the level of Production Insurance guarantee and acres planted, resulting in financing of 70%-75% of the cost of production. The CLP can provide greater operating capital and longer repayment terms than the Advance Payment Program.

Crops covered include:

Grains and oilseeds: corn, soybeans, winter and spring wheat, barley, oats and mixed grain, canola, seed corn, white beans, coloured beans.

Processing vegetables: cucumbers, green peas, sweet corn, green and wax beans, butternut squash, cauliflower, cabbage, red beets, carrots, tomatoes, banana and bell peppers, lima beans and potatoes.

Others: apples, grapes, sugar beets and various tobacco crops.

Up to $400,000 can be rolled or transferred into the Advance Payment Program storage component ($100,000 interest free) with repayment extended to September of the following year.

Further information

ACC Farmers Financial
100 Stone Rd. W., Ste 101, Guelph, ON N1G 5L3
Phone: (519) 766-0544
Phone toll-free:1-(888) 278-8807
Fax: (519) 766-9775
E-mail: agcorp@accfinancial.ca
Web site: www.accfarmersfinancial.ca

Agriculture and Agri-Food Canada (AAFC)

Agriculture and Agri-Food Canada is a federal government department that supports agricultural productivity and trade, the stabilizing of farm incomes, encourages research and development, and is responsible for the inspection and regulation of animals and plant-life forms.

Growing Forward 2 (GF2)

Growing Forward 2 (GF2) replaces the original Growing Forward initiative and became operational on April 1, 2013. It is a policy framework for Canada's agricultural and agri-food sector with a $3 billion dollar investment by federal, provincial and territorial governments. Of that amount, $2 billion will be cost-shared on a 60:40 basis for programs delivered by provinces and territories, and $1 billion for federally delivered strategic initiatives and the foundation for government agricultural programs and services. Cost-shared investments under GF2 will increase by 50% over the funding offered under the original Growing Forward Program and provincial and territorial governments will have greater flexibility to tailor the new programs to their local needs.

GF2 will be operational until March 31, 2018.

The programs under GF2 are intended to focus on innovation, competitiveness and market development to ensure Canadian producers and processors have the tools and resources they need to continue to innovate and capitalize on emerging market opportunities. GF2 will also include an effective suite of Business Risk Management (BRM) programs to help farmers in managing risk due to severe market volatility and disaster situations.

Canadian Agricultural Loans Act (CALA) Program

The Canadian Agricultural Loans Act (CALA) Program replaces the Farm Improvement and Marketing Cooperatives Loans Act (FIMCLA).

Loans can be for up to $500,000 for land and the construction or improvement of buildings and up to $350,000 for all other purposes. The maximum term is 10 years, with 15 years for loans on land purchases. Interest can be paid on a floating rate which is the lender's prime rate plus a maximum of 1%. For loans on a fixed-term rate using a formula based on the lender's residential mortgage rate plus a maximum of 1%.

Loans under the CALA can be obtained from chartered banks, trust companies, Alberta treasury branches, loan companies, credit unions, insurance companies, caisses populaires and other designated organizations.

The farmer must pay a fee to have the loan registered and guaranteed under the CALA. This fee is 0.85% of the amount of the loan. The lender may also charge an administration fee of 0.25% of the amount of the loan up to a maximum of $250.

Loans must be used in the applicant's farming operation and can be used to purchase:

- equipment
- building/construction
- land
- livestock
- shares in a farming operation. The program is open to beginning or start-up farmers, existing farmers together with those taking over a family farm.

Assistance of up to $3 million can also be provided to farmer co-operatives with over 50% farmer ownership.

Application should be made through financial institutions listed above.

CALA Administration Office
Financial Guarantee Programs Division
Agriculture and Agri-Food Canada
1341 Baseline Rd., Tower 7 , Ottawa, ON, K1A 0C9
Phone toll-free: 1-(888) 346-2511
Fax: (613) 773-2020
E-mail: fgp-pgf@agr.gc.ca
Web site: www.agr.gc.ca/cala

Advance Payments Program (APP)

The Advance Payments Program (APP) provides cash advances with an interest-free feature on the first $100,000 to eligible producers to store eligible crops after harvest allowing them to market the crops later in the season when market conditions may result in better prices and thereby encourage the orderly marketing of the crop. In February 2008, coverage was extended to cover livestock and a number of other crop types.

The program is available to all producers of field crops grown in Canada, which are storable in their natural state, together with producers of maple syrup and honey.

The Minister of Agriculture and Agri-Food Canada guarantees advances through eligible administrators (producer organizations) who administer the program on behalf of their members. The overall maximum advance guarantee per producer or partnership or co-operative is $400,000 for crops. The advance guarantee cannot exceed 50% of the expected average farm gate price for the crop year. For each producer, Agriculture and Agri-Food Canada pays the interest on the first $100,000 of advances. Producers repay their advance on a predetermined basis as the crop is sold throughout the year but the period for repayment cannot exceed 18 months.

In early 2009, an amendment was added to enable cattle and hog producers to be exempt from making any repayments to their 2008-09 APP advances prior to September 30th, 2010.

Agriculture and Agri-Food Canada
Financial Guarantee Programs Division
1341 Baseline Road, Tower 7, 7th Floor
Ottawa ON K1A 0C5
Phone toll-free: 1-(888) 346-2511

Farm Debt Mediation Service (FDMS)

The free Farm Debt Mediation Service provides counselling and mediation services to farmers who may be having trouble repaying their debts. Further information can be obtained toll-free by phone at: 1-(866) 452-5556.

Newfoundland & Labrador:
Fisheries Loan Guarantee Program

The Fisheries Loan Guarantee Program was created to support the Province's independent fish harvesting industry. It provides government guaranteed loans of up to $2 million through local financial institutions. Loans are usually at prime rate plus 1.0% or 1.5% and can be for a term of between 10 and 20 years in the case of purchasing new vessels. For used vessels, the repayment is calculated based on the estimated remaining useful life of the vessel; as determined by an appraisal.

Funds can be used for the purchase of new or used fishing vessels or to purchase new engines or equipment to improve existing vessels. Under certain circumstances, funds can also be used to re-finance existing loans which had previously been obtained from processors or other third parties.

In order to be eligible for assistance under this program, applicants should be Canadian citizens and/or have their enterprises registered with the Province. They should be full-time fish harvesters and be the registered owner of a commercial fishing vessel together with the necessary licenses. They should also be able to demonstrate their ability to re-pay the loan and to demonstrate that they are commercially viable and have a satisfactory credit record.

Applicants under this program are required to make a down payment of 10% for the purchase price of vessels and 15% for engines, equipment and rebuilding/repairs. They should also be able to provide security for the loan in the form of a promissory note and/or mortgages against the vessel or equipment.

Dept. of Innovation, Business and Rural Development
Government of Newfoundland and Labrador
P O Box 8700,
St. John's, NL A1B 4J6
Phone: (709) 729-7003
Fax: (709) 729-5124

Prince Edward Island
Department of Fisheries, Aquaculture and Rural Development

The Prince Edward Island Department of Fisheries, Aquaculture and Rural Development offers several assistance programs.

Low Interest Loan Program for Fishers

Announced in September 2007, a low interest loan program was made available to fishers experiencing financial difficulties because of declining lobster landings and rising costs. Fishers in Lobster Fishing Areas 25 and 26A with net cash positions less than $40,000 are eligible for loans on their fishing related debts. The program will be administered by the Prince Edward Island Lending Agency.

The loans carry 4% interest rates over five years. Eligible expenses which can be consolidated under this program must be attributed to the fishery. The maximum individual loan amount will be $200,000.

The program will not provide low interest loans for new entrants into the fishery. Loans will not be made to fishers in such cases where their financial situation has deteriorated beyond the point of long-term viability, regardless of a low interest rate.

Further Information

Department of Fisheries, Aquaculture and Rural Development
PO Box 1180, 548 Main St. Montague PE C0A 1R0
Phone: (902) 838-0635
Phone toll-free: 1-(877) 407-0187
Fax: (902) 838-0975
Web site: http://www.gov.pe.ca/fard/index.php3?number=1002204&lang=E

PEI Department of Agriculture

Future Farmer Assistance Program

The Future Farmer Assistance Program encourages new Prince Edward Island farmers to develop successful commercial farm operations by providing an interest rebate on loans.

There are seven components to the program:

- facilitating and coaching assistance by a program advisor;
- skills assessment and development of a personal learning plan;
- business planning;
- skills development and training ;
- business risk management; and,
- understanding analytical laboratory results.

Further Information

PEI Department of Agriculture
Jones Building, 11 Kent Street
PO Box 2000
Charlottetown, PE C1A 7N8
Phone: (902) 368-4145
Fax: (902) 368-4846

Nova Scotia Farm Loan Board

The Nova Scotia Farm Loan Board is a credit agency that lends to farm operators in rural Nova Scotia. It is an agricultural development agency serving the needs of agriculture and forestry through the provision of long-term credit at fixed interest rates.

FarmNEXT Program

The objective of the FramNEXT Program is to encourage new Nova Scotian farmers to purchase and develop successful farm operations or for succession projects. Applicants must be 19 years and older. They must be involved in Nova Scotia farm businesses (single proprietorship, partnership or corporation) with minimum annual sales of $10,000..

In the case of start-ups, benefits of up to $30,000 can be assigned to the loan and in the case of succession the amount is $20,000.

Small Business Loan Guarantee Program

The Small Business Loan Guarantee Program was already covered earlier in this chapter. It enables credit unions to deliver financial assistance to establish new business, grow existing business and empower entrepreneurs with the support they need to create employment for themselves and others.

The Nova Scotia Farm Loan Board has partnered with this program and can provide financing of up to $500,000 in the form of term loans, working capital and lines of credit for those who would like to start a business, purchase a business or expand an existing business.

Loans can be in the form of term loans, lines of credit or working capital.

Further Information

Program Coordinator
Nova Scotia Farm Loan Board
Nova Scotia Department of Agriculture and Fisheries
P.O. Box 890
Truro, NS B2N 5G6
Phone: (902) 893-6506
Fax: (902) 895-7693
Web site: http://www.gov.ns.ca/agri/farmlb/

Nova Scotia Farm Loan Board
Kentville Agricultural Centre
32 Main Street, Kentville, NS B4N 1J5
Phone: (902) 679-6009
Fax: (902) 679-4997

Nova Scotia: Fisheries and Aquaculture Loan Board

The Fisheries and Aquaculture Loan Board provides loans to fishers, associations of fishers or companies in two principal areas.

Vessel Loans

The board will provide loans for vessels less than 25 years old and of over 22 feet in length. Loans can be used for:

- purchasing or building a fishing vessel;
- purchasing and installing engines/equipment/electronics; and/or,
- technical modifications.

A deposit for 10% of the loan amount is required and personal guarantees are required. Repayment schedule depends upon the age of the vessel and can vary from 20 years for a new vessel to 6 years for a vessel that is between 19 and 25 years old. For diesel engines and technical modifications, it is 8 years and 5 years for equipment or electronics.

Aquaculture Loans

The board will provide loans to sustain aquaculture in the following areas:

- finfish;
- shellfish; and,
- seaplants.

Loans can be used for:

- salmonoid seed stock;
- shellfish seed/spat;
- collection materials, grow-out equipment and materials; and,

- rafts, buoys, floatation devices, anchors, nets, cages for finfish grow-out, small boats, outboard motors and onboard gear handling devices.

A deposit for 10% of the loan amount is required and personal guarantees are required plus a chattel mortgage on equipment.

The loan repayment schedules are as follows.

Finfish fry: upon harvest.

Finfish equipment: up to 10 years.

Mussel spat: upon harvest.

Mussel equipment: up to 10 years.

Oyster spat: upon harvest.

Oyster equipment: up to 15 years.

Licence Loan Program

The Licence Loan Program provides loans to purchase a fishing licence. Loans can be for a maximum term of 20 years with interest rates set quarterly but fixed for the term of the loan. A personal guarantee is taken on all loans.

Loans are available for eligible independent fishers who:

- have never held a licence in the commercial fishery (New Entrant), or;
- are current commercial fishery licence holders who wish to diversify into a species for which they have never held a licence (New Species).

Financing is available to purchase a licence only or licence and associated gear. Where a vessel purchase forms part of the licence package, the vessel is to be included on the same Licence Loan Application.

An applicant must have a Fishing Masters Class certificate or five years experience as captain of a vessel or in the case of a new entrant, meet Department of Fisheries and Oceans eligibility requirements.

A detailed five year business plan must be submitted with the application. Required deposit of 5% is required for a new entrant licence. Required deposit for a new species licence only or licence and associated gear loan is a minimum of 10%.

Further Information

Nova Scotia Fisheries and Aquaculture Loan Board
P.O. Box 890
Truro, NS B2N 5G6
Phone: (902) 896-4800
Fax: (902) 896-4812
Web site: http://www.gov.ns.ca/fish//

New Brunswick:
Department of Agricultural, Aquaculture and Fisheries

Business Risk Management Programs

There are three programs under Business Risk Management.

AgriInvest: to help producers protect their margin from small declines or provide funds for investment to reduce risks or improve profitability. Each year, producers can make a deposit into an AgriInvest account, and receive a matching contribution from federal and provincial governments.

AgriStability: provides assistance when a producer's current year program margin falls below 85% of the producer's historical reference margin.

Agricultural Insurance: provides farmers with financial protection against production losses caused by natural perils, such as drought, flood, hail, frost, excessive moisture and insects.

Agricultural Loans

The Agricultural Development Board can provide loans for projects that are deemed strategic to provincial agricultural strategies. These loans are designed to complement other sources of lending such as Farm Credit Canada and financial institutions.

The business plan must show reasonable chances of viability and must demonstrate that a demand exists for the product and the applicant must have acceptable agricultural knowledge and business skills, and an acceptable credit history.

The project must fit with the province's sector strategies in terms of impact on agricultural land, jobs, export sales, markets, etc.., and acceptable security must be provided for the proposed financing. The applicant must have an acceptable amount of equity in the business.

Direct loans are amortized for up to 20 years, at the provincial interest lending rate.

Agricultural Loan Guarantees

The Agricultural Development Board can provide loan guarantees to financial institutions, on a portion of a line of credit, for working capital requirements. The guarantees are typically for up to a maximum of 80% of line of credit, and usually for a period of up to 3 years.

The business plan must show reasonable chances of viability and must demonstrate that a demand exists for the product and the applicant must have acceptable agricultural knowledge and business skills, and an acceptable credit history.

The project must fit with the province's sector strategies in terms of impact on agricultural land, jobs, export sales, markets, etc.., and acceptable security must be provided for the proposed financing. The applicant must have an acceptable amount of equity in the business. This program provides a guarantee, to financial institutions, on a portion of a line of credit, for working capital requirements.

The guarantee is typically for up to a maximum of 80% of line of credit, and usually for a period of up to 3 years. The loan guarantee fee of 1.5% of the amount guaranteed is paid at the beginning of each year.

New Entrant Farmer Loan Program

The New Entrant Farmer Loan Program is one in which the Agricultural Development Board can provide financial assistance, in the form of loans, to persons entering into the agriculture sector. The program is designed to assist in the purchase of a farm and can complement other sources of lending such as Farm Credit Canada and other financial institutions.

Applicant must have 6 years of post-secondary education and work experience on a farming operation. Their business plan must show reasonable chances of viability and must demonstrate that a demand exists for the product and acceptable security must be provided for the proposed financing.

Loans can be for up to 100% of the appraised value of security, to a maximum amount of $750,000 and can be amortized over 20 years at provincial lending rate. Payments are interest only during the first four years and with blended payments of interest and principal thereafter.

During the first 4 years of loan, the New Entrant farmer may apply for an additional loan for expansion or improvement of up to $750,000.

Value-Added and Niche Production Assistance for Agriculture, Aquaculture and Fisheries

The Program is designed to assist small-scale agri-businesses and primary producers to expand or diversify into value-added or niche production and to enable them to implement and adopt processes and technologies that reduce production costs, add value, improve product quality and address emerging challenges to the sector. It is also designed to facilitate the development of new products which will enable agri-food businesses to improve their competitive position and address consumer preferences.

This sub-program is available to agricultural producers, partnerships and incorporated companies carrying out agricultural operations in New Brunswick. Individual applicants must be nineteen years of age or older. It covers:

- process automation;
- process improvement;
- technology adoption; and,
- value chain development.

Perennial Crop Establishment Loan Program

The Perennial Crop Establishment Loan Program is offered by the Agricultural Development Board and can provide financial assistance, in the form of loans, to persons wishing to establish a perennial crop. It can finance up to 75% of the enhanced value and can be amortized for up to 10 years at the provincial lending rate; with no loan interest payments during the first 5 years of the loan.

Livestock Incentive Loan Program

The Livestock Incentive Loan Program can guarantee loans to financial institutions for farmers purchasing and raising livestock. Applicant must invest at least 10% equity in the project and loans can be for $75,000 with guarantees of up to 90% of the loan.

The term of the guarantee will be up to 18 months for the purchase of feeder livestock and up to 7 years for the purchase of breeding livestock.

New Land Purchase Program

The New Land Purchase Program is offered by the Agricultural Development Board. It can purchase eligible land and lease it to an applicant for a period of up to six years. The applicant agrees to purchase the land at the end of the lease.

The proposed land has not had any agricultural crop produced or harvested during the previous 2 years, excluding unimproved forage land. The business plan must show reasonable chances of viability and must demonstrate that a demand exists for the product and the applicant must have acceptable agricultural knowledge and business skills, and an acceptable credit history.

During the first two years, annual lease payments are deferred based on the equivalent of the annual provincial lending rate and the lease amount. The client must agree to purchase the land at the end of 6 years

Agri-Food Market Development Program

The Agri-Food Market Development Program provides assistance to build and enhance domestic market channels to increase the sale and consumption of New Brunswick-produced agri-food products within the province. It is open to individuals agricultural or agri-food enterprises marketing New Brunswick agri-food products and associations or organizations representing an agricultural commodity or agriculture marketing group. It will also assist businesses that partner with the New Brunswick agri-food industry to promote the sale and consumption of New Brunswick agri-food products

There are five elements:

- road signage;
- promotion;
- agri-tourism;
- new product development/market launch; and,
- marketing groups and organizations for establishment and capacity building.

Aquaculture Loans and Loan Guarantees

The Fisheries and Aquaculture Development Board provides financial assistance in the form of loans and loan guarantees for aquaculture production and related services. Project must fit with policies with regard to the impact on marine resources, jobs, export sales, markets, etc.

The program is designed to complement other sources of lending and financial institutions and applicants must invest, or have invested about 20% equity in the project and acceptable security must be provided for the proposed financing.

Direct loans: may be provided to finance viable projects for the purchase or construction of various aquaculture capital costs such as equipment and buildings. Loan payments in the shellfish sector can be customized to correspond with the development of the project.

Loan guarantees: may be provided on a portion of lines of credit for inventory and feed expenses, sharing the financial risk with financial institutions

The applicant must have acceptable knowledge of aquaculture and business skills, and an acceptable credit history. Their business plan must show that the project is viable and that a demand exists for the product.

A 1.5% service fee is charged annually based on the principal amount of a guaranteed loan outstanding.

Loans for Commercial Fishing

Loans are available to fishermen, groups of fishermen, companies, partnerships, co-operatives and associations of fishermen for:

- new vessel construction;
- major refits or overhaul of existing vessels;
- the purchase of used fishing vessels;
- new onboard equipment; or,
- for purposes deemed to be in aid of and to encourage the establishment or development of fisheries in the Province of New Brunswick.

It should be noted that expenses relating to the normal maintenance and repair of vessels and equipment are not eligible.

Applicants must have about 20% equity invested in the business. Interest is charged on loans as follows:

For equity of 29% or less: prime plus 3.5%
For equity of 30% to 39%: prime plus 2.5%
For equity of 40% or more: prime plus 1.5%.

New Entrant Fisheries Loans

The Fisheries and Aquaculture Development Board provides financial assistance in the form of loans to a new entrant who has never owned a vessel-based commercial fishing license.

The business plan must show reasonable chances of viability and must demonstrate that a demand exists for the product and the applicant must have acceptable fishing and business skills, and an acceptable credit history.

The applicant must invest, or have invested, 5% of the amount of the loan, which can be used for the construction, purchase or repairs of commercial fishing vessels, as well as for the replacement of motors and fishing equipment. However, normal maintenance of vessels, such as annual repairs and equipment replacement, are not eligible.

Further Information

Agricultural Research Station (Experimental Farm)
P. O. Box 6000
Fredericton, NB E3B 5H1
Phone: (506) 453-2666
Phone toll-free : 1-(888) 622-4742
Fax : (506) 453-7170

Ontario: Tile Loan Program

The Tile Loan program is a partnership between municipalities and the province. It allows agricultural property owners to access loan funds to finance 75% of the cost of the tile drainage work on their agricultural land. Loans can be for a maximum of $50,000 per year and can be for 10 year terms and carry a fixed interest rate of 6%.

Ontario Ministry of Agriculture and Food (OMAF)
1 Stone Road West
Guelph, ON N1G 4Y2
Phone: (519) 826-3100
Phone toll-free: 1-(888) 466-2372
Web site: www.omafra.gov.on.ca

Ontario: ACC Farmers Financial

Advance Payments Program (APP)

Coverage includes eighty varieties of crops and livestock in Ontario. Producers must be enrolled in either Production Insurance or AgriStability to apply to the program. It should be noted that farm-fed crops are not eligible.

Producers can receive a cash advance on up to 50% of the expected average market price of the agricultural product or commodity. Producers can access up to $400,000 of financing with the first $100,000 interest-free and next $300,000 at bank prime.

Up to 18 months of financing available if used with advance payments program for crops in storage. Cash advances are repaid as the agricultural product is sold or when producers are entitled to a payment under a Business Risk Management (BRM) program.

Livestock Advances: are based on number of animals currently on the farm times a set dollar amount per animal or per cwt. The program covers beef, hogs and sheep.

Field crops: include barley, canola, coloured beans, corn, flue-cured tobacco, mixed grain, oats, rye, seed corn, soybeans, spelt, white beans, winter and spring wheat

Berry crops: include strawberries, raspberries, blueberries and cranberries.

Coverage is also available for:

- fresh market vegetables
- greenhouse vegetables
- greenhouse cut flowers and potted plants
- fresh market grapes and tender fruits
- processing grapes
- sugar beets
- deciduous trees and container shrubs.

Commodity Loan Program (CLP)

This Program provides operating funds for crop inputs up to $750,000. The interest rate is bank prime. Loans are available at different times throughout the year, depending on the crops included in the loan. Loans are available as early as December for winter wheat and March through June 30 for spring crops.

It is repaid by Direct Debit to account at financial institution when crops are designated for feeding on the farm. Crops must be insured through Production Insurance.

Approved loan advances are based on both the level of Production Insurance guarantee and acres planted, resulting in financing of 70%-75% of the cost of production. The CLP can provide greater operating capital and longer repayment terms than the Advance Payment Program.

Crops covered include:

Grains and oilseeds: corn, soybeans, winter and spring wheat, barley, oats and mixed grain, canola, seed corn, white beans, coloured beans.

Processing vegetables: cucumbers, green peas, sweet corn, green and wax beans, butternut squash, cauliflower, cabbage, red beets, carrots, tomatoes, banana and bell peppers, lima beans and potatoes.

Others: apples, grapes, sugar beets and various tobacco crops.

Up to $400,000 can be rolled or transferred into the Advance Payment Program storage component ($100,000 interest free) with repayment extended to September of the following year.

Further information

ACC Farmers Financial
100 Stone Rd. W., Ste 101
Guelph, ON N1G 5L3
Phone: (519) 766-0544
Phone toll-free:1-(888) 278-8807
Fax: (519) 766-9775
E-mail: agcorp@accfinancial.ca
Web site: www.accfarmersfinancial.ca

Ontario Cattlemen's Association (OCA)

The Ontario Cattlemen's Association (OCA) was formed in 1976 to act as a lobby group for the industry. It also has two financial programs which may be of interest to cattlemen.

Ontario Beef Breeder Loan Program

The Ontario Beef Breeder Loan Program provides loans to Ontario cow or calf producers to expand their beef herds. The program allows producer co-ops to obtain credit from lenders and then extend financing to eligible Ontario producers. The program applies to breeding females of commercial breeding value intended for beef production.

To be eligible for the program:

- members must pay an annual fee to the co-operative;
- eligible cattle are vaccinated bred females or open heifers; and,
- members deposit 15% of their own funds into an assurance account before receiving a purchase order.

The maximum loan is $50,000 with a term of 5 years for each purchase order. If a producer has owned and calved out less than 20 cows in the previous year, the maximum loan is $25,000 the first year.

Ontario Feeder Cattle Loan Guarantee Program

The Ontario Feeder Cattle Loan Guarantee Program is a loan guarantee to incorporated feeder cattle co-operatives in Ontario. The co-operatives then provide financing to members to purchase cattle for feeding.

A member deposits 5% of the amount of a purchase order into the co-operative's assurance account.

The maximum loan amount is $250,000 and loans must be repaid within 12 months. If a producer has fed less than 100 head of cattle in the previous 12 months, maximum loan is $50,000.

Further Information

Ontario Cattlemen's Association
130 Malcolm Rd.
Guelph, ON N1K 1B1
Phone: (519) 367-5590
Fax: (519) 824-9101
Web sire: www.cattle.guelph.on.ca

Manitoba Agricultural Services Corporation (MASC)

The Manitoba Agricultural Services Corporation (MASC) is a Manitoba Crown corporation which offers a number of financial assistance programs to farmers.

Renewable interest terms are now available for 1, 2, 3, 4 and 5-year terms on loans to purchase long-term assets or breeding livestock. At the end of the selected term, the borrower can renew for another short-term or select a fixed long-term rate. Fixed interest rates for up to 25 years are still available with no prepayment penalties.

MASC clients can benefit from General Purpose Mortgages, which will expedite the approval turnaround times on loans for existing clients. With this multi-draw mortgage, clients can borrow up to 80% (90% for young farmers) of the market value of their collateral, and are allowed to subsequently borrow up to this amount without new security registrations or associated legal costs.

Direct Loans Program

The Direct Loans Program is open to individuals, joint farm units, partnerships, corporations or cooperatives and provides funding for:

- the purchase of land or buildings;
- the purchase of new or used agricultural equipment;
- construction or renovation of farm buildings (including housing for up to $225,000);
- breeding stock;
- debt consolidation;
- supply-managed quota and share financing;
- finance start-up shares in New-Generation Co-ops; and,
- purchase shares in a farming corporation for the purpose of farm transfer or primary agricultural production.

In general financing will cover up to 80% of the appraised value of the assets; up to a maximum of maximum of $2.0 million for individuals, partnerships, corporations, or co-operatives. Loan terms can be for up to 25 years.

In 2011, a General Purpose Mortgage was added as part of the Direct Loans program. It can expedite the approval turnaround times on subsequent loans for existing customers. With this multi-draw mortgage, customers can borrow up to 80% of the market value of their collateral, and are allowed to subsequently borrow up to this amount without new security registrations or associated legal costs. Young farmers can borrow up to 90% of the market value of their collateral.

Bridging Generations Initiative (BGI)

The MASC Bridging Generations Initiative (BGI) aims to help young farmers; aged 18 - 39 to secure their future. It has several components:

Flexible Financing: enables young farmers to opt for either 90% financing or 5 years of interest-only payments on MASC loans; thereby significantly reducing the down payment required for the purchase of a farm, or ease the cash flow pressures during a young farmer's critical start-up period.

Young Farmer Rebate (YFR): farmers aged 18-39 are eligible to receive a rebate of up to 2% of the amount of principal of the loan for the first five years; up to a maximum of $15,000.

Management Training Credit: provides a lifetime credit of up to $12,500 ($2,500 per year maximum) to young producers who participate in annual training together with a 1% credit on the the first $250,000 principal amount of the loan for the first five years.

Bridging Generations Mortgage Guarantee: assists young and retiring farmers with intergenerational farm transfers, with guarantees to a maximum of $250,000 for the purposes of taking over a farm operation. To qualify total off-farm income including that of a spouse cannot exceed $125,000 and net worth cannot exceed $1.5 million.

Environmental Enhancement Loan Program

The 2006 Manitoba Budget announced the introduction of the Environmental Enhancement Loan Program to help farmers increase the environmental performance of their land.

The Environmental Enhancement Loans are offered through the Manitoba Agricultural Services Corporation (MASC). The maximum loan is $150,000 with repayment terms of up to 15 years. MASC's regular eligibility criteria, such as limitations on net worth, have been waived for this loan program. As a result, Environmental Enhancements Loans provide financing at reasonable fixed interest rates and are available to all Manitoba producers planning to participate in environmental incentive programs.

The program focuses on providing loan assistance for projects such as improved manure storage, handling and treatment, relocation of livestock and horticulture facilities, and other environmental initiatives involving substantial capital commitment.

Alternate Energy Loans

Alternate Energy Loans are offered to encourage the local production of ethanol, bio-diesel and capturing wind energy projects. In 2011, maximum loan levels have been increased to $900,000 for individuals and up to $1.8 million for partnerships and corporations. Borrowers will also be eligible for a 1% credit on the amount of the loan as a management training credit.

Stocker Loans

This Program helps finance 100% of the purchase price of feed livestock. It specifies that cattle purchased under the program must be sold within 12 months of purchase and breeding heifers within 9 months. In 2011, the maximum assistance was increased to $300,000.

To qualify total off-farm income including that of a spouse cannot exceed $125,000 and net worth cannot exceed $1.35 million.

Wastewater Management (WM) Loans

Wastewater Management (WM) loans are available for the total of the Certified Installer's invoice, for amounts of up to $20,000. It offers five or ten-year repayment terms, with an interest rate set at MASC's lending rate for the selected term as at the date of application. Loan payments are made through monthly pre-authorized deductions from an account at a financial institution. WM loans can be repaid in full at any time with no prepayment penalties.

MASC's Manure Management Loans

MASC's Manure Management Loans are designed to finance the engineering and construction of new manure storage facilities, repair or improvement of existing storage facilities, and the engineering and construction of new treatment projects. During the construction period (maximum of two years), the MML borrower will make interest-only payments. When the project is completed, the MML borrower is required to assign the full MMFAP grant to MASC, which will be applied to the loan. The outstanding balance will then be re-amortized over the remainder of the loan's 10-year repayment term.

Manitoba Livestock Associations Loan Guarantees

Manitoba Livestock Associations Loan Guarantees program helps Manitoba residents establish livestock cattle associations. Funds borrowed by the association from participating lending institutions to purchase feeder cattle and breeder cattle are secured by a government guarantee. MASC will guarantee the lender repayment of 25% of the loan outstanding to the maximum guaranteed loan limit of $5 million per association.

Applicants must be 18 years of age, a resident of Manitoba, own or lease a farm in Manitoba and have facilities to care for livestock. The associations must have a minimum of 15 members.

299

Members of a feeder association must deposit 5% of their authorized loan limit into the association's assurance fund. Members of a breeder association must deposit 10% of their authorized loan limit into the association's assurance fund.

Onsite Wastewater Management (WM) Systems Loan Program

The Onsite Wastewater Management Systems (WM) loan program provides a loan of up to $20,000 for the costs of phasing out a rural sewage ejector and installing a disposal field that complies with the new Onsite Wastewater Management Systems Regulations.

Operating Credit Guarantee for Agriculture

This program provides 25% guarantees for new operating lines of credit made by participating lending institutions. These guarantees can be for up to $700,000 for individuals and $700,000 to $1 million for partnerships, corporations or cooperatives.

The loans that are the subject of these guarantees must be repaid at the end of the production cycle and cannot carry interest in excess of prime plus 1.5%.

Rural Entrepreneur Assistance (REA)

The Rural Entrepreneur Assistance (REA) Program provides loan guarantees to financial institutions that are prepared to offer full-time, small and home-based businesses in rural Manitoba with the financial support they need to be successful. Enhancements to the program were made in November 2006.

Loans can be used for the purchase of fixed assets, inventory and/or working capital. Loan money cannot be used to pay existing debts of the company or any individual, nor can loans be transferred. Effective November 2006, loans can also be used to provide loan guarantees for the purchase of existing businesses.

The program is available to businesses located in Manitoba, outside of Winnipeg. Only small businesses with $2.0 million or less in annual income/sales are eligible. Applicants must contribute 20% of the total project cost in the form of cash, land, buildings, equipment, inventory and/or other assets that would be used in the business.

The maximum net worth to be eligible under the direct loan program was increased from $775,000 to $850,000, effective November 27, 2006.

Businesses not eligible include: insurance, real estate, financial, professional and consulting services and restaurants, those engaged in primary harvesting of resources, primary agriculture, those intending to purchase a currently operating existing business or those intending only to renovate or make cosmetic changes to buildings.

Under the REA Program, the province will guarantee individual business loans. Effective November 2006, the term for loan guarantees had been extended for up to ten years and the loan maximum was increased to $200,000.

Rural Small Business (RSB) Operating Credit Guarantees

The Rural Small Business Operating Credit Guarantee (RSB) program provides guarantees on lines of credit obtained from participating lending institutions. The maximum amount that can be guaranteed is $200,000. The loans that are guaranteed can be used for purchases of inventory, financing of receivables, and to cover the costs of most other common day-to-day business expenses. The maximum interest that can be charged for such loans is the commercial prime rate plus 2%.

To qualify for the RSB program applicants must be:

- 18 years of age or older and a resident in Manitoba;
- the owner-operator or majority shareholder of the business (with at least 20% equity);
- located in rural Manitoba (outside of Winnipeg), and must provide full-time employment for at least one individual (1,500+ hours of employment per year); and,
- the business must have annual sales or income of less than $2 million.

Further Information

MASC Corporate Lending Head Office
Unit 100 - 1525 First Street S.
Brandon, MB R7A 7A1
Phone: (204) 726-6850
Fax: (204) 726-6849
Web site: http://www.masc.mb.ca/

Saskatchewan Agriculture

Saskatchewan Agriculture offers several programs which may be of interest to farmers in the Province.

Livestock Loan Guarantee (LLG) Program

The Livestock Loan Guarantee (LLG) program allows producers in a feeder cattle or bison association to obtain alternative financing to purchase livestock or construct or expand feedlot facilities. Some producers also use the program as a management tool to generate cash flow through retained ownership of livestock. The specific areas covered by the program are as follows.

Cattle Feeder Option

The Cattle Feeder Option allows feedlot operators (one feedlot member and a minimum of 10 feeder members) direct access to the Livestock Loan Guarantee program which will guarantee the lender 25% of the loan amount owing at the time of first default. It is open to individual members or feedlot members (i.e., producers or corporations).

The loan limits per individual feeder member are as follows:

First year	$100,000
2nd Year	$200,000
3rd Year	$300,000

Cattle Breeder Options

The Cattle Breeder Options helps Saskatchewan residents establish production associations and to borrow funds on the strength of a government guarantee to the lender and the association's assurance fund. These animals may be fed or pastured on member farms or in custom feedlots or pastures. The maximum that any member may borrow under both options is $300,000.

The loan limits per member are as follows:

Feeder Cattle

First year	$100,000
2nd	$150,000
3rd	$200,000

Individual Cattle Feeder Option

Under this option, the Government will guarantee 25% of loans amount outstanding at the time of first default. It applies to heifers and steers and covers amounts between $500,000 and $3 million. Loans must be repaid within 12 months of date of purchase or when feeders are sold (whichever comes first).

Sheep Feeder Options

The Government will guarantee 25% of loan amounts outstanding at the time of first default.

The feeder option applies to wethers and ewes and the loan limits per member are as follows

First year	$25,000
2nd Year	$70,000
3rd Year	$100,000

The maximum loan limit per feeder association is $4 million.

Sheep Breeder Options

The breeder option applies to pregnant females under four years of age and non-pregnant females under four years of age with a lamb(s) at foot. Breeder loans must be repaid within four years from the date of purchase, with 25 per cent annual payments due on the anniversary date, or when the lambs are sold, whichever comes first. Tthe loan limits per member are as follows

First year	$35,000
2nd Year	$70,000
3rd Year	$100,000

The maximum loan limit per breeder association is $4 million.

Bison Feeder Option

The Government will guarantee 25% of loan amounts outstanding at the time of first default.

This option applies to bison feeder bulls and feeder heifers under two years of age. The maximum loan limits are as follows:

First year	$50,000
2nd year	$100,000
3rd and following years	$100,000

Loans must be repaid within 18 months of date of purchase or when bison are sold; whichever comes first. The maximum loan limit per feeder association is $5 million

Bison Breeder Option

The Bison Breeder Option applies to pregnant females under eight years of age, pregnant or non-pregnant females under eight years of age with a calf at foot or a member's own pregnant heifers.
The maximum loan limits are as follows:

First year	$50,000
2nd year	$75,000
3rd and following years	$125,000

Loans must be repaid within six years from the date of purchase. The maximum loan limit per feeder association is $6 million

Feedlot Construction Option

This option provides loan guarantees to lenders that finance the construction or expansion of feedlot facilities for cattle, bison or sheep. Loans can be used for site improvements, building materials, labour costs and equipment that is to be permanently attached to the feedlot site or building. Loans can be for between $50,000 and $3 million with terms of over 10 years, but the maximum that can be covered by the guarantee is 25% of the loan to a maximum of $750,000 and a term of up to 10 years.

Further Information

Financial Programs Branch, Ministry of Agriculture
Room 329 - 3085 Albert St. Regina SK S4S 0B1
Phone: (306) 787-6425 Phone toll-free: 1-(866) 457-2377
Fax: (306) 798-3042

Alberta - Agriculture Financial Services Corporation (AFSC)

Agriculture Financial Services Corporation (AFSC) is a provincial Crown corporation which has merged with the Alberta Opportunity Company (AOC). Its Commercial Loan Program was previously covered in Chapter 6.

AFSC reports directly to the Alberta Minister of Agriculture, Food and Rural Development. It is partly funded by the government but also has many alliances with private sector companies.

Alberta Farm Loan Program

The Alberta Farm Loan Program can provide loans of up to $5 million to purchase equipment, land, machinery, breeding livestock, production quota, and shares in a farming company. Loans can be used to improve land, complete repairs, and renovate or construct buildings (including livestock facilities, barns, and housing.) Loans can also be used to assist with financial restructuring, restoring working capital or investing in a Value Added Agribusiness, but not for operating loans or feeder loans. Loans can be for terms of up to 20 years at fixed interest rates and can be paid off in full at any time without penalty.

Beginning Farmer Incentive: provides a reduction in interest rates of 1.5% for the first five years to beginning farmers with a net worth of under $500,000, however the maximum loan that can be obtained is $500,000. Couples applying jointly could increase the minimum loan to $1 million.

Value Added & Agribusiness Program (VAAP)

The Value Added & Agribusiness Program (VAAP) can provide loans of up to $5 million to help start, expand, purchase, or upgrade facilities, equipment, or other capital assets. The program can cover working capital, including training costs, that support new or expanded operations or products for value added or agribusiness enterprises and change of ownership.

Loan repayment can be for up to 20 years at a fixed interest rate but they can be paid in full at any time without penalty.

Specific Loan Guarantee Program (SLGP)

The Specific Loan Guarantee Program (SLGP) is open to primary producers, associated business, and agricultural or commercial enterprises. Guarantees can be for up to $5 million and for up to 100% of a loan. Guarantees could also be in the form of a letter of credit, bid bonds, or performance guarantees.

Capital Sourcing Program

The Capital Sourcing Program is designed to encourage the expansion of agriculture, agri-business and small business enterprises by making it convenient for business owners to find the capital they need through other Lenders. Basically, AFSC works with other financial institutions that are able to provide financial support to business owners. Services can be provided as a stand-alone fee-based service, or as part of other programs.

Revolving Loan Program

The Revolving Loan Program provides a consistent source of capital to individuals and companies involved in primary agriculture. It is available to Canadian citizens or landed immigrants with satisfactory credit ratings, who meet Alberta residency requirements and who are primary agriculture producers. It provides financing for the acquisition of assets or payment of liabilities or expenses necessary for starting, expanding or operating a farm. The maximum amount that can be loaned is $5 million with terms of 12, 24 and 36 months; with an option to renew. The loan is secured by real property.

AgriStability Program and Growing Forward 2

Effective April 1, 2013, changes were made to the AgriStability Program as a result of the new Growing Forward 2 Agreement between Alberta and the Federal Government

AgriStability provides effective whole-farm business risk management coverage for farming operations that experience severe margin declines resulting from production losses, price declines, increases in input costs, and market interruptions. The program will continue to meet these objectives under Growing Forward 2, however, some program elements will change.

Office Locations

Web site: www.afsc.ca
Phone toll-free: 1-(877) 899-2372
AFCS maintains business loan offices throughout Alberta:

AIRDRIE
Agriculture Centre
97 East Lake Ramp NE
Airdrie AB   T4A 0C3
Phone: (403) 948-8543
Fax: (403)948-1418

ATHABASCA
Provincial Building
100 - 4903 - 50th Street
Athabasca AB T9S 1E2
Phone: (780) 675-4007
Fax: (780) 675-3827

BARRHEAD
Provincial Building Main Floor
6203 - 49th Street
Barrhead AB T7N 1A4
Phone: (780) 674-8216
Fax: (780) 674-8362

BROOKS
Provincial Building
220 - 4th Avenue W
Brooks AB T1R 0E9
Phone: (403) 362-1262
Fax: (403) 362-8078

CALGARY
Deerfoot Atrium North
Suite 150, 6815 - 8th Street NE
Calgary AB T2E 7H7
Phone: (403) 297-6281
Fax: (403) 297-8461

CAMROSE
Bag 5000
4910 - 52nd. Street
Camrose AB T4V 4E8
Phone: (780) 679-1229
Fax: (780) 679-1300

CARDSTON
Provincial Building
576 Main Street
Cardston AB T0K 0K0
Phone: (403) 653-5138
Fax: (403) 653-5156

CASTOR
4902 - 50th Avenue
Castor AB
T0C 0X0
Phone: (403) 882-3770
Fax: (403) 882-2746

CLARESHOLM
Provincial Building
109 - 46th Avenue W
Claresholm AB T0L 0T0
Phone: (403) 625-1462
Fax: (403) 625-2862

DRUMHELLER
Box 2319
111 Railway Avenue West
Drumheller AB T0J 0Y0
Phone: (403) 823-3042
Fax: (403) 823-5083

EDMONTON
Room 100 J.G. O'Donoghue Building
7000-113 Street
Edmonton, AB T6H 5T6
Phone: (780) 427-2140
Fax: (780) 415-1218

EDSON
PO Box 11
Provincial Building
111 54 Street
Edson, AB T7E 1T2
Phone: (780) 723-8233
Fax:(780) 723-8575

FAIRVIEW
Provincial Building 2nd Floor
10209 - 109th Street
Fairview AB T0H 1L0
Phone: (780) 835-4975
Fax: (780) 835-5834

FALHER
M.D. Building. 701 Main Street
Falher AB T0H 1M0
Phone: (780) 837-2521
Fax: (780) 837-8223

FOREMOST
Box 37
218 Main Street
Foremost AB T0K 0X0
Phone: (403) 867-3666
Fax: (403) 867-2038

FORT VERMILION
5101 River Road
Fort Vermilion AB
T0H 1N0
Phone: (780) 927-3715
Fax: (780) 927-3838

GRANDE PRAIRIE
102 - 10625 Westside Drive
Grande Prairie, AB
T8V 8E6
Phone: (780) 538-5220
Fax: (780) 538-5260

GRIMSHAW
5306 - 50th Street
Grimshaw AB T0H 1W0
Phone: (780) 332-4494
Fax: (780) 332-1044

HANNA
Provincial Building
401 Centre Street
Hanna AB T0J 1P0
Phone: (403) 854-5525
Fax: (403) 854-2590

HIGH PRAIRIE
Provincial Building
Bag 1259
5226 - 53rd Avenue
High Prairie AB T0G 1E0
Phone: (780) 523-6507
Fax: (780) 523-6569

HIGH RIVER
129 - 4th Avenue SW
High River AB T1V 1M4
Phone: (403) 652-8313
Fax: (403) 652-8306

LACOMBE CENTRAL OFFICE
5718 - 56 Avenue
Lacombe, AB T4L 1B1
Phone: (403) 782-8200

LACOMBE DISTRICT OFFICE
Bay 105 - 4425 Heritage Way
Lacombe AB
T4L 2P4
Phone: (403) 782-6800
Fax: (403) 782-6753

LAMONT
5014 - 50th Avenue
Lamont AB T0B 2R0
Phone: (780) 895-2459
Fax: (780) 895-7755

LEDUC
6547 Sparrow Drive
Leduc AB T0B 2R0
Phone: (780) 986-0999
Fax: (780) 986-1085

LETHBRIDGE REGIONAL OFFICE
County of Lethbridge Building
200 - 905 - 4th Ave S.
Lethbridge AB T1J 0P4
Phone: (403) 381-5102
Fax: (403) 381-5178

LIOYDMINSTER (part time location)
Phone: (780) 853-8260
Fax: (780) 853-1982

MANNING
116 - 4th Avenue SW
Manning AB T0H 2M0
Phone: (780) 836-3573
Fax: (780) 836-2844

MEDICINE HAT
111 - 7 Strachan Bay SE
Medicine Hat, AB
T1B 4Y2
Phone: (403) 488-4508
Fax: (403) 488-4518

OLDS
Provincial Building
101 - 5030 - 50th Street
Olds AB T4H 1S1
Phone: (403) 556-4334
Fax: (403) 556-4255

OYEN
201 Main Street
Oyen AB T0J 2J0
Phone: (403) 664-3677
Fax: (403) 624-6483

PEACE RIVER
Bag 900, 23, 9809 - 98th Avenue
Peace River, AB T8S 1J5
Phone: (780) 617-7225
Fax: (780) 624-6493

PONOKA
Provincial Building
103 - 5110 - 49th Avenue
Ponoka AB T4J 1S1
Phone: (403) 783-7011
Fax: (403) 783-7925

PROVOST
Provincial Building
5419 - 44th Street
Provost AB T0B 3S0
Phone: (780) 753-2150
Fax: (780) 753-2876

RED DEER REGIONAL OFFICE
Unit #1 - 7710 Gaetz Avenue
Red Deer, AB T4P 2A5
Phone: (403) 340-5326
Fax: (403) 340-7004

RIMBEY
Provincial Building
5025 - 55th Street
Rimbey AB T0C 2J0
Phone: (403) 843-4516
Fax: (403) 843-4150

SEDGEWICK
Box 266
4701 - 48th Avenue
Sedgewick AB T0B 4C0
Phone: (780) 384-3880
Fax: (780) 384-2156

SMOKY LAKE
Provincial Building
108 Wheatland Avenue
Smoky Lake AB T0A 3C0
Phone: (780) 656-3644
Fax: (780) 656-3669

SPIRIT RIVER
Provincial Building
1st Floor 4602 - 50th Street
Spirit River AB T0H 3G0
Phone: (780) 864-3896
Fax: (780) 864-2529

ST. PAUL
Provincial Building
5025 - 49th Avenue
St. Paul AB T0A 3A4
Phone: (780) 645-6453
Fax: (780) 645-2848

STETTLER
Bag 600, 5020 50th Street
Stettler AB T0C 2L0
Phone: (403) 740-4209
Fax: (403) 740-4210

STONY PLAIN
Provincial Building
4709 - 44th Avenue
Stony Plain AB T7Z 1N4
Phone: (780) 963-4720
Fax: (780) 963-1251

STRATHMORE
325 - 3rd Avenue
Strathmore AB T1P 1B4
Phone: (403) 934-3616
Fax: (403) 934-5018

TABER
Provincial Building
5011 - 49th Avenue
Taber AB T1G 1V9
Phone: (403) 223-7920
Fax: (403) 223-7985

THORHILD
County Administration Building
801 - 1st Street
Thorhild AB T0A 3J0
Phone: (780) 398-3933
Fax: (780) 398-2087

THREE HILLS
Provincial Building
160 - 3rd Avenue S
Three Hills AB T0M 2A0
Phone: (403) 443-8515
Fax: (403) 443-7519

VALLEYVIEW
Provincial Building
5102 - 50th Avenue
Valleyview AB T0H 3N0
Phone: (780) 524-3838
Fax: (780) 524-4565

VEGREVILLE
Vinet's Village Mall
Suite 138, 4925 - 50th Avenue
Vegreville AB T9C 1S6
Phone: (780) 603-2332
Fax: (780) 632-3385

VERMILION
Provincial Building
4701 - 52nd Street
Vermilion AB T9X 1J9
Phone: (780) 853-8266
Fax: (780) 853-1982

VULCAN
102 - 1st Street S
Vulcan AB T0L 2B0
Phone: (403) 485-5141
Fax: (403) 485-2947

WAINWRIGHT
Provincial Building
810 - 14th Avenue
Wainwright AB T9W 1R2
Phone: (780) 842-7542
Fax: (780) 842-4948

WESTLOCK
Provincial Building
2 - 10003 - 100th Street
Westlock AB T2P 2E8
Phone: (780) 349-4529
Fax: (780) 349-5240

9

Preparations

Some Preliminary Steps

There are a number of legitimate steps that you can take to show your company in the best light possible before you approach your bank manager. These should be taken before you even start to prepare your documentation to support a loan application.

If your company has a large amount of shareholder debt; especially if this is to yourself as the sole owner, you should be converting this into long term debt. This will significantly improve the company's working capital position (current assets minus current liabilities).

The same technique should be adopted with other short term loans. If possible, try to convert these into long term debt.

An alternative is to convert shareholder loans into shares. Obviously, this is only possible if the company has been incorporated. Such a manoeuvre can significantly improve your debt to equity ratio - something which your bank manager will be looking at closely.

Make sure that the rates you have used for depreciation of capital assets are the most favourable. The rates you employ do not have to be identical to those set down by the Canada Revenue Agency (unless the statements are being used for filing with your tax return but seek your accountant's advice first).

If machinery or equipment has a long life expectancy, then use rates reflecting that expectancy and point this out in footnotes to your statement.

Push to collect outstanding invoices before the date of your financial statement. Cash in the bank looks a lot better than accounts receivable, especially those over 90 days.

The professional advice of a good accountant can pay handsomely in "tidying things up" before you start putting your proposal together.

Preparing for a Loan Application

About 80% of the businesspeople who approach a bank for a loan are turned away [1]. This is not because the bank will not loan them money - it is simply because they have not made the preparations to apply for a loan.

In this context, it should be noted that a previous volume in this series was devoted to the preparation of the business plan as a financing document.

The banker needs information; facts and figures: past, present and future. He wants to know how you run your company; who you are; how long you have been at it; how dedicated you are to your business and so on.

Basically, the banker needs to know everything that a well prepared business plan would tell him. In addition to this, he is looking for some specific information which may not have been included in your plan, such as personal information and a personal financial statement.

Your bank manager will want to see a statement of your accounts receivable, which has been aged. In other words, he will want to know the names of the accounts to whom you owe money and how much. He will want these figures on a "current basis" for the past 30 days; for the period 31-60 days; 61-90 days, together with those that are over 90 days.

He may also want to see your accounts payable on the same basis. It may be wise not to offer this information unless it is specifically requested.

A list of inventory will be essential if inventory financing is being sought. It would also be very useful in other circumstances as well. Also, a schedule of equipment should be prepared; especially if such equipment has any significant value. In some cases, it may be helpful to have a customer list and even a list of suppliers (which could be useful credit references).

Chapter 9
Preparations

In some instances (especially retail), it could be useful to have a copy of your lease handy - even if it remains in your briefcase during the discussions.

It is a good idea to prepare a financial proposal (in addition to your overall business plan), which shows specifically why you need the money and what you will use it for. Above all, show your banker how he is going to get his money back! Show him your projections and how the loan is to be serviced and paid off.

Include any way of showing your banker how secure the bank's money will be. If there are assets that can be pledged or personal guarantees - then, your task in obtaining a loan will be that much easier. List them so that your manager can see them.

Remember - banks love collateral! They also love guarantees! But also remember that a guarantor of a loan has been described as a fool with a pen in his hand! Guarantees are fine when all is well, but if things go sour - they can come back to haunt the guarantor in the middle of the night! Be careful!

In fairness to the banks, one of the reasons for requesting personal guarantees is to prevent the owners from draining the company of cash by way of excessive salaries or dividends and then leaving the bank with an empty barrel! As you can imagine, the banks have acquired a few empty barrels in their day!

The bank may also reason that, if you are not willing to put your personal assets on the line, then the bank shouldn't bother about putting its assets on the line either.

Make sure that when you borrow - you borrow enough to cover whatever you have in mind. There is nothing worse than finding that you have run out of funds to achieve your objective and that all your assets are tied up as collateral. You could end up having very little room to manoeuvre.

Be open with your banker. Don't hide a lot of dust under the rug - because it is going to come out sooner or later. Every business has its weaknesses and its problems. Don't make these a surprise. Invite him to visit your premises and show him what is going on. Remember that you are selling him on the idea of supporting your business!

Banks love to lend money when the risk is low. It may behove the business owner to borrow from a bank when he does not need the money; just to establish a good credit rating!

When you can show your banker that you don't really need his money, he will come chasing after you with wheelbarrows full of it. Show him that you really need it and he will retire like a tortoise - into his shell! Banks are always willing to lend money to people who don't need it! Indeed, Mark Twain once observed that there are bankers who will loan you an umbrella when the sun is shining but want it back when the rain comes!

Shop for your banker! Look around and enquire in your business community, to find out who the best commercial bankers are in your area.

The best bank is not necessarily the nearest bank!

The best bank manager is the one that understands small business and that you can get along with.

If you end up dealing with a commercial banking branch that is located at a distance from your business; you might consider opening another account with the same bank at a nearby branch to handle your day-to-day deposits and other requirements.

Another clever tactic is to establish both yourself and your business with the bank and get to know them well; especially the manager, months in advance of making any kind of loan application. Have lunch with your bank manager. The nice thing about it is that he will probably want to pay the bill!

Just as in selling, it is harder for somebody to say: "no!", if he likes you and has been doing business with you for a while. Bank managers are human, believe it or not!

Don't forget to ask for an appointment when you want to discuss a loan with your manager. Also, dress well; just as you would when you go to make an important sale.

If the bank says: "no"; ask why your application has been turned down. Listen carefully and if it was for some reason that can be corrected - correct it and try again! Don't give up! If you can't get what you want at one bank, try another! Even within the same banks there are tremendous differences between branches.

Discretionary Limits

Before you go charging into your local bank in search of a loan, it may be useful to know that different managers have different ceilings on the amount of money that they are authorized to lend. The banks do not generally advertise these figures and the following information, although a little dated, may be useful.

Assistant managers have discretionary limits of $25,000 to $35,000. Senior Assistant Managers run at about $50,000 and Branch Managers at $100,000. [2]

Discretionary limits will also vary according to the size of the branch. The smaller the branch; the lower the limit.

Try to discreetly find out if you are talking to the right person at the bank. If your request is above the limit of the person you are talking to; you may be wasting your time.

NOTES

[1] Discussion during last program in the series: *Frontrunners*, TV Ontario

[2] *Chartered Bank Financing of Small Business In Canada* - University of Western Ontario

Chapter 9
Preparations

10

The Banker's Viewpoint

View from the Banker's Side of the Desk

As was noted previously, there is a great deal of misunderstanding between the small business community and the banks. It may be useful to take a look from the banker's side of the desk and try to understand his concerns before approaching him for money.

Don Allan stated: "banks are - first, last and always businesses... The bank manager is responsible for generating a profit at his branch." One of the basic problems is that "small business loans represent a low profit clientele" [1].

The plain truth of the matter is that banks generally make more money on loans to purchase cars, mortgage houses etc., than in loaning money to small business with the associated high risks and administration costs. This is compounded by the fact that many bankers do not have the training to be instant experts in your market area.

"Banks like to look at a proven track record" according to John Bowden, vice-president of the Canadian Imperial Bank of Commerce [2].

George Klein, President of Management Graphics was quoted as saying in reference to software developers: "The banks don't like to finance ideas" [2].

The banker is looking for his "Three C's". He is looking to the small business owner's "character"; to the "capacity" (or, as some put it the "cash flow") of the business to generate the funds to both service and repay the loan and for "capital" or assets to secure the loan.

The reader may muse that the word "collateral" also begins with a "C" and indeed this is often added as a fourth "C"!

Sometimes a fifth "C" is also added. This relates to the "conditions" such as the economy or external factors relating to the industry that the business belongs to.

Thus, the adverse effects of the Canada-U.S. Free Trade Agreement on certain business sectors have become an important condition for some bankers and are the reason for quite a number of loan rejections if reports in the press are to be believed.

You must do a selling job on your banker to convince him that you know what you are doing; that the bank's money is safe and that the bank will be repaid (with interest!).As in any other selling job, you should get to know your customer well - what his needs are; what his problems are and what he is looking for.

Banker's Credit Review

Now that you have a general idea of what is going on in the banker's mind, it may be useful to take a peak over the banker's shoulder and see what he is scribbling on his scratch pad as he asks questions!

The manager will be evaluating you on your capability to manage the business. He will assess your experience and level of training or education in relation to the business that you are operating. He will be probing your technical skills and your ability to run your company i.e., your administrative skills and your ability to plan and make decisions.

The banker will evaluate you as a good manager. This can be assisted by a well prepared business plan and financial statements that are right up to date (even if they are "preliminary").

The banker will also be probing into how well you know your business and his "market niche". He will evaluate your level of general business awareness; of where the economy is heading or of new government policies.

The banker really wants to see if you read the financial papers and havn't got your head buried in the sand.

The banker will be closely watching your personality. He will look at your appearance and how you dress; how you communicate; your level of self-confidence and how committed you are to the business.

The banker is looking to see how motivated you are and how hard you will drive yourself to achieve your goals.

The banker wants to know about your company; how it got to where it is and what its future earnings prospects are. He will evaluate the realism of these projections and whether they will enable the company to repay the loan.

In performing a loan evaluation, the banker wants facts and figures. He needs to know how stable the business is.

The bank manager will look at the market for the company's products. He will access future growth and he will want to know about the competition. He will look at the effectiveness of the company's distribution methods.

The banker is also going to examine the general economic environment for your company's products and any external influences (such as free trade) which might have a positive or negative effect on the market.

Bankers' Favourite Financial Ratios

When reviewing any loan application, your banker is almost certain to look at the three ratios in making his evaluation.

The banker will examine your firm's debt to equity ratio. If it is in the range of 1:1; he is likely to be satisfied. If it is 2:1; it is becoming a little chancy. If it is 3:1 or more; then there is a problem. Too much debt relative to equity is frequently the reason given for rejecting a loan application.

The banker will look at your company's current ratio i.e., the total of its current assets (cash, accounts receivable, prepaid expenses, inventory etc.) by current liabilities (accounts payable, shareholder loans, other loans, taxes payable etc.). If this ratio is 1:1 it is borderline. A ratio of 2:1 would be considered good and 3:1 excellent.

The banker will examine your company's quick ratio i.e., the value of assets that can quickly be converted into cash. It is calculated by eliminating inventory from current assets in the calculation of current ratio. If the ratio is 1:1 or better (such as 2:1) then there should be no problem. However, if the ratio is much less than 1:1, there is likely to be trouble. In addition, the banker will look at the rate of turnover of your accounts receivable and the turnover of inventory. How quickly is your company able to turn over its inventory and incoming cash to make money?

He will be examining your company's debt position carefully and look at profits. He will also look at the return your company has offered on investment (see *Your Guide to Preparing a Plan to Raise Money for Your Own Business* which can be purchased securely online at *www.ProductivePublications.ca*).

If your business plan has been properly prepared, you should be able to answer most questions concerning financing ratios, market potential and earnings potential.

Collateral

Collateral provides the banker with a security net if things go wrong. This is something which every banker will address in the course of preparing his credit review.

It is an area where many start-ups have difficulty. If both you and your company have no assets or other security to offer; the answer to a loan application is almost certain to be negative.

How much is the banker looking for? It depends somewhat on the size of your business. The smaller the business; the greater the proportion of collateral relative to the size of the loan.

A Canadian study found that the average bank collateral demanded of start-ups was 431% (yes - over four times!) of the amount of the loan [3]. Banks looked to entrepreneurs themselves for most of this amount - 374% from personal assets with the balance from the business

Established businesses fared a little better. Those with sales of under $250,000 required total collateral coverage of 313%.

Those between $1/4 and 1/2 million the coverage was still 251%. Even for companies with sales in excess of $2 million, the coverage was 200%, or double the amount being requested!

A study, released in 1994, by the Canadian Federation of Independent Business found that the average security to loan ratio on business lending was 3.25:1.

It is no wonder that 70% of Canadian business owners complain about excessive collateral demands by the banks!

There is not much alternative; especially if you really need the loan! There are, however, a number of things that can be done to minimize the exposure.

Firstly, negotiate all collateral requirements. Don't just say "yes" and sign the dotted line. Unfortunately, most business owners do this. It is a mistake! Try to negotiate to give up as little as you can.

If the bank is demanding that life insurance policies be signed over to them, make sure that any such amounts are in excess of what has already been arranged for your family in the event of death. In other words, make sure that the bank doesn't get a chance to make your widow or orphans poor!!

Make sure that your RRSPs are not included. Even though it is against the law to assign RRSPs to lenders, some financial institutions try to get around this by inserting conditions to force RRSPs to be dissolved in the event that the business fails.

If they do manage to corner you on this point, make sure that any amount you promise on RRSP dissolution is net after your personal tax liabilities. The last thing you want, after everything has gone wrong, is for the Canada Revenue Agency to crucify you personally!

A wise move, if you own a home is to consider transferring registration to your spouse and to try to avoid posting the home as a guarantee. You can bet the bank will want it so they can lay their hands on it if things go sour.

Try and avoid having your spouse co-sign any deal. If you have to, then make sure that you stay on good terms with the spouse!

The advice of a good lawyer and accountant should be obtained before you sign yourself away to the bank! Remember, the question of guarantees should be a matter of negotiation between yourself and your banker.

Banker's Assessment

The banker gathers most of the information he needs from you through the interview process and from your business plan. However, you can also expect your banker to check you out as thoroughly as he can. He will almost certainly conduct a credit check; both on your business as well as you - the owner. He may call some of your suppliers and have a report prepared by a credit bureau.

The assessment stage normally takes a couple of days and if there is any delay, it is usually because inadequate information was provided.

The Final Steps

If the assessment by your bank manager is favourable, your file will normally be passed "up the ladder" to the next level of authority for approval. If it is granted, you will be invited to sign the legal paperwork including the loan agreement.

Read the agreement carefully. Bankers tend to become paranoid if you request any changes, but you should still know what you are getting into.

You will also be requested to sign the documents posting any guarantees and those relating to collateral. Read these exceptionally carefully and, if necessary, seek your own legal advice.

In the event that your application is turned down, try to find out why (in as nice a way as possible!). This may provide some clues on what has to be changed before you approach another bank; or indeed if it is worthwhile making such an approach.

NOTES

[1] *Banking and Small Business*, a 1982 study for the CFIB by Don Allen

[2] The Financial Post, September 21, 1985

[3] *Chartered Bank Financing of Small Business in Canada*, University of Western Ontario

11

The True Costs

The Costs of Borrowing

What is all this little exercise going to cost? Well, there are a number of costs - direct and indirect.

Banks have entered the era of the service charge as you well know! Charges are even being applied for processing loan applications. These fees vary from bank to bank but generally range $100-200. This is a direct cost. Another direct cost is the interest charged on your loan or operating line. Generally, it will range anywhere from 0.5% to 3% above the prime lending rate set every week by the Bank of Canada. The average usually lies around 1.5% to 1.6% above prime. The more risky the loan; the higher the premium that will be charged.

There are also indirect costs. These are the potential costs to the company and to yourself in the event that things go wrong. They can be tremendously high.

Many a small business owner has a home and practically everything else of value to a bank. This is a sobering thought which you should consider carefully before dashing into a bank for money.

Giving up some ownership in the company, in the form of equity, might end up being much cheaper in the long run than borrowing from a bank!

Other Services for Which Banks Charge

Aside from a choice of a bewildering array of cheque colours and decorations (for which the consumer pays dearly!); banks do offer some cash management services, which may be of assistance to the business owner and may save money.

One of the most common services offered by banks is payroll. Another is the management of accounts receivable and accounts payable.

Some banks offer same day automated funds transfer to a designated account; thereby accelerating cash inflow and allowing surplus funds to be placed into interest bearing accounts. Investment of short term cash balances can also be placed in T-Bills or term deposits and can generate interest over the years.

Some will offer "lock box" transfers in which customers in a specified area of the country are requested to send their cheques to a certain local post office box address. This is serviced by the bank in that area, which ensures prompt depositing of accounts receivable. This is only practical if the volume of business justifies it.

One area in which banks are not necessarily improving, is in reducing the lengths of their teller line-ups. However, there is hope in electronic banking capabilities which can reduce the number of times you have to visit your bank.

Most of the major banks offer electronic banking so you can make transfers and pay bills online. This also allows statements to be run off, as required and assists in reconciliation, as needed.

Electronic banking can be a real time-saver and you should give it serious consideration if you are not already using it.

The Importance of Maintaining a Good Relationship

Bankers are optimists; although it may not seem so at times! They hope that once they have you on the hook, that they will be able to continue to do business over many years and that you will develop into one of their loyal customers.

Once you've obtained your loan, try to stay on good terms with your bankers. Keep them fed with monthly or quarterly statements and lists of accounts receivable. They are likely to ask for these anyway - but make sure that they receive the information on time. Tell them the good news and let them know when things are going badly.

If you have an operating line; make sure that it changes - don't let it sit there. Bankers expect it to go up and down. If at all possible try to "rest the line" once a year at least i.e., pay off the loan, especially after you receive your money following periods of high selling activity.

Your banker is often an observant creature and will continue to watch your business even after the loan arrangements have been put to bed. If problems arise in repaying loans; late payments or overdrafts you may find that you have got your banker's full attention once again! The same may be true, if credit reporting agencies find that your company is experiencing trouble in paying its bills.

In addition to continually monitoring the health of your business, your banker will want to formally review your loan once a year. This may necessitate revisions to your business plan and your projections. Go to the necessary trouble. You want your banker to know that you are professional and are adapting plans in response to changes in market conditions.

Concluding Comments on Banks

Banks, trust companies and credit unions represent the most likely source of obtaining debt financing in Canada. If the banks refuse to finance your small business or project, probably the most useful thing that they can do is to provide a letter stating that they will not fund it. They may be reluctant, but armed with it, you can approach some of the government sources for funding. Most want evidence that the commercial banks would not support your venture.

Chapter 11
The True Costs

12

Factoring

Factoring as a Method of Borrowing

Factoring is not commonly used for business financing. This was revealed in a 1985 survey conducted by Dun & Bradstreet on 1,060 American companies. It found that only 7% used factoring as a means of financing. Having said that, about 75% of businesses in the apparel trade use factors, according to Mark Perna, President of Accord Business Credit.

The total of all factoring in Canada during 2010 has been estimated at $4.95 billion.

The financing of accounts receivable was discussed earlier in this book. Under that arrangement, your receivables were assigned to the bank but actually remained the property of your business. This would continue, so long as the bank was satisfied with the relationship. Should it fall apart, the bank has the right by law to go to your company's customers and collect the monies owing directly.

In the case of factoring, your business sells its accounts receivable to a third party - known as a "factor". The latter takes on the responsibility of collecting the money owing.

The factoring company assumes the risk that the customer will pay his bill.

If the customer fails to pay after a specified period of time (usually 90 days); the factor pays your business or credits your account even though the factor has not received payment.

Obviously, the factoring company will examine the credit of your customers very closely and if the credit is not satisfactory, may refuse to factor those particular accounts. You are still free to sell to such accounts at your own risk.

In practice, you would normally perform a credit check (through the factor) on the customer to ensure that the credit standing is satisfactory even before the goods are shipped and invoiced. This reduces the possibility of the factor refusing to accept certain invoices.

In order to reduce risks, factors will maintain credit checking operations; together with their own collection facilities. This is the biggest advantage factors offer, since many small businesses do not have the staff or the time to do this on their own. Collecting on overdue bills is also a very time consuming and unpleasant task.

Methods of Payment

There are two methods by which the customer can pay for the goods received from your small business.

The first, is direct payment to the factor. Basically, you inform your customer that payment should be made directly to the factor.

Under the second, payment is made to your business, and you endorse the cheques in favour of the factor. You can carefully camouflage such endorsements to prevent your customers from knowing they are actually paying their bills to a factor.

Method of Financing

There are two types of factoring. The first, is the element of factoring itself. The second, is the borrowing of funds against the accounts that have been factored.

The first type is for the factor to collect on the monies owing. Normal trade credit is for 30 days, although many customers attempt to stretch this out for longer. When a customer makes payment, the factor credits your business with the amount less its factoring fee. This fee normally ranges between 1% and 3%.

For argument's sake, assume that the fee is 2% and the invoice is for $1,000. When payment is received, $980 ($1,000 less 2%) is credited to your business account. If for any reason, the customer fails to pay, the factor will still credit your business account after a specified period of time; usually 90 days. In the above example, the $980 would be credited and the factoring company would absorb the loss.

The fee which the factor charges is obviously a function of the quality of the accounts of your business; their size and the volume of business. Should your business leave the funds with the factor beyond the period when they were collected, interest would be paid on the monies in the account.

The second type of factoring involves borrowing against the invoices which you have sold to the factor. The borrowing can be for a higher percentage of the receivables than offered by the banks. Thus, a factor will frequently lend money against 90% of the value of your receivables, as opposed to the 60% to 75% normally offered by the banks.

The factor will hold 10% in reserve.

In the above example, your business would be entitled to borrow up to an additional 90% of the $1,000 from the factor. The interest charged for such borrowing is usually 2% to 3% above prime. The amount of this interest is usually deducted in calculating the cash advance. The arithmetic on the example is as follows:

```
Invoice amount                          $1,000.00
Reserve (10%)                              100.00
Factor's fee (2%)                           20.00
Interest $880 @ 14% x 45 days               15.19
Cash Advance                               864.81
Release of Reserve after payment           100.00
Total finally realized from sale           964.81
```

In this example, the total factoring cost to your business is about 3.5% over the 45 day period; or about 28.5% on an annualized basis. In looking at these figures you must remember that the factor is assuming all the risk - as opposed to the banks which assume no risk!

Advantages and Disadvantages

The big advantage of factoring for your business is the credit checking facility. The factor is set up to perform large numbers of credit checks and has the staff and resources to do it properly. This function can be time consuming for you and subject to errors; especially if your staff are careless in conducting checks. Another big advantage is that your business is always going to receive its money. If the customer does not pay, that becomes the factor's problem for collection.

Factoring provides your business with immediate cash when the sale is made. You do not have to wait until your customer decides to pull his cheque book out of the drawer and write up a cheque. Also, the amount of cash advanced by a factor against receivables is likely to be higher than that offered by the banks.

The big disadvantage of factoring is the cost! The factor is in the business to make money and you have to pay for the advantages that the factor has to offer. Another disadvantage is that factoring may affect your relationship with your bank for other borrowing. Consultation with your banker would be advisable before any agreement is reached.

Be warned that some of your customers may attach stigma against your business if you are using a factor, especially when payments must be made directly to the factor. Customers may question the financial stability of your business, even if such fears are totally unfounded.

Finance factors generally have a lending range of between $50,000 to $10 million. So, if your sales are under $50,000 you may be better off approaching your bank to seek financing against your accounts receivable.

Who Can Factor

Factoring started in the garment and textile industries. It is now accepted in a much wider variety of business activities such as wholesale, manufacturing, building supply, etc.

Where to Find Factors

The simplest way of finding factors is to consult the yellow pages of any major city in Canada. There are about 45 companies engaged in factoring in Canada. You can also contact Factors Chain International which is a worldwide organizations that links 252 factors in 61 countries:

Factors Chain International
Keizersgracht 559
1017 DR Amsterdam
The Netherlands
Phone: +31-20-6270306
Fax: +31-20-6257628
E-mail address: fci@fci.nl

The next chapter on export financing will also provide the contact information for many factoring companies.

Confirming

Confirming has only very limited application to small business. It is used to finance payables on raw materials and semi-finished goods, especially if they are being imported and subject to lengthy delivery times.

Since assignments or liens are not normally required on the goods, the financial standing of the business and its supplier must be very good.

The few confirming houses in Canada are associated with financial companies involved with import and export finance or with some of the chartered banks.

13

Export Financing

Export Development Canada (EDC)

The name of the Export Development Corporation (EDC) was changed to Export Development Canada (EDC) in November 2001. At the same time, a new mandate requires that any projects that receive EDC funding must first be evaluated to determine if they will adversely affect the environment.

EDC is a Crown corporation which was formed to help Canadian exporters compete internationally. It is governed by a Board of Directors composed of representatives of both the public and private sectors and reports to Parliament through the Minister of International Trade.

EDC provides a wide range of financial and risk management services.

Financing for Canadian Companies

EDC offers domestic financing in a number of areas.

Export Guarantee Program: provides guarantees to financial institutions to support export-related activities and/or foreign investments. Guarantees on loans can be used:

- to finance work in progress and inventory related to specific or multiple export contracts;
- to finance on-going export-related working capital needs;
- to finance the purchase of equipment or other expenses related to export activities;
- to provide support to allow Canadian companies looking to expand their business by making business investments outside Canada;

- to finance foreign-domiciled inventory which must consist of finished goods for which the exporter has unencumbered legal title; and,
- to free up working capital by using the security of foreign receivables and an EDC guarantee to the applicant's bank to increase an operating line of credit.

The coverage available can be for up to 100% for loans where Canadian companies are making direct investments abroad; up to 90% for guaranteed amounts up to and including $500,000; up to 75% for guaranteed amounts greater than $500,000 and up to $10 million.

Supplier Financing Arrangements: are tailored towards small- and medium-sized export contracts. Under a note purchase arrangement, EDC can buy promissory notes issued to the business by the foreign buyer related to the sale of Canadian goods and services. This reduces the risk of non-payment and increases access to cash. In practice, these arrangements are used for contracts with simple payment terms and with repayment terms of up to two years.

Project Finance: provides structuring expertise and direct financing of complex, large-scale global projects when the project sponsor needs to build, expand or acquire a project. It specialises in the following key sectors: energy; telecom and infrastructure; and mining, metals, and resources.

EDC can assist in mobilizing capital dictated by the needs of the project. EDC's role is typically that of an advisor, arranger and underwriter. EDC can provide assistance in relation to a project's technical, environmental or documentation needs.

EDC can also provide financing for smaller scale projects, acquisitions and the financing of assets.

To be considered, projects must demonstrate an economic benefit to Canada.

Financing for Foreign Buyers

Loans: provides foreign buyers with the funds necessary to finance the purchase of Canadian goods and/or services. Such loans, usually for up to two years, can be made directly by EDC or through another financial institution. EDC may also participate in corporate loan syndications and club deals to meet the need for consolidated financing.

Loans are made based on credit quality, general market conditions, and the length of repayment terms being considered. Also, an exposure fee may be charged in connection with EDC's export financing, consistent with OECD guidelines.

Lines of Credit: where EDC lends money to a foreign bank, institution, or purchaser, which then uses this money to loan the necessary funds to foreign purchasers of Canadian goods and services.

Bank Guarantee Program: provides cover to Canadian and international banks financing the sale of Canadian exports to customers in developing markets.

Foreign Investment Financing

EDC can offer mid-sized Canadian businesses with lending to purchase foreign equipment and facilities as well as for the possible acquisition of a foreign company. Typically financing involves amounts in excess of $1 million. Any foreign affiliates would be required to provide secured guarantees for a loan or the Canadian parent would need to supply a guarantee normally in the form of a lien on Canadian assets.

Bonding and Guarantees

Buyers frequently ask for bonds to be posted to guarantee on bids to insure performance or to secure advance and progress payments. EDC can offer assistance and advice in this area.

Account Performance Security Guarantee: provides a 100% guarantee to the bank for a bond posted on behalf of the Canadian contractor. This helps to free up the working capital that would otherwise be needed to supply security to the banks as collateral for posting the bond.

Domestic Surety Bonding and Bank Guarantees: EDC provides risk sharing reinsurance capacity to the contractor's surety company for up to 100% of the bond liability amount. It will also provide bank guarantees for domestic business and this will assist businesses by replacing collateral required by banks. The guarantees themselves are issued by private sector surety companies (which in turn are re-insured by EDC). Further information can be obtained from:

The Surety Association of Canada
6299 Airport Road, Suite 709
Mississauga, ON L4V 1N3
Phone: (905) 677-1353   Fax: (905) 677-3345
E-mail: surety@suretycanada.com
Web site: www.surety-canada.com

Foreign Exchange Facility Guarantee (FXG): enables Canadian companies to free up working capital on the purchase of forward contracts from their financial institutions. Most institutions require collateral equivalent to 15% of a contract's value to cover against foreign exchange fluctuations. On the other hand, this Facility enables exporters to lock in the exchange rates as protection against foreign currency fluctuations. Essentially, EDC guarantees the collateral amount, thereby making financial institutions forego their 15% freeze on funds. The cost of the Guarantee is based on several factors including exporter risks and forward contract-specific factors.

Surety Bond Insurance: is designed to protect surety companies from losses in the event that a customer demands payment against a surety bond. This provides help to businesses that require bonding for their international contracts.

Insurance

EDC offers insurance in a number of areas.

Accounts Receivable Insurance (ARI): offers credit insurance for accounts receivable for up to 90% of their value.

Single Buyer Insurance: is designed for the occasional exporter or for those selling to a customer in a new market. It covers up to 90% losses due to non-payment after the customer has accepted the goods. Such non-payment could be due to factors such as bankruptcy, insolvency, currency conversion and transfer, war, revolution or insurrection. It will cover unlimited sales of up to $250,000 (US) to one customer for up to six months.

Performance Security Insurance (PSI): offers protection of up to 95% against losses if a foreign buyer makes a wrongful call on a bond (standby irrevocable letters of credit or letters of guarantee).

Contract Frustration Insurance (CFI): provides coverage for up to 90% of losses incurred on specific export contracts involving capital goods, service contracts or projects.

Political Risk Insurance (PRI): helps to protect assets abroad by covering up to 90% of any losses.

Domestic Credit Insurance: provides re-insurance facilities (for domestic receivables) to private insurance companies. Support is available until March 12, 2013 and applies to both exporting and non-exporting companies in all sectors with the caveat that all transactions must be creditworthy and supported by a viable business model. It should be noted that this type of insurance is not supplied directly by EDC but by the insurance companies in the private sector listed below:

Atradius Credit Insurance N.V.
Canadian Head Office
83 Little Bridge Street, Unit 12
Almonte, ON K0A 1A0
Phone: (613) 256-9134
Fax: (613) 256-9133
E-mail: info.ca@atradius.com

Atradius Credit Insurance N.V.
Mississagua Office
1 City Centre Drive, Suite 310
Mississauga, ON L5B 1M2
Phone: (905) 897 5959
Fax: (905) 897 8659
E-mail: info.ca@atradius.com

Atradius Credit Insurance N.V
White Rock - British Columbia Office
304 - 1360 Fir Street
Duncan, BC V4B 4B2
Phone: (778) 294-0627
Fax: (778) 294-0627
E-mail: douglas.roff@atradius.com

Coface S.A.
251 Consumers Road, Suite 910
Toronto, ON M2J 4R3
Phone: (647) 426-4730
Fax: (647) 426-1879

Coface S.A.
1375 Trans-Canada Highway, Suite 430
Dorval, QC H9P 2W8
Phone: (514) 696-5661
Fax: (514) 696-8550
E-mail: info@coface.ca

Euler Hermes
1, place des Saisons
F-92048 Paris La-Défense Cedex
France
Phone: + 33 1 8411 5000
Fax: + 33 1 8411 5117

Executive Risk Insurance Services Ltd.
36 Toronto Street, Suite 500
Toronto, ON M5C 2C5
Phone: (416) 979-3600
Fax: (416) 979-8337

The Guarantee Company of North America
4950 Yonge Street, Suite 1400
Toronto, ON M2N 6K1
Phone: (416) 223-9580
Phone toll-free: 1-(800) 268-6617

The Guarantee Company of North America
Montreal:
Phone: (514) 866-6351
Phone toll-free: 1-(800) 361-8603

The Guarantee Company of North America
Halifax:
Phone: (902) 425-4700
Phone toll-free: 1-(800) 565-0013

The Guarantee Company of North America
Vancouver:
Phone: (604) 687-7688
Phone toll-free: 1-(800) 663-2022

The Guarantee Company of North America
Québec City:
Phone: (418) 652-1676
Phone toll-free: 1-(800) 463-5350

The Guarantee Company of North America
Woodstock
Phone: (519) 539-868
Phone toll-free: 1-(800) 265-4262

The Guarantee Company of North America
Edmonton:
Phone: (780) 424-2266
Phone toll-free: 1-(800) 268-9957

Chartis Insurance Company of Canada
666 Burrard Street, Suite 1100
Vancouver BC V6C 2X8
Phone toll-free: 1-(800) 663-0231
Fax: (604) 691-2939

Chartis Insurance Company of Canada
145 Wellington Street West
Toronto, ON M5J 1H8
Phone toll-free: 1-(800) 387-4481
Fax: (416) 977-2743

Chartis Insurance Company of Canada
2000 McGill College Avenue, Suite 1200
Montreal, QC H3A 3H3
Phone toll-free: 1-(800) 361-7211
Fax: (514) 978-5357

Credit Profiles

EXPORT*Check*: which permits a credit check of 64 million companies in 70 countries. For as little as $30, companies can find out whether EDC considers their foreign buyer insurable.

Further Information

Head Office
Export Development Canada
150 Slater St., Ottawa, ON K1A 1K3
Phone: (613) 598-2500
Fax: (613)598-3811
Web site: http://www.edc.ca

EDC Regional Offices

Vancouver Office
1055 Dunsmuir Street
Suite 400, Bentall Four
P.O. Box 49086
Vancouver, BC V7X 1G4
Phone: (604) 638-6950
Fax: (604) 638-6955

Calgary Office
308-4th Avenue S.W.
Calgary, AB T2P 0H7
Phone: (403) 817-6700
Fax: (403) 817-6701

Edmonton Office
Suite 1000, 10180-101st Street
Edmonton, AB T5J 3S4
Phone: (780) 801-5402
Fax: (780) 801-5333

Regina Office:
Suite 300, 1914 Hamilton Street
Regina SK S4P 3N6
Phone: (306)586-1727
Fax: (306) 586-1725

Winnipeg Office
Commodity Exchange Tour
Suite 2075 - 360 Main Street
Winnipeg, MB R3C 3Z3
Phone: (204) 975-5090
Fax: (204) 975-5094

Toronto Office
Suite 3120 - 155 Wellington Street West
Toronto, ON M5V 3L3
Phone: (416) 349-6515
Fax: (416) 349-6516

Mississauga Office
Suite 805 - 1 City Centre Drive
Mississauga ON L5B 1M2
Phone: (905) 366-0300
Fax: (905) 366-0332

London Office
Suite 1512 - 148 Fullerton Street
London, ON N6A 5P3
Phone: (519) 963-5400
Fax: (519) 963-5407

Ottawa Office
150 Slater Street
Ottawa, ON K1A 1K3
Phone: (613) 598-2500
Fax: (613)598-3811

Windsor Office:
3270 Electricity Dr., Suite 209
Walker Industrial Park
Windsor ON N8W 5J1
Phone: (519) 974-7674
Fax: (519) 974-9753

Montreal Office
Suite 4520 - 800 Victoria Square
P.O. Box 124, Tour de la Bourse
Montreal, QC H4Z 1C3
Phone: (514) 908-9200
Fax: (514) 878-9891

Québec City Office
Suite 1340, 2875 Boulevard Laurier
Ste-Foy, QC G1V 2M2
Phone: (418) 577-7400
Fax: (418) 577-7419

Drummondville
1412 Jean Berchmans Michaud Street
Drummondville QC J2C 7V3
Phone: (819) 475-2587
Fax: (819) 475-2408

Ville Saint-Laurent Office:
9900 Cavendish Boulevard, Suite 201
Saint-Laurent QC H4M 2V2
Phone: (514) 215-7200
Fax: (514) 215-7201

Moncton Office
735 Main Street, Suite 400
Moncton, NB E1C 1E5
Phone: (506) 851-6066
Fax: (506) 851-6406

Halifax Office
Suite 1605
1969 Upper Water Street, Tower 2
Halifax NS B3J 3R7
Phone: (902) 450-7600
Phone toll-free: 1-(888) 332-3343
Fax: (902) 450-7601

St. John's Office
90 O'Leary Avenue
St. John's, NF A1B 2C7
Phone: (709) 772-8808
Fax: (709) 772-8693

Northstar Trade Finance Inc.

Northstar is an innovative export financing company which was formed to assist small Canadian companies in expanding into international markets.

A $150,000 start-up loan was provided by Western Economic Diversification Canada and Export Development Canada (EDC) is a partner.

Northstar's shareholders are the Bank of Montreal, Royal Bank, HSBC Bank Canada, National Bank and the Government of British Columbia together with Shepherd Trust.

Buyer Financing for Canadian Exporters

Northstar enables Canadian exporters financing in support of their bids for small and medium-size export transactions around the world by financing term paper: This can be a valuable tool when selling overseas since Canadian exporters can include financing from Northstar as part of their marketing package. Such buyer financing is available for large sales (up to $5 million) as well as for sales of relatively low dollar value. Funds are payable to the exporter directly, and Northstar assumes the buyer risk.

Financing provided to the buyers is non-recourse to the Canadian exporter provided the exporter has fulfilled his obligation under the contract of sale with the buyer.

Exporters receive payment in full from Northstar within ten days of shipment and the exporter's lines of credit are not affected by Northstar's financing. Loan applications are usually processed within ten business days of submitting a complete application.

It should be noted that there are no Letters of Credit involved in Northstar's transactions, and no receivables to be discounted. Interest rates can be fixed or variable. Amortization payments are equal, allowing the foreign importer to know the exact funding cost and budget accordingly.

Floor Plan Financing

Northstar also offers a Floor Plan Financing option for Canadian exporters. This provides a direct loan to the foreign distributor, while the exporter is paid upon shipment of the goods. The distributor repays Northstar when the goods are sold, or in 360 days; whichever occurs first.

The big advantage for small and medium-sized Canadian exporters is that Northstar assumes the buyer risk and, as exporters, they receive payment within 30 days of shipment. Their lines of credit are not affected by Northstar's financing. Exporters can also include an indication of interest by Northstar as a valuable marketing tool in selling their products; which places them on the same footing as their larger competitors.

Northstar maintains recourse to the exporter for the performance of the exporter's sales contract with the buyer.

Foreign customers must be credit-worthy and be resident in a country belonging to the Organization for Economic Cooperation and Development (OECD) or another country acceptable to Northstar and EDC.

Applications are processed within seven business days. Exporters pay a non-refundable application fee of $300 plus GST, together with a 1-1/4% administration fee on the value of the export sale. In addition, an insurance premium must be paid for every successful transaction. This varies according to country and buyer credit risk.

The rate of loan interest for the foreign buyer is at competitive rates. Loans can carry variable rates of interest if necessary. Foreign buyers must also assume any legal and out-of-pocket expenses they incur.

Further Information

Northstar Trade Finance Inc.
PO Box 49058
Suite 833, Three Bentall Centre
595 Burrard Street
Vancouver, BC V7X 1C4
Phone: (604) 664-5828
Fax: (604) 664-5838
Toll-free: 1-(800) 663-9288
Web site: www.nstfglobal.com

Calgary Branch Office:
First Canadian Centre
6th Floor, Banff Room
350-7th Ave SW
Calgary, AB T2P 3N9
Phone: (403) 366-2030
Fax: (403) 366-2127

Toronto Branch Office:
Suite 501, 1 University Avenue
Toronto, ON M5J 2P1
Phone: (416) 861-8224
Fax: (416) 861-8233

Montréal Branch Office:
4269 St. Catherine St. W.
Montréal, QC H3Z 1P7
Phone: (514) 874-3366
Fax: (514) 874-8428

Accord Financial Corp.

Accord Financial Corp. offers several products that may be of interest to Canadian importers and exporters; especially those involved with apparel, textiles, footwear and other "soft goods". It commands about a 40% share of the non-recourse factoring market in Canada and generally provides credit and collection facilities to companies that are already well financed. (Non-recourse financing is one in which payment is made from the product being financed as opposed to repayment being made from other assets of the borrower.) Since the financing provided is "off-balance sheet", it does not affect the other lines of credit that a business has with its bank.

Export Factoring to the US and Overseas: provides credit and collection services for Canadian exporters both for the US and 65 countries worldwide. This can help overcome some of the difficulties experienced by Canadian exporters; especially when it comes to language and cultural differences plus the challenge of working in different time zones. To facilitate these services, Accord maintains an international credit department to handle overseas business. In addition, it has links with over 100 international factoring companies.

Factoring USA Receivables to Canada: helps foreign buyers by providing import factoring. Accord guarantees the credit-worthiness of customers and virtually becomes a collection department for all sales to the US that are make on credit terms with 100% credit guarantees and no deductibles!

Asset-Based Financing: provides flexible financing for inventory, equipment, rolling stock and tax credits for scientific research and experimental development into maximum funding. It is offered to a wide range of industries including automotive, apparel, appliances, business services, consumer goods, electronics, employment, energy, food, footwear, furniture, industrial goods and services, lumber, media, packaging, paper, printing, retail, textiles, transportation and many others.

ExportEasePlus: combines Export Development Canada's (EDC's) receivables insurance with Accord's financing and receivables management services. It takes advantage of their global network to provide Canadian clients exporting overseas with all-inclusive receivables insurance, financing, reporting and management on a cost efficient basis.

Accord Financial Corp.
77 Bloor Street West, Suite 1803
Toronto, ON M5S 1M2
Phone: (416) 961-0304
Fax: (416) 961-9443
E-mail: bshapiro@accordfinancial.com
Web site: www.accordfinancial.com

Accord Financial Corp.
3500 de Maisonneuve West, Suite 1510
Montreal, QC H3Z 3C1
Phone: (514) 866-8433
Fax: (514) 954-1836
Web site: www.accordcredit.com

Exportbank

Exportbank is a service of elanbancorp and is designed to address the needs of smaller or first time exporters It works in conjunction with Accounts Receivable Insurance offered by Export Development Canada (EDC) and funds receivables through factoring or invoice discounting for amounts of between $5,000 and $5 million per month. Advances can be made for up to 90% of the receivable's value. It has associated offices in the US and 14 countries worldwide.

Receivables in the following areas can be funded:

* products
* services
* royalties
* intellectual property
* arts and culture
* tourism.

Exportbank helps by providing immediate cash since most commercial invoices are not paid for 30 to 90 days. It should be noted that Exportbank's activities are not restricted to exporters; indeed, any business with cash flow funding problems can apply.

Exportbank
elanbancorp
398 Avenue Road
Cambridge, ON N1R 5S4
Toll-free phone: 1-(800) 808-8802
Toll-free fax: 1-(800) 598-6222
Web site: www.exportbank.ca

Maple Trade Finance

Maple Trade Finance works with Export Development Canada (EDC) to offer factoring for EDC-insured foreign invoices.

Maple Trade Finance also finances receivables; offers support for purchasing materials with its contract financing and supply chain financing. In addition, it can enable companies to obtain their Scientific, Research & Experimental Development (SR&ED) tax credits much sooner through Maple Trade Finance's claim financing.

Maple Trade Finance - Head Office	Maple Trade Finance - Eastern Ontario
5475 Spring Garden Rd., 7th Floor	340 Albert Street, Suite 1300
Halifax, NS B3J 3T2	Ottawa, ON K1R 7Y6
Phone: (902) 444-5566	Phone: (613) 751-4443
Phone toll-free: 1-(866) 444-6555	Phone toll-free: 1-(888) 868-4658
Fax: (902) 444-5567	Fax toll-free: 1-(877) 655-5567
E-mail: info@mapletradefinance.ca	
Web site: www.mapletradefinance.ca	

Maple Trade Finance -
Greater Toronto Area
2 Robert Speck Pkwy., Suite 280
Mississauga, ON L4Z 1H8
Phone: (905) 232-1683
Phone toll-free: 1-(866) 444-6555
Fax toll-free: 1-(877) 655-5567

Maple Trade Finance - Western Region
604 Columbia Street, Suite 406
New Westminster, BC V3M 1A5
Phone: (604) 656-6460
Phone toll-free: 1-(866)-444-6555
Fax: (877) 655-5567

Société Financière Maple - Québec Region
1939 Boulevard de Maisonneuve Ouest
Montreal, QC H3H 1K3
Phone: (514) 285-7810
Phone toll-free: 1-(888) 868-4658
Fax toll-free: 1-(877) 655-5567

Jebco International Corporation

Jebco International Corporation is a financial institution specializing in commercial loans and accounts receivable management, with clients situated in Québec, Ontario, and the United States. Export Development Canada in conjunction with the Jebco Accounts Receivable Policy, offers an all-inclusive package that combines receivables management with accounts receivable insurance.

Jebco has a special program with the Canadian Export Development Corporation (EDC) that provides a preferred method of operation and preferred rates. This applies to all foreign receivables generated outside of Canada.

Jebco International Corporation
6700 Cote de Liesse, Suite 402
Montreal, QC H4T 2B5
Phone: (514) 341-9788
Fax: (514) 341-4431
E-mail: info@jebcointernational.com
Web site: www.jebcointernational.com

353

HSBC

HSBC is Canada's largest foreign bank and also has a presence in 82 other countries. It works with Export Development Canada's insurance and provides a trade invoice non-recourse financing facility to let business clients enhance their ability to grow their international export sales, obtain quicker access to working capital and liquidity through their own receivables base.

Through its international branches, HSBC can help coordinate export credit insurance; contracts, bonding and guarantees; pre-shipment financing; and trade invoice discounting. For importers HSBC can help with letters of credit, documentary collections, shipping guarantees or airway bill releases, and import financing.

Trade Invoice Non-Recourse Financing Facility (TINRFF): signed in April 2008 by Export Development Canada (EDC) and HSBC Bank Canada, this agreement will assist exporters in the following ways:

- to obtain discount up to 100% of the portion of the exporter's open-account receivable that is covered by EDC;
- to minimize the commercial and political risk exposure of doing business in many foreign markets;
- to improve the exporter's working capital by converting receivables and invoices to cash; and,
- enhance the exporter's quality of credit management.

HSBC has 180 offices throughout Canada. To discuss international and supply chain needs, phone toll-free: 1-(866) 808-4722.

National Bank of Canada: NatExport

The National Bank of Canada can offer factoring of foreign and domestic receivables under its NatExport division. It works in conjunction with the insurance policies of Export Development Canada (EDC) and provides factoring for export accounts receivables. This helps to eliminate the risks associated with following up and collecting receivables, and considerably improves cash flow.

National Bank of Canada
600, rue de La Gauchetière Ouest, 5th Floor
Montreal, QC H3B 4L3
Phone toll-free: 1-(866) 283-2957
Web site: http://www.bnc.ca

Brome Financial Corporation

Brome Financial Corporation can complement or replace the services offered by traditional financial institutions for small and medium-sized businesses. It offers the following services:

* single invoice discounting
* asset-based lending
* accounts receivable management.

Brome Financial Corporation
550 Sherbrooke West, suite 700, Tour Est
Montreal, QC, H3A 1B9
Phone: (514) 842-2975
Phone toll-free: 1-(888) 878-9485
Fax: (514) 842-2050
Fax toll-free: 1-(877) 644-9828
Web site: http://www.bromecapital.com/en/default.idigit

Desjardins: Factoring - Export D

The Export D facility enables businesses to obtain immediate cash by selling all or part of their accounts receivable of up to 365 days. The amount received is net after discount and administrative fees have been deducted. Export Development Canada will insure foreign receivables of small and medium-sized businesses when they use the factoring service offered by Desjardins.

Desjardins has numerous Business Centres throughout Québec and one in Ontario. For further information phone toll-free: 1-(800) 508-2874.

BNP Paribas SA

BNP Paribas SA operates in over 80 countries, and has 202,000 employees predominantly located in Europe, North America and Asia. Export Development Canada will insure foreign receivables factored by BNP Paribas.

BNP Paribas
1981 McGill College Avenue
Montreal, QC H3A 2W8
Phone: (514) 285-6000
Fax: (514) 285-6278

BNP Paribas
1230, 335 - 8th Avenue SW
Calgary, AB T2P 1C9
Phone: (403) 691-8800
Fax: (403) 691-8890

BNP Paribas
155, Wellington Street West, Suite 3110
RBC Centre, P.O. Box 149
Toronto, ON M5V 3H1
Phone: (416) 365-9600
Fax: (416) 947-0086

Canadian Commercial Corporation (CCC)

Canadian Commercial Corporation (CCC) is a federal Crown corporation established to assist in the development of trade between Canada and other nations. It offers a wide range of services designed to help exporters conclude sales, principally to foreign governments and international agencies. It assumes the role of prime contractor, takes part in negotiations and signs contracts respectively with the customer and the supplier. It also follows through on other aspects of the sale, including collection of accounts receivable from customers and the payment to suppliers.

CCC's participation on behalf of the Government of Canada normally guarantees performance of the contract. This enhances the supplier's credibility while increasing the customer's confidence.

Since 1946, CCC has helped Canadian exporters capture more than $30 billion in export sales. About 80% of its clients are small and medium-sized businesses.

It should be noted that all defence purchases made by the US military which are in excess of $100,000 must be contracted through CCC.

Canadian Commercial Corporation (Head Office)
50 O'Connor Street, 11th. Fl.
Ottawa, ON K1A 0S6
Phone: (613) 996-0034
Phone toll-free: 1-(800) 748-8191
Fax: (613) 995-2121
E-mail: info@ccc.ca
Web Site: http://www.ccc.ca

Canada Economic Development (CED) for Québec Regions

Canada Economic Development (CED) is a major player in Québec's economic development and a leading partner of Small and Medium-Sized Enterprises (SMEs) and their support organizations.

Market or Export

Designed to help increase market share, work within value chains or penetrate new markets.

The program is open to SMEs and organizations operating facilities or engaged in commercial activities; non-profit organizations; organizations dedicated to commercialization and exports; and, business associations. It is not open to retail businesses.

Projects are reviewed based on specific criteria:

- anticipated results of the project;
- viability of the business or organization;
- the technical and financial management capacity;
- partner contributions in financial resources or professional services; and,
- the level of risk.

Examples of activities that are acceptable include:

- development of distribution network;
- purchase of equipment, computer tools and technology;
- prototyping, proof of concept, demonstration, technology showcases;
- implementation of a commercialization strategy;
- patent or license purchase;
- certification activities;
- management capacity building
- recruitment of specialized resources;
- associations, alliances and partnerships;
- knowledge transfer;
- strategy development;
- development of business leads and searching for funding;
- networking
- consulting and guidance services; and,
- information services.

Assistance can be in the form of repayable contributions or non-repayable contributions of up to 50% of authorized costs for SMEs and 90% for NPOs..

Authorized costs are defined as all those directly related to the project, deemed reasonable and essential to its completion. Restrictions may apply in certain cases.

Further Information

Head Office

Economic Development Agency of Canada for the Regions of Québec
Dominion Square Building
1255 Peel St., Suite 900
Montréal, Quebec H3B 2T9
Phone: (514) 283-6412
Phone toll-free: 1-(866) 385-6412
Fax: (514) 283-3302
Web site: http://www.dec-ced.gc.ca

Abitibi-Témiscamingue
906 5th Avenue, Val-d'Or, QC J9P 1B9
Phone: (819) 825-5260
Toll-free:1-(800) 567-6451
Fax: (819) 825-3245

Bas-Saint-Laurent
2 Saint-Germain Street East, Suite 310
Rimouski, QC G5L 8T7
Phone: (418) 722-3282
Toll-free phone: 1-(800) 463-9073
Fax: (418) 722-3285

Centre-du-Québec
1100 René-Lévesque Boulevard, Suite 105
Drummondville, QC J2C 5W4
Phone: (819) 478-4664
Toll-free phone: 1-(800) 567-1418
Fax: (819) 478-4666

Québec – Chaudière-Appalaches
2954 Laurier Blvd., Suite 030
Québec QC G1V 4T2
Phone: (418) 648-4826
Toll-free phone: 1-(800) 463-5204
Fax: (418) 648-7291

Côte-Nord
701 Laure Blvd, Suite 202B
P.O. Box 698, Sept-Îles, QC G4R 4K9
Phone: (418) 968-3426
Toll-free phone: 1-(800) 463-1707
Fax: (418) 968-0806

Eastern Townships
202 Wellington Street North, Suite 100
Sherbrooke, QC J1H 5C6
Phone: (819) 564-5904
Toll-free phone: 1-(800) 567-6084
Fax: (819) 564-5912

Gaspésie — Îles-de-la-Madeleine
Place Jacques-Cartier
120 de la Reine Street 3rd Floor
Gaspé QC G4X 2S1
Phone: (418) 368-5870
Toll-free phone: 1-(866) 368-0044
Fax: (418) 368-6256

Île-de-Montréal
3340 de l'Assomption Blvd.
Montréal, QC H1N 3S4
Phone: (514) 283-2500
Fax: (514) 496-8310

Laval, Laurentides, Lanaudière
2990 Pierre-Péladeau Avenue, Suite 410
Laval QC H7T 3B3
Phone: (450) 973-6844
Toll-free phone: 1-(800) 430-6844
Fax: (450) 973-6851

Mauricie
Immeuble Bourg du Fleuve
25 des Forges Street, Suite 413
Trois-Rivières, QC G9A 2G4
Phone: (819) 371-5182
Toll-free phone: 1-(800) 567-8637
Fax: (819) 371-5186

Montérégie
101 Roland-Therrien Blvd., Suite 400
Longueuil QC J4H 4B9
Phone: (450) 928-4088
Toll-free phone: 1-(800) 284-0335
Fax: (450) 928-4097

Nord-du-Québec
1255 Peel Street, Suite 900
Montréal QC H3B 2T9
Phone: (514) 283-8131
Toll-free phone: 1-(800) 561-0633
Fax: (514) 283-3637

Outaouais
259 Saint-Joseph Blvd, Suite 202
Gatineau, QC J8Y 6T1
Phone: (819) 994-7442
Toll-free phone: 1-(800) 561-4353
Fax: (819) 994-7846

Saguenay--Lac-Saint-Jean
100 Saint-Joseph Street South, Suite 203
Alma QC G8B 7A6
Phone: (418) 668-3084
Toll-free phone: 1-(800) 463-9808
Fax: (418) 668-7584

Québec City
Place Iberville IV
2954 Laurier Blvd., Suite 030
Québec, QC G1V 4T2
Phone: (418) 648-4826
Phone toll-free:1-(800) 463-5204
Fax: (418) 648-7291

Investissement Québec (IQ)

Established in mid-1998, Investissement Québec (IQ) has a mandate to assist innovative, new economy businesses.

Financing of R&D for Exporting Businesses

For companies engaged in exporting, scientific research and experimental development (SRED) activities giving rise to refundable tax credits under the tax laws of Québec and Canada. If revenues from international exports are at least $5 million or account for at least 15% of its total revenues.

Investissement Québec can provide a loan guarantee, i.e., a repayment guarantee on the net loss of a loan granted by a financial institution. The minimum amount of the loan guarantee provided by Investissement Québec to exporting businesses is $50,000 to finance scientific research and experimental development (SRED) activities. The loan guarantee covers 85% of the net loss and the maximum duration of the financial assistance is two years. The maximum loan amount, $500,000 provided by the financial institution can cover up to 75% of the cost of the project.

Interest rates are set by the financial institution and interest is payable to the financial institution from the first loan disbursement.

Investissement Québec - Head Office
413, Saint-Jacques, office 500
Montréal, QC H2Y 1N9
Phone: (514) 873-4375
Fax: (514) 873-5786
Web site: www.investquebec.com

Branch Offices

Investissement Québec
4805, boul. Lapinière, bureau 4100
Brossard QC J4Z 0G2
Phone: (450) 676-2123

Investissement Québec
500, ave. Daigneault
Case postale 1360, suite 10 A
Chandler, QC G0C 1K0
Phone: (418) 689-2549

Investissement Québec
230, boul. Saint-Joseph
Gatineau QC J8Y 3X4
Phone: 819 772-3211

Investissement Québec
3300, boulevard de la Côte-Vertu, bureau 210
Montréal QC H4R 2B7
Phone: (514) 873-1401

Investissement Québec
Montréal (East)
7100 Jean-Talon Street East, suite 1250
Montréal, QC H1M 3S3
Phone: (514) 873-9292

Investissement Québec
Région ouest de Montréal
413, rue Saint-Jacques, bureau 500
Montréal QC H2Y 1N9
Phone: (514) 873-4375

Investissement Québec
1200, route de l'Église, bureau 500
Québec QC G1V 5A3
Phone: (418) 643-5172

Investissement Québec
70 St-Germain Street East
3rd floor, suite 100
Rimouski, QC G5L 8B3
Phone: (418) 727-3582

Investissement Québec
454, ave. Arnaud
Sept-îles, QC G4R 3A9
Phone: (418) 964-8160

Investissement Québec
3950, boulevard Harvey, 2e étage
Saguenay QC G7X 8L6
Phone: (418) 695-7865

Investissement Québec
100 Laviolette Street, 3rd floor
Trois-Rivières, QC G9A 5S9
Phone: (819) 371-6012

Investissement Québec
1100, boul. René-Lévesque, bureau 102
Drummondville QC J2C 5W4
Phone: (819) 478-9675

Investissement Québec
3030 Le Carrefour Boulevard, suite 902
Laval, QC H7T 2P5
Phone: (450) 680-6161

Investissement Québec
170, Principale, suite 202
Rouyn-Noranda, QC J9X 4P7
Phone: (819) 763-3300

Investissement Québec
11535 First Avenue, suite 303
Saint-Georges, QC G5Y 7H5
Phone: (418) 222-5768

Investissement Québec
200 Belvédère Street North
3rd floor, suite 3.10
Sherbrooke, QC J1H 4A9
Phone: (819) 820-3224

Partnership Between National Bank and Investissement Québec to assist exporters

In July 2004, the National Bank and Investissement Québec announced a partnership to help exporters. Under the agreement, both entities will offer a comprehensive solution to help Quebec companies be more competitive abroad.

National Bank will offer businesses term loans to finance up to 100% of the cost of equipment, machinery, technology or any other project-related expenses. Exporters making such investments must do so with the intention of improving their productivity and, consequently, their competitiveness abroad. Investissement Québec will assume part of the risk by guaranteeing the Bank's loan.

In addition, a foreign exchange line will be offered so that businesses can use it to protect themselves against exchange rate fluctuations. This should help them control their profit margins and avoid unforeseen situations. As partner, Investissement Québec will assume a portion of the risk of loss for the Bank.

Further information can be obtained from Investissement Québec or branches of the National Bank.

National Bank of Canada Inc.
600 De la Gauchetiere St W
Montréal, QC H3B 4L2
Phone: (514) 394-5000
Phone toll-free: 1-(888) 835-6281
Fax: (514) 394-4339
Web site:: http://www.nbc.ca

Export Québec

Launched on November 8, 2011, Export Québec was allocated $60 million over three years to support businesses in, among other things; in conducting market studies outside Québec and preparing and implementing, international business plans; and, recruiting international business specialists.

Export Québec also helps Québec businesses to become known in 26 business centres in 21 countries through an incubator network. That service is provided under an agreement with Entreprise Rhone-Alpes International. Exports account for 45% of GDP, making them one of the main drivers of the Quebec economy.

Budget 2012-2013 allocated $34.9 million over three years, to continue government efforts regarding Québec exports; enable Export Québec to support new sectors, namely, the manufacturing, fashion and clothing, forestry and biofood sectors; and, multiply business opportunities through the network of Quebec offices abroad. The Budget also introduced a refundable tax credit pertaining to the diversification of markets of Québec manufacturing companies; ensure the leadership of the Centre de la francophonie des Ameriques; and, make adjustments to the tax credit for the production of multimedia titles.

Programme Exportation (PE)

Programme Exportation is a new program to help Québec companies operate in a highly competitive environment. It can provide financial assistance and is flexible and responsive to the changing business environment and the nature of promotional activities abroad.

The goal of the program is to support Quebec businesses for the development and diversification of their export markets and to:

- encourage Québec businesses adopt a structured approach to export,
- persevere in promising markets; and,
- promote the emergence of partnerships between Québec companies and foreign companies in order to create global value chains.

The program is open to Québec companies in the private sector as well as non-financial cooperatives, non-profit organizations (NPOs), educational organizations and educational institutions in Québec.

The program is not open to companies that offer personal services; wholesale trade, retail trade; accommodation or restoration.

Eligible activities are those which promote the expansion of their business outside Québec and may take the following forms:

- study of markets outside Québec;
- business plan and marketing outside Quebec (design and implementation);
- strengthening the international marketing function and use of e-business for export;
- prospecting mission;
- trade show (visitor or exhibitor);
- compliance work for border control measures;
- negotiation of partnerships and alliances with foreign partners;
- use an incubator for international service;

- pre-development steps up a subsidiary and a joint venture, or procedures prior to the acquisition of a company outside of Quebec, to the extent that such investment would have economic benefits for the province;
- hiring a specialist for international affairs;
- home buyers or foreign partners; or,
- preparing a proposal invitation to obtain a major overseas contract.

Financial aid is in the form of a grant of up to 40% of eligible expenses up to a maximum of $100, 000 per project. In the case of a project of hiring a specialist or international affairs, the maximum amount can reach $20,000.

Industrial Agreements Programs (PAI)

Industrial Agreements Programs (PAI) between Québec and some parts of Europe are designed to to promote industrial partnerships, technology and services between small and medium sized businesses.

At the time of writing, agreements had been established with the following areas:

- Catalonia (Spain),
- Bavaria (Germany),
- Lombardy (Italy)
- the regions of Wallonia , Flanders and Brussels (Belgium).

UBIFRANCE / QUÉBEC program

The UBIFRANCE / QUÉBEC program is a France-Québec agreement for industrial cooperation that aims to promote the negotiation and conclusion of partnership agreements between small and medium French and Quebec businesses. The program can cover the preparation of a mission, the cost of transatlantic transportation, living expenses and intercity transportation in France.

The program is not open to companies distributing products; trading houses; service companies, cultural enterprises, professional or industry associations; universities and colleges; research centers;
departments; governmental or quasi-governmental organizations.

A lump sum of $1,500 per person is allowed for logistical support to the achievement of the mission. A company can make a maximum of two trips per project. The maximum number of projects is three in total.

Further Information

Ministère des Relations internationales,
de la Francophonie et du Commerce extérieur
380, rue Saint-Antoine Ouest, 5e étage
Montréal QC   H2Y 3X7
Phone: (514) 499-2181
Fax: (514) 873-0776
E-mail address: exportquebecmri.gouv.qc.ca

Manufacturiers et exportateurs du Québec

The Manufacturiers et exportateurs du Québec is a non-profit organization with a mission to improve the business environment; help manufacturing and export companies to become more competitive on local and international markets, through its leadership, expertise and network, and the strength of its members.

Manufacturiers et exportateurs du Quebec is a division of Canadian Manufacturers and Exporters, the largest business and industrial association in Canada, founded in 1871.

Thus, Budget 2012-2013 provided $600,000 over three years to support a special agreement between Export Québec and Manufacturiers et exportateurs du Quebec, for the purpose of developing specific export processes for businesses with a high potential for internationalization; continuous sharing of strategic information on the needs of manufacturing companies and their financial situation; and, undertaking projects to assist companies in target markets.

The agreement will enable companies to showcase their know-how regarding, for example, the quality of their labour force, their ability to innovate and their creativity.

Export Québec has already began supporting Québec businesses in the fashion and clothing sector, and assisting them in their international development efforts.

The Québec Budget for 2012-2013 provides for an envelope of $2 million in 2012-2013 and $1 million for 2013-2014 and 2014-2015 under the Export Program of the Ministere du Developpement economique, de l'Innovation et de l'Exportation. This funding will enable Export Québec to step up its support for businesses in the fashion and clothing sector that wish to make inroads abroad by participating in events and developing promotional activities to showcase their creations. Export Québec will be able to draw on the best business practices in this sector.

14

Leasing

What is Meant by Leasing?

Leasing is one method of financing your business, especially in the area of vehicles, computers and office equipment.

Leasing in Canada has gained tremendous popularity within the last few years and now accounts for 10% to 12% of all new equipment purchases; up from 4% just a few years ago.

According to the Equipment Leasors Association of Canada, leasing in Canada still lags far behind the United States where it accounts for 25% to 30% of all new equipment purchases.

Under a leasing arrangement, the leasing company owns the asset. Your business gets to use the asset for a monthly or quarterly charge. There are three basic varieties of the leasing arrangement.

The First Type of Arrangement

In one type, your business does not build up any equity in the equipment leased. At the end of a lease, you return the asset to the leasing company which then disposes of it.

This arrangement is known as a "fixed-in lease", "closed-end lease", "walk-away lease", "operating lease" or "net lease".

Because of the leasing company's responsibility to dispose of the asset, it is exposed to the risk that the asset will be mistreated whilst it is being leased. For this reason, some leasing companies charge more to compensate for any losses.

In cases of excessive abuse, the leasing company may require extra payment to compensate for reduced value.

Such leases for vehicles are likely to contain a stipulation relating to the number of kilometres that can be driven. Any amounts over the maximum will be subject to an extra charge on a per kilometre basis. This can be expensive to your business if the limits are greatly exceeded.

It is also difficult to get out of this type of lease before its termination date.

The Second Type of Arrangement

Another type of lease allows your business to build up equity ownership in the equipment leased.

At the end of the lease, the asset is sold either to the business or to a third party for a pre-determined amount known as the "buy-back".

This type of lease is known as an "open-end lease", "buy-back lease", "capital lease" or "financed lease".

The party entering into the lease guarantees this final price. If the asset is sold for less than the buy-back price, then your business must make up the difference. If it is sold for more, the profit goes to your business (where it may be subject to tax - check with your accountant).

This type of lease is usually fairly easy to get out of before it expires. The "buy-back" is simply calculated at any given point in time in accordance with a pre-determined schedule. Most leasing periods are for between 12 and 48 months; although other periods exist on the market.

In the case of these "open-end leases", it is frequently possible to obtain lease extensions which essentially reduce the ultimate buy-back price.

The Third Type of Arrangement

There are hybrid leases which combine some of the features of both "open" and "closed-end" leases.

Maintenance and Repair

Maintenance and repair of the equipment can either be the responsibility of the leasing company or the responsibility of your business.

In most car leases, your business would be responsible for maintenance and repairs.

For office equipment such as typewriters, photocopiers, etc., the leasing company will frequently take responsibility for the repair and maintenance. In the latter case, a maintenance charge is added to the basic lease rates.

It should be noted that full-service leases for vehicles are becoming more widely available in North America. Some of these are not directly tied into the lease and can be entered into separately. Thus, one of the major oil companies in Canada is offering a fleet program, which in reality is only a semi-maintenance program. This allows for discounts on parts and gas; includes warranties on maintenance work; provides all the billing information and eliminates unauthorized purchases by employees [1].

Insurance

In some instances (especially with vehicles), your business will be required to carry insurance on the asset. Some leasing companies offer insurance as part of their service to the customer, however, the rates may or may not be competitive.

The Leasing Company's Viewpoint

The leasing company owns the asset and is able to use the capital cost allowance for tax purposes. It also charges your business interest for the money that is tied up in the asset.

Should your business fail or stop making lease payments; the leasing company will simply come in and remove the equipment which legally belongs to it. At that point, their risk is reduced to the difference between the price that they can obtain when they sell the used equipment and the amount of principal still outstanding on the lease.

It is for this reason that the leasing company prefers to lease equipment that will have a marketable value in the event of something going wrong. Therefore, you may find leasing companies reluctant to enter into agreements involving high technology products which may become obsolete very quickly.

Advantages of Leasing

There are a number of advantages of leasing for the small business.

Firstly, it helps you to conserve working capital. Your company does not have to lay out cash for the outright purchase of the asset and can use those funds for day-to-day expenses and operations.

Comparing leasing to equipment purchased on a financing plan; your payments are generally lower under the leasing arrangement. Also, most leases cover 100% of the equipment cost, including delivery, which is unlikely to be the case under a financing plan.

Secondly, leasing does not affect your firm's ability to borrow from your bank or other sources. The lease does not tie up any of your assets as collateral, simply because the asset does not legally belong to your business in the first place.

Thirdly, your business can charge lease payments as operating expenses; thereby reducing taxes more than would have been possible by claiming capital cost allowances (under normal circumstances). Term of your lease can also be geared to life expectancy of equipment.

Interest rates charged on leases are usually fixed at the time they are entered into. You know exactly in advance what its cost is going to be. This can be an advantage if the lease is signed at a time of low interest rates; because the rate is locked in. The converse is true at times of high interest rates.

Some leases are available with floating rates, however, these are less common.

An advantage, touted by leasing companies, is protection against obsolescence. In this high tech era, many pieces of equipment become rapidly outdated. Leasing permits trading up to a new piece of equipment; thereby keeping an edge over competitors.

Leasing allows your business to make equipment "sing for its supper", or pay its own way. The additional monthly revenue generated from the use of a new piece of leased equipment will frequently exceed the monthly leasing charges.

In the case of automobiles, some big leasing companies have such enormous buying power that it permits them to obtain discounts that can be passed on to their customers.

Leasing is usually available, even in poor economic times, if your business has a good credit rating. This may not necessarily be the case with bank loans, which can become as scarce as hen's teeth when the economy is falling out of the sky and your bank manager is hiding under his desk!

Disadvantages of Leasing

If leasing is so wonderful, why isn't everyone using it? Well, it certainly has gained a tremendous amount of popularity over the last 20 years. In fact leasing in Canada is now a multi-billion dollar industry. There are, however, some disadvantages.

The first is cost. The leasing company is not doing it for free and charges interest on the money that is tied up in the asset.

Equipment that is leased will cost more than if it is purchased outright, however, there are tax advantages in writing off the leasing expenses.

The second is that, unless there is a buy-back provision at the end of the lease, your business will relinquish the equipment on termination of the lease and have nothing to show for it after all those payments!

On the other hand, if there is a buy-back, the equipment may fall short of the buy-back price when it is sold and your business will be held liable for the difference. This could happen in the case of a vehicle which has been poorly maintained or has clocked up a very large number of kilometres.

In the case of a closed end lease, a vehicle which has exceeded the pre-set mileage limit will be subject to a surcharge based on a per kilometre usage.

Under a lease, your business does not own the asset, so it cannot be used as collateral for any other form of borrowing.

It is easy to get caught up in the sales talk about wanting to avoid obsolescence. Is a talking photocopier better than one that does not talk? Is there really any very significant competitive advantage in having the latest this or that?

If you lease at a fixed rate when rates are high - you may be stuck until the lease expires. This would not be the case with a loan which has floating interest rates. On the other hand, leases do exist which carry floating interest rates.

The Lease or Purchase Decision

To come to a decision as to whether to lease or purchase a particular piece of equipment, you must weigh the pros and cons.

If your business has plenty of cash, leasing may not make sense because of the interest charges. On the other hand, if cash is tight, leasing makes a lot of sense.

In some cyclical types of businesses (where the cycles are of one or two year durations), leasing could be advantageous. Such might apply if your company has a major contract for a specified period of time or a certain project that will have a finite length. Staff and equipment may only be needed for a one or two year period.

Your monthly payments on a lease may be less than installment payments for a loan. This is particularly so for cars and trucks. The lease payments are based on the difference between the projected wholesale value at the end of the lease and the initial value. In the case of installment payments, the full value of the equipment has to be paid off.

To counter this advantage which leasing has over borrowing, the banks (which are prohibited by law from leasing, although they hope to get into this area when the Bank Act is revised) have introduced a guaranteed buy-back value for vehicles.

Under this arrangement, the banks simply finance the difference between the purchase price of your vehicle and the guaranteed buy-back price. Since this price spread is smaller, your monthly payments are correspondingly smaller. There is, however, a small interest premium that you have to pay in order to enjoy this privilege.

Frequently, a loan will require a certain percentage down payment in advance e.g., 20%. A lease frequently requires only an initial cash layout for the first and last month's payments.

In some instances, two months payments are required by way of deposit. Incidentally, no interest is paid on lease deposits. Personal guarantees may also be requested, especially for small companies or those at the start-up stage.

In coming to a final decision, it would be wise to consult an accountant or other professional who can provide some unbiased advice, especially with regard to the "real" benefits to the business and to the "true" costs after taxes are taken into account.

Sale-Leasebacks

Sale-Leaseback is a process by which an asset is sold to a third party who then leases it back.

This lease financing technique is commonly used with buildings and major pieces of equipment with a ready second-hand market, such as oil rigs or aircraft. It is a technique that can be used by established companies that need cash.

According to a study prepared by consultants Brimmer and Co., lease financing in the United States has reached a point where it has become the most important source of funds to support purchases of capital equipment [2]. Such funds can also be used for working capital.

The disadvantage of this technique is that, if there is no buy-back provision, your company loses its asset by converting it into cash. If the cash is used wisely, however, your company may be able to expand much more rapidly and in the long run achieve a much greater value than if it had simply retained the asset. Of course, if the cash is not used wisely, the converse holds true!

If a buy-back provision can be negotiated, your business may be able to re-purchase at some later date (maybe 10 to 20 years hence) at a pre-determined price. Hopefully, your company can work itself into a strong enough cash position prior to that date in order to repurchase the property.

The sale leaseback technique is particularly useful if your company is in a capital intensive industry. It enables you to convert your assets into working capital, which can be used for further expansion.

The technique can also be used if your company is in financial trouble. It can provide badly needed cash.

How to Locate Leasing Companies

Aside from those listed above, most leasing companies advertise themselves in the yellow pages.

Many equipment sales reps are willing to arrange leasing and have ready-made plans available. Some office equipment firms run their own leasing divisions to support the leasing of their own products.

In the case of sale-leasebacks, try approaching people in the real estate area. Many large corporations are entering this field and there are wealthy private individuals or trusts who may be willing to become involved.

You may also want to consider purchasing equipment in your own name or in the name of a private leasing company and lease the equipment to your company. Take care to make sure that sales taxes are not paid twice!

15

Mortgaging

"If you have an urge to write something that will live forever, sign a mortgage." (Evan Esar: 20,000 Quips & Quotes)

Chattel Mortgaging

Chattel mortgaging is the process of pledging a chattel for a loan.

The chattels can be in various forms. One of the most common is equipment e.g., machine tools. Another is inventory, where items are readily identifiable by means of serial numbers. In this type of arrangement, the lender holds a lien on the chattels, whilst the borrower still holds title to them.

Chattel mortgages are far less common than regular mortgages on real estate. This is because of the high risk associated with assets that can be moved (possibly in the middle of the night!) and which may have low resale values in the event of business failure. On account of this, interest rates are frequently very high.

Sometimes chattel mortgages can be arranged as part of an overall financing package. Only a few mortgage and finance companies will enter into them. Those that do, appear to be reluctant and many will not finance what they consider small amounts of under $1/2 million.

The best way to find companies in your local area is to consult your yellow pages under "mortgages" or by consulting your bank.

Commercial Real Estate Mortgages

If your business owns any real estate in which it has built up equity, financing is certainly possible by means of a mortgage on the property.

If there is already an existing first mortgage that is below the market value of the property (which is normally the case), it may be possible to place a second or even a third mortgage on the property.

Since the risk increases with a second and is even greater with a third; the business owner can expect interest rates to increase in proportion to the risk.

There are a large number of companies and private individuals in the mortgage market. These include most of the chartered banks, trust and loan companies, insurance companies and credit unions.

Contact can also be made through "matchmakers" or mortgage brokers who will match deals for a fee which can range from 0.5% to 5.0% according to the size and complexity. According to Statistics Canada there were 391 such brokers operating in Canada.

Your yellow pages or classified section in your local newspaper will provide many names.

16

Planning and Financing
From the Public & Private Sectors

A Summary of This Book

This is was a practical book, full of advice and suggestions on how you can successfully raise debt financing for your business. It covered 373 loan programs, sub-programs and initiatives in both the public and private sectors. It includes 843 contact addresses, phone and fax numbers together with Web sites, where available.

It provided you with a brief history of banking and describes the structure of the Canadian banking industry. It told you about the types of loans which banks offer. This 2013/2014 Edition has been revised to cover loans and guarantees provided by the federal, provincial and territorial governments and their agencies or private sector partners. It described loans for exporting and for businesses involved with agriculture, agrifoods, aquaculture and fisheries. It also covered micro loans and loan circles which you can access through a number of non-governmental organizations.

This book also showed you what to do before you approach your bank manager in order to present your business in the best light. It told you how your bank manager evaluates deals.

It showed you how factoring of accounts receivable can be used for financing as well as chattel mortgages. Leasing can help you reduce cash outlay and is considered as a form of debt financing. It showed you the advantages and disadvantages.

Planning Preparations

Your Guide to Preparing a Plan to Raise Money for Your Own Business shows you how to structure your deal and whether debt or equity would be the most appropriate.

It is a practical, step-by-step guide to preparing a business plan you can use to raise financing. It shows you how to address the concerns of investors or lenders. It covers points you will need to consider before starting and shows how your plan should be structured and provides an example.

Learn what to do after finishing your plan and how to use it effectively. A good plan will not guarantee financing, however, it is an essential first step in the search. Without it, you will not get your foot into the door of finance.

The 2013/2014 edition has been revised and restructured. It now includes chapters on strategic planning and the importance of using spreadsheets in the planning process. It covers premises and equipment and how to use your plan as a dynamic document.

There are chapters on time management and project management. It emphasizes the importance of the Internet and e-commerce and discusses the tricky balancing act of disintermediation, when you sell direct to the end-user and cut out the middleman.

It will help you prepare an advertising and marketing strategy as well as preparing a human resource plan. It also suggests ways of printing your plan and presenting it to potential investors or lenders. It covers some of presentation software packages that could help you. Finally, it reviews off-the-shelf software packages that you could use to prepare your own plan from scratch.

It contains a wealth of knowledge accumulated over many years. You owe it to yourself to read it before you embark on preparing a plan for your own business.

Financing from Formal & Informal Venture Capitalists

Your Guide to Raising Venture Capital for Your Own Business in Canada is designed to assist you in the search for the formal venture capitalist and to show where the informal investor or "angel" hides.

It has been completely updated and revised for 2013/2014 to reflect the many changes that have taken place since the last edition was published in 2012.

You will find that it is a gold mine of information if you are raising venture capital in Canada. It shows you how to do it yourself. It discusses the structure of the industry; what venture capitalists are looking for and how they evaluate deals. It tells you how to contact them and provides 544 addresses. It reviews 86 upcoming venture capital conferences and supplies the necessary contact information.

Find out what informal investors or "angels" can offer and how to find them. You can see if corporate angels, immigrant investors and intermediaries can be of assistance. Labour-sponsored venture capital corporations have sprung up all over the country. Most of them have money to invest and may be the answer in your search for capital.

You are given hints on negotiating with investors and some words of caution in dealing with angels.

Ways to Finance Your Business By Selling a Piece of the Pie

This book shows you how to finance business growth by selling a piece of the pie. Find out what's involved in selling shares to the public and the advantages together with the disadvantages. This book covers the Canadian exchanges and their listing requirements as well as London's Alternative Investment Market (AIM) and one of the US exchanges, NASDAQ.

Learn how employee stock ownership plans work and how they can be used to raise capital; together with the advantages and disadvantages. Find out how some of the provincial governments will help.

Take a look at franchising as a method for financing growth. Consider some of the factors that you will need to take into account. It includes a section on private placements and on stock options as they relate to the Toronto Venture Exchange.

This book has been completely revised for 2013/2014. It includes a broader review of major world stock markets, the indexes and the types of shares that are publicly traded.

Government Financing

Your Guide to Government Financial Assistance for Business is available in 13 volumes; one for each of the ten provinces and the three territories. Each of these covers all the federal programs and all the provincial or territorial programs relating to that specific province or territory. They can be purchased separately or as a set.

Each volume provides details of specific programs; what they offer by way of assistance; the eligibility requirements and contact information, including e-mail addresses and web sites.

These editions have been published annually since 1993 and cover hundreds of federal and provincial programs, sub-programs and other initiatives that relate to for-profit companies operating in each if the provinces ans territories. It describes each program; the eligibility requirements together with the application process. Each provide hundreds of contact addresses, phone and fax numbers together with Web sites.

Financing is constantly in a state of flux. New programs and initiatives are announced every year and others fade away without any fanfare. For this reason, this guide is updated you annually. It is a monumental task but readers appreciate getting the latest information.

If you are looking to finance a business in any province or territory, this is the place to start. You can save yourself countless hours of searching for the programs that are best suited to your needs. Whether you are at the start-up stage or wish to expand an existing business, you will benefit greatly from knowing what is available and how to make quick contact with the program managers. It's all here at your fingertips!

Export Financing

Your Guide to Canadian Export Financing examines techniques for financing exports. It reviews the latest government assistance programs for exporting at both federal and provincial levels across Canada. It has been completely revised and updated for 2013/2014 to reflect the many changes that have taken place since the last edition, written in 2012.

Addresses, phone numbers e-mail and Internet sites or web pages are provided so you can contact the various departments directly.

This edition contains a chapter on sources of marketing information that will be useful to exporters.

This book is an excellent introduction to export financing for Canadians.

More Information on Software for Small Business

If you want to get a better handle on what kind of software will help you run your business, you should consider another book I wrote a couple of years ago called: ***Software for Small Business: A Review of the Latest Windows Programs to Help You Improve Business Efficiency and Productivity - 2011 Edition*** which you can purchase from Productive Publications. It is not an instructional book on how to use programs, but rather, it is a "concept book" that lets you know what software is available and what it will do for you. I have designed it to help you make informed decisions on what types and brands of software to purchase for your business.

Further Information

These financing guides and the software book can be purchased at the publisher's Web site at: ***www.productivepublications.ca*** or from the order desk by toll-free phone at: 1-(877) 879-2669.

PRODUCTIVE PUBLICATIONS

Our 28th Year Publishing Non-Fiction Books
to Help You Meet the Challenges of the Digital Age

Other Great Books to Help You!
Check Them Out!

You will find brief outlines in the following pages but for more details and chapter contents, visit our Web sites as follows:
USA and Overseas: *www.ProductivePublications.com*
Canada: *www.ProductivePublications.ca*

You can order using a credit card as follows:
Order Desk USA and Canada Phone Toll-Free: 1-(877) 879-2669
Fax Order Form on the last page to: (416) 322-7434
Enquiries Phone: (416) 483-0634
Place Secure Orders Online at:
USA and Overseas: *www.ProductivePublications.com*
Canada: *www.ProductivePublications.ca*

E-mail orders to: *ProductivePublications@rogers.com*

Snail Mail Orders to: Productive Publications
                              P. O. Box 7200, Station A
                              Toronto, ON M5W 1X8 Canada

Courier Orders to: Productive Publications
                              7-B Pleasant Blvd., #1210
                              Toronto, ON M4T 1K2 Canada

**eBook Publishing
for Beginners**

**How to Make Money
Selling Your Digital
Books Online**

**By: Learn2succeed.com
Incorporated**

Barclay's Capital has suggested that a quarter of all worldwide book sales in 2015 will be made up of eBooks. This is wake-up call to publishers who are still trapped in the print-on-paper world. It also has ramifications for bookstores, libraries and the book supply chain .

112 pages; Softcover; ISBN: 978-1-55270-456-1   CIP
Canada: $19.99 US: $19.99 UK: $12.59

**Desktop Publishing
for Beginners**

**How to Create Great
Looking Brochures,
Books and Documents**

**By: Learn2succeed.com
Incorporated**

This book will introduce you to desktop publishing and shows you how you can create your own brochures, books and documents. It is s, although some are available for the Macintosh.

114 pages; Softcover; ISBN: 978-1-55270-455-4   CIP
Canada: $19.99 US: $19.99 UK: $12.59

**Gold Investing
for Beginners**

**An Opportunity for Huge
Gains or a Bubble About
to Burst?**

**By: Learn2succeed.com
Incorporated**

Find out about the major factors which influence the price of gold and determine for yourself whether a gold bubble has developed and is about to burst or whether investing in gold still offers an opportunity to make huge gains.

134 page; Softcover, ISBN: 978-1-55270-445   CIP
Canada $19.99 US: $19.99 UK: $12.59

**Stock Market Investing
for Beginners**

**How to Increase Your
Wealth in Uncertain Times**

**By: Learn2succeed.com
Incorporated**

Written for people who are fed up with the paltry interest their bank pays on their savings accounts as well as those who are sadly disillusioned with the lackluster performance of their investment advisors. Everything you need to know to get started.

164 pages, Softcover; ISBN: 978-1-55270-446-2   CIP
Canada: $24.95 US: $24.95 UK: $15.79

**For details visit our Canadian Web site: *www.ProductivePublications.ca*
American Web site: *www.ProductivePublications.com*
Order securely online or mail the order form at the end of this catalogue
Phone our Order Desk toll-free at: 1-(877) 879-2669**

Digital Photography for Beginners

How to Create Great Photos for Fun or Profit

By: Learn2succeed.com Incorporated

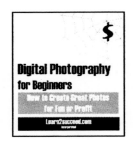

If you want to become a digital shutterbug, the place to start is by reading this excellent introduction which tries to explain everything in plain, non-technical terms.

98 pages; Softcover; ISBN: 978-1-55270-447-9 CIP
Canada $17.99 US: $1799 UK: $11.39

Time Management for Beginners

How to Get the Most Out of Every Day

By: Learn2succeed.com Incorporated

There is a saying that some people count time, while others make time count. This book is about making time count. It's about managing your time effectively so that you can get the most out of each and every day of your life.

114 pages; Softcover, ISBN: 978-1-55270-453-0 CIP
Canada: $19.99 US: $19.99 UK: $12.59

Steps to Choosing the Right Computer for Your Home or Business

A No-Nonsense Guide Which Cuts Through All the Hype

By: Learn2succeed.com Incorporated

Read this book **before** you purchase a new computer. It leads you through all factors you should consider. Computer store sales people are more interested in making a commission than on selling you what you need. This book will help. Softcover;

96 pages; Softcover, ISBN: 978-1-55270-454-7 CIP
Canada: $17.99 US: $1799 UK: $11.39

Food Poisoning and Waterborne Illness

How to Prevent 1.8 Million Deaths Every Year

By: Learn2succeed.com Incorporated

Figures from the World Health Organization and the Government of Ghana, suggest that between 1.8 million and 2.2 million deaths occur every year due to food poisoning and waterborne illness. There are many ways to significantly reduce the death rate. You will find out why governments are reluctant to regulate or take steps to meet the challenge.

116 pages, Softcover; ISBN 978-1-55270-449-3 CIP
Canada: $19.99 US: $19.99 UK: $12.59

For details visit our Canadian Web site: *www.ProductivePublications.ca*
American Web site: *www.ProductivePublications.com*
Order securely online or mail the order form at the end of this catalogue
Phone our Order Desk toll-free at: 1-(877) 879-2669

Page 2

**Business Start-Up
for Beginners**

**How to Become
Your Own Boss**

**By: Learn2succeed.com
Incorporated**

If you have ever dreamed of starting your own business and becoming your own boss, you've taken the first important step by selecting this book. It will show you what it takes to become an entrepreneur and how to find ideas to start your own business. You will have to acquire a lot of skills very quickly and this book will alert you to some of the things you will need to know and provide you with a lot of insight, based on first-hand experience.

116 pages, Softcover; ISBN 978-1-55270-444-8; CIP
Canada: $19.99 US: $19.99 UK: $12.59

**Bank Financing
for Beginners**

**How to Borrow Money to
Grow Your Business**

**By: Learn2succeed.com
Incorporated**

This book should definitely be on your reading list before you go charging into you bank in search of a business loan. Credit conditions may be tight, but this book should increase your chances of securing a bank loan.

114 pages; Softcover; ISBN: 978-1-55270-459-2 CIP
Canada: $19.99 US: $19.99 UK: $12.59

**Venture Capital Financing
for Beginners**

**How to Raise Equity
Capital from Venture
Capitalists and Angels**

**By: Learn2succeed.com
Incorporated**

If you are already in business or about to start a business, this book will help you raise equity capital from traditional venture capitalists or from "angels".

110 pages; Softcover, ISBN: 978-1-55270-458-5 CIP
Canada: $19.99 US: $19.99 UK: $12.59

**Public Speaking
for Beginners**

**How to Communicate
Effectively in the
Digital Age**

**By: Learn2succeed.com
Incorporated**

The King's Speech, drew attention to public speaking by someone with a disability. Even if you don't have a disorder, speaking in public can still be a challenge. This book will help you communicate effectively with your audience.

78 pages; Softcover; ISBN: 978-1-55270-452-3 CIP
Canada: $15.99 US: $15.99 UK: £9.99

**For details visit our Canadian Web site: *www.ProductivePublications.ca*
American Web site: *www.ProductivePublications.com*
Order securely online or mail the order form at the end of this catalogue
Phone our Order Desk toll-free at: 1-(877) 879-2669**

Your Guide to Raising Venture Capital for Your Own Business in Canada

Revised and Updated 2013-2014 Edition

By: Iain Williamson

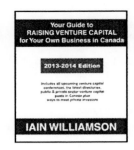

This book is a gold mine of information if you are raising venture capital in Canada. It shows you how to do it yourself. Lean about the structure of the industry; what venture capitalists are looking for and how they evaluate deals. You are given tips on the negotiating with them. It lists 86 conferences and provides 544 contact addresses. Find out what angel investors are looking for and how they could help you.

248 pages, softcover; ISBN 978-1-55270-667-1   CIP
ISSN 1191-0534   Canada: $74.95

Your Guide to Arranging Bank & Debt Financing for Your Own Business in Canada

Revised and Updated 2013-2014 Edition

By: Iain Williamson

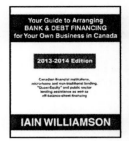

Learn the secrets of successful debt financing in Canada. Find out who the players are. Covers 373 loan programs and includes 843 contact addresses. How to prepare your company before you approach lenders. Find out how your loan application is evaluated. Can factoring or leasing help you? The author has many years of experience in bank financing and leasing and his book will help you in your quest for a loan.

386 pages, softcover; ISBN 978-1-55270-668-8   CIP
ISSN 1191-0542 Canada: $81.95

Your Guide to Financing Business Growth by Selling a Piece of the Pie

What's involved in going public; employee share ownership plans and franchising in Canada

Revised and Updated 2013-2014 Edition

By: Iain Williamson

A critical examination of three methods of growing your business by using other peoples' money. How to sell shares to the public or to your employees. Covers the Canadian stock exchanges and their listing requirements. Includes sections on London's Alternative Investing Market (AIM) and on NASDAQ in the US. What's involved in establishing an Employee Share Ownership Plan (ESOP). How to expand through franchising. The author was a financial analyst in the Canadian stockbrokerage business for five years.

162 pages, softcover; ISBN 978-1-55270-669-5 CIP
ISSN 1191-0488: Canada: $46.95

Your Guide to Canadian Export Financing: Successful Techniques for Financing Your Exports from Canada

Revised 2013-2014 Edition

By: Iain Williamson

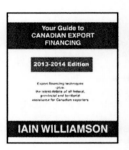

Provides you with practical techniques for financing your exports. Get details of all provincial, territorial and federal assistance programs that help you export including addresses and phone numbers to steer you in the right direction. Includes a chapter on insurance and sources of marketing information for exporters. The author is a consultant and entrepreneur who knows the practical side of importing and exporting.

300 pages, softcover; ISBN 978-1-55270-670-1   CIP
ISSN: 1191-047X Canada: $58.95

For details visit our Canadian Web site: *www.ProductivePublications.ca*
American Web site: *www.ProductivePublications.com*
Order securely online or mail the order form at the end of this catalogue
Phone our Order Desk toll-free at: 1-(877) 879-2669

Your Guide to Starting & Self-Financing Your Own Business in Canada

Revised 2013-2014 Edition

By: Iain Williamson

This 2013-2014 Edition has been updated to reflect the many changes that have taken place in the sources of marketing information. Shows you how to operate a business out of your home. How to use computers and the Web to run your business more efficiently. Covers web authoring software and how to sell online with your own e-commerce site or through eBay; as an Amazon Merchant or through online classifieds. Helps you determine how much money you <u>really</u> need and whether you can self-finance your own business to compete in the digital age.

362 pages, softcover; ISBN 978-1-55270-665-7   CIP
ISSN 1191-0518 Canada: $56.95

Your Guide to Preparing a Plan to Raise Money for Your Own Business

Revised 2013-2014 Edition

By: Iain Williamson

A good business plan is essential to succeed in your quest for financing. Contains a step-by-step guide to create your own winning plan. Computer software you can use. Find out how spreadsheets can help you. Learn how to address the concerns of investors or lenders. Tips on structuring your plan. Contains a sample plan as an example. Computer software to help you make great presentations to investors or lenders.

310 pages, softcover, ISBN 978-1-55270-666-4   CIP
ISSN 1191-0496 Canada: $46.95

Your Guide to Government Financial Assistance for Business

(Separate Editions-one for each Province & Territory)

Revised 2013-2014 Editions

By: Iain Williamson

Business financing in Canada is in a constant state of flux. New government programs are continually being introduced. Old ones are often amended or discontinued with little publicity. These books will provide you with the latest information on all Federal and Provincial/Territorial programs that specifically relate to each area. Author, Iain Williamson, of Entrepreneurial Business Consultants of Canada, has over 30 years experience as a stock market financial analyst and as owner-manager of his own companies.

$89.95 ea. Softcover; CIP.   Title & ISBN See list on right ➜

Your Guide to Government Financial Assistance for Business In...

EDITION	ISBN	PAGES
Newfoundland & Labrador	9781552706718	304
Prince Edward Island	9781552706725	273
Nova Scotia	9781552706732	308
New Brunswick	9781552706749	278
Quebec	9781552706756	312
Ontario	9781552706763	376
Manitoba	9781552706770	314
Saskatchewan	9781552706787	306
Alberta	9781552706794	306
British Columbia	9781552706800	286
The Yukon	9781552706817	256
The Northwest Territories	9781552706824	246
The Nunavut	9781552706831	248

Please specify Province or Territory when ordering. All titles are $89.95 each.

For details visit our Canadian Web site: *www.ProductivePublications.ca*
American Web site: *www.ProductivePublications.com*
Order securely online or mail the order form at the end of this catalogue
Phone our Order Desk toll-free at: 1-(877) 879-2669

Steps to Opening a Successful Web Store

The Basics of How to Set-Up Shop in Cyberspace

By: Learn2succeed.com Incorporated

How to find products to sell, research the market and open your own e-commerce Web site. Use online and offline advertising to drive traffic. Consider selling at eBay auctions at your own eBay store. Review the advantages of running your business from home and how to set it up. Learn how to select the best computer hardware and software. Establish your marketing strategy, prepare your marketing plan and incorporate it into your business plan. Calculate how much will it cost to start.

154 pages, softcover; ISBN 978-1-55270-357-1 CIP
Canada: $24.95 US: $24.95 UK: £15.79

Steps to Starting a Successful Retail Business

How to Find a Niche and Turn it Into a Money Machine

By: Learn2succeed.com Incorporated

Where to get ideas and direct import your own merchandise. How to research your market. Covers legal structures and tax permits. The importance of location and the hazards of lease renewals. Your store layout, fixturing, signage, lighting and window displays. Hire staff and reduce shoplifting. Use planogramming to fine-tune your operation. How to advertise and use direct marketing to augment your sales. Use e-commerce on the Web to extend your reach.

144 pages, softcover; ISBN 978-1-55270-359-5 CIP
Canada: $24.95 US: $24.95 UK: £15.79

Steps to Starting a Successful Import Business

How to Find Products, Bring Them into the Country and Make Money Selling Them

By: Learn2succeed.com Incorporated

Provides the basic knowledge you need to set up and start your own importing business and how to make money selling the products you import. How to find products to import and then do the research to find out whether you can sell them in your local market. How to pay for imports plus freight alternatives for importing your goods and what's involved with customs clearance. Look at some of the advantages of warehousing and bonded warehousing. How to use advertising, direct marketing and e-commerce to sell your imports.

148 pages, softcover, ISBN 978-1-55270-358-8 CIP
Canada: $24.95 US: $24.95 UK: £15.79

Direct Marketing for Beginners

How to Cut Out the Middleman and Sell Direct to Consumers

By: Learn2succeed.com Incorporated

Cut out the middleman and increase your profit margins. Review different methods of direct marketing and learn how to create your own Web site, attract visitors and conduct e-commerce. Take a look at permission-based e-mail and e-newsletters. Learn how to sell at auctions on eBay and set up your own eBay store. How to prepare your marketing plan. Review the laws and regulations which govern advertising and marketing together with the do-no-call lists.

160 pages, softcover; ISBN 978-1-55270-352-6 CIP
Canada: $24.95 US: $24.95 UK: £15.79

For details visit our Canadian Web site: *www.ProductivePublications.ca*
American Web site: *www.ProductivePublications.com*
Order securely online or mail the order form at the end of this catalogue
Phone our Order Desk toll-free at: 1-(877) 879-2669

Home-Based Business for Beginners

How to Start a Business on a Shoestring from Your Own Home

By: Learn2succeed.com Incorporated

If you want to run your own business out of your home, this book will provide you with all the information you need to get started. Learn about the tax and other advantages of running a home-based business. But also be alerted to some of the disadvantages including finding good employees and your legal liabilities. You will learn where to find products or services to sell and how to develop your own products. Then get help in finding out if there is a market for what you have to offer.

156 pages, softcover; ISBN 978-1-55270-353-3 CIP
Canada: $24.95 US: $24.95 UK: £15.79

Part-Time Business for Beginners

Successful Ways to Augment Your Income While Working for Someone Else

By: Learn2succeed.com Incorporated

When you are working for someone else, you probably don't want them to know you have set up your own business, so you will be given some tips on how to keep it secret. How to develop a business idea and figure out if there is a market for the product or service you have selected. Learn how to advertise and sell it. Create your own Web site and open your own Web store. Sell merchandise at eBay auctions or by opening your own eBay store. Learn about legal structures for your part-time business and government sales tax permits.

152 pages, softcover; ISBN 978-1-55270-354-0 CIP
Canada: $24.95 US: $24.95 UK: £15.79

Business Financing for Beginners

Where to Find Money to Grow Your Business

By: Learn2succeed.com Incorporated

Find out how much money you really need. How to finance during different stages of business growth; all the way from relatives and friends,to informal investors or angels. What the venture capitalists can offer and hints on negotiating with them including the due diligence process, term sheets and the legal agreement. Types of loans and how to prepare before you apply. Take a look at factoring, leasing and how to sell shares through an Initial Public Offering (IPO). What's involved in Employee Share Ownership Plans (ESOPs).

146 pages, softcover, ISBN 978-1-55270-355-7 CIP
Canada: $24.95 US: $24.95 UK: £15.79

Seven Basic Steps to Start-Up Business Success

Find a Need, Conduct Research Prepare Your Plan, Locate Financing, Start Operations, Advertise and Monitor Your Progress

By: Learn2succeed.com Inc.

Find out what people want and where to get great ideas. How to conduct market research and prepare a business plan. Decide between debt or equity. Where to find informal investors or how to get bank financing. Consider the legal form of your business, registration for sales taxes and how to protect your trademarks. Take a look at different marketinga and advertising techniques. How to use permission-based e-mail and e-newsletters. Review your progress and be prepared to change your strategy.

158 pages, softcover, ISBN 978-1-55270-360-1 CIP
Canada: $24.95 US: $24.95 UK: £15.79

**For details visit our Canadian Web site: *www.ProductivePublications.ca*
American Web site: *www.ProductivePublications.com*
Order securely online or mail the order form at the end of this catalogue
Phone our Order Desk toll-free at: 1-(877) 879-2669**

Streaming Video and Audio for Business

New Ways to Communicate with Your Customers, Employees and Shareholders Over the Internet

By: Learn2succeed.com Incorporated

This timely book looks at new ways for businesses to communicate over the Internet using video and audio. It includes advice on the equipment and software required, together with tips on content creation.

140 pages, softcover; ISBN 978-1-55270-302-1 CIP
Canada: $24.95 US: $24.95 UK: £15.79

Corporate Video Production on a Shoestring

Improve Your Communications with Your Customers, Employees and Shareholders

By: Learn2succeed.com Incorporated

Inexpensive digital camcorders offer great opportunities to improve communications with customers, employees and shareholders. This book covers the equipment and software required together with tips on post-production editing and hints on creating great content.

116 pages, softcover; ISBN 978-1-55270-303-8 CIP
Canada: $24.95 US: $24.95 UK: £15.79

e-Business for Beginners

How to Build a Web Site that Brings in the Dough

By: Learn2succeed.com Incorporated

Written for both new and existing businesses, this book introduces you to business on the Internet. It shows you how to create your own Web site, conduct e-commerce, attract customers and get paid. Reviews Web authoring and e-commerce software. How to make your Web site user-friendly and perform search engine optimization.

184 pages, softcover; ISBN 978-1-55270-280-2 CIP
Canada: $29.95 US: $29.95 UK: £18.99

Web Marketing for Small & Home-Based Businesses:

How to Advertise and Sell Your Products Online

By: Learn2succeed.com Incorporated

This book shows you how to advertise and sell your products or services on the Web. Learn the basics of e-commerce and some of the challenges facing online merchants. Find out about search engines and how to improve your listings with them. Keep you name in front of your customers with permission-based e-mail and electronic newsletters. Don't forget the importance of referrals. How to use traditional marketing to drive traffic to your site. Find out about the importance of web links and associate programs.

132 pages, softcover; ISBN 978-1-55270-119-5 CIP
Canada: $24.95 US: $24.95 UK: £15.79

For details visit our Canadian Web site: *www.ProductivePublications.ca*
American Web site: *www.ProductivePublications.com*
Order securely online or mail the order form at the end of this catalogue
Phone our Order Desk toll-free at: 1-(877) 879-2669

**Business Planning
for Beginners**

**Find Out How Much Money
You Will Need to
Run Your Business**

By: Learn2succeed.com
Incorporated

Covers your operational, marketing and advertising plans. Examines the impact of the Internet. Covers human resource requirements and sub-contracting, automation or computerization to minimize staffing requirements. Set strategic objectives and calculate how much money you will need. Covers the manufacturing, service, retail and construction businesses. Printing your plan. How to use it as a financing document and make effective presentations to potential investors or lenders.

150 pages, softcover, ISBN 978-1-55270-356-4   CIP
Canada: $24.95 US: $24.95 UK: £15.79

**Advertising for
Beginners**

**Successful Web and
Online Advertising
in the Digital Age**

By: Learn2succeed.com
Incorporated

This book emphasises less expensive forms of advertising such as direct mail, print media, yellow pages, signage, trade shows, telemarketing and fax broadcasting. Less emphasis is placed on broadcast media, since this tends to be expensive and often beyond the budget of smaller companies. It shows you how to establish an effective Web presence and how to use offline media to drive traffic to your Web site. Learn how to prepare your advertising plan and the standards and laws which apply to advertising and privacy.

146 pages, softcover; ISBN 978-1-55270-351-9   CIP
Canada: $24.95 US: $24.95 UK: £15.79

**Steps to Starting a
Recession-Proof Business**

**Where to Find Ideas and
How to Start**

By: Learn2succeed.com
Incorporated

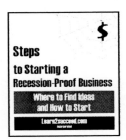

Recessions are tough times to start a business and it is imperative to choose one that will survive. This book provides a lot of tips on finding areas which will survive and prosper during a severe economic downturn. It also shows readers how to set up their business and keep their start-up costs to a minimum.

141 pages, softcover; ISBN 978-1-55270-381-6   CIP
Canada: $24.95 US: $24.95 UK: £15.79

**Self-Employment
for Beginners**

**How to Create Your Own
Job in a Recession**

By: Learn2succeed.com
Incorporated

With huge increases in job losses, many people are finding it impossible to find work. Students who are graduating from school, college or university are facing challenges like never before. This book will guide all of them through the process of working for themselves; where to get ideas and how to go about it. It is full of practical tips.

140 pages, softcover; ISBN 978-1-55270-382-3   CIP
Canada: $24.95 US: $24.95 UK: £15.79

**For details visit our Canadian Web site: *www.ProductivePublications.ca*
American Web site: *www.ProductivePublications.com*
Order securely online or mail the order form at the end of this catalogue
Phone our Order Desk toll-free at: 1-(877) 879-2669**

**eBay for Beginners
in Canada**

**How to Buy and
Sell at Auctions**

**By: Learn2succeed.com
Incorporated**

This timely book will help every Canadian who wants to buy and sell on eBay. It covers issues specific to Canada (unlike most other books which are written for Americans). Selling on eBay is probably one of the easiest ways for you to earn extra income, yet many people do not know how to go about it. This book will provide you with the basic knowledge to get started with a very small investment.

146 pages, softcover, ISBN 978-1-55270-326-7 CIP
Canada: $24.95 US: $24.95 UK: £15.79

**Steps to Starting
a Successful eBay
Business in Canada**

**Your Path to
Financial Independence**

**By: Learn2succeed.com
Incorporated**

This book will help every Canadian who wants to start a business using eBay. It outlines 12 basic steps for success and covers issues specific to Canada (unlike most other books which are written for Americans). Welcome to the World's Largest Auction! Learn how eBay started; how big it has grown and the basics of selling by auction on eBay.

142 pages, softcover, ISBN 978-1-55270-327-4 CIP
Canada: $24.95 US: $24.95 UK: £15.79

**eBay Your Own
Home-based Business**

**Practical Steps to Achieve
Financial Independence**

**By: Learn2succeed.com
Incorporated**

Written in non-technical language, this book will help you make effective use of eBay to run your own home-based business and make money. You can operate either as a part-time or full-time business. It is written from a Canadian perspective and shows you how to get started with a very small investment. This book starts with an eBay primer and tells you what you can sell and how auctions work. It also shows you the role of eBay in the product cycle
.

182 pages, softcover, ISBN 978-1-55270-329-8 CIP
Canada: $29.95 US: $29.95 UK: £18.99

**Expand Your Canadian
Business Using eBay**

**Everything Managers
Need to Know to Start
Successfully**

**By: Learn2succeed.com
Incorporated**

Written in non-technical language, this book will help every Canadian small business person make effective use of eBay to increase their sales to domestic and foreign markets. It covers issues specific to Canadians (unlike most other books which are written for Americans). Selling on eBay is probably one of the easiest ways to test new products and sell-off excess inventory or end-of-line goods, yet many Canadian businesspeople do not know how to go about it. This book will provide them with the basic knowledge to get started with a very small investment.

226 pages, softcover, ISBN 978-1-55270-328-1 CIP
Canada: $34.95 US: $34.95 UK: £21.99

**For details visit our Canadian Web site: *www.ProductivePublications.ca*
American Web site: *www.ProductivePublications.com*
Order securely online or mail the order form at the end of this catalogue
Phone our Order Desk toll-free at: 1-(877) 879-2669**

Page 10

The Small Business Guide to Increasing Your Sales Using eBay

Easy Ways to Expand into Domestic and Foreign Markets

By: Learn2succeed.com Incorporated

Written in non-technical language, this book will demonstrate eBay's role in the product cycle so that every business can make effective use of eBay to increase their sales in domestic and foreign markets. How to list products for auction and get paid. How to open an eBay Store. How to get positive feedback and integrate eBay into existing operations.

138 pages, softcover, ISBN 978-1-55270-251-2   CIP
Canada: $24.95 US: $24.95 UK: £15.79

Start Your Own Successful Home-Based Business Using eBay

Everything You Need to Know to Get Started

By: Learn2succeed.com Incorporated

How to start your own full-time or part-time home-based business using eBay. How to register your business, find products, conduct research, list your items for auctions, open an eBay Store and get paid. How to select the right computer hardware and software to help you. The importance of getting positive feedback.

226 pages, softcover, ISBN 978-1-55270-250-5   CIP
Canada: $29.95 US: $29.95 UK: £18.99

Inexpensive E-Commerce Solutions for Small & Home-Based Businesses:

You Don't Have to Spend a Fortune to Start Selling Online

By: Learn2succeed.com Incorporated

This book is a great place to start if you want to learn about inexpensive e-commerce solutions for your small or home-based business. Find out how to do it inexpensively for about $100 per month. You don't have to spend a fortune to start selling online!

130 pages, softcover;; ISBN 978-1-55270-118--8   CIP
Canada: $24.95 US: $24.95 UK: £15.79

Fundamentals of Effective Online Selling

Use the Power of the Internet to Increase Your Sales

By: Learn2succeed.com Incorporated

How to advertise and sell your products or services on the Web. The basics of online selling and some of the challenges facing online merchants. How to use the Web for your market research and how to prepare your Web marketing plan. Take a tour of inexpensive software to establish your own e-commerce Web site. This book will provide you with all the information you need to start increasing your online sales.

206 pages, softcover; ISBN: 978-1-55270-210-9   CIP
Canada: $29.95 US: $29.95 UK: £18.99

For details visit our Canadian Web site: *www.ProductivePublications.ca*
American Web site: *www.ProductivePublications.com*
Order securely online or mail the order form at the end of this catalogue
Phone our Order Desk toll-free at: 1-(877) 879-2669

Page 11

Inexpensive Ways to Start Your Own Successful Home-Based E-Commerce Business

How to Set Up Your Business, Select Products & Start Selling Online for Well Under $2,000

By: Learn2succeed.com Inc.

How to start your own online business. Where to get ideas and how to check them out. How to plan your business. How much money will you need? How to get financing. How to advertise and sell your products or services on the Web. The basics of online selling and some of the challenges facing online merchants. How to use the Web for your market research and how to prepare your Web marketing plan.

328 pages, softcover; ISBN 978-1-55270-203-1   CIP
Canada: $39.95; USA: $39.95; UK: £25.19

Steps to Starting a Successful Business in the Digital Age

How to Use the Latest Technology to Turn Your Ideas into Money

By: Learn2succeed.com Incorporated

This book will help everyone who wants to start a business in the digital age. It outlines 10 basic steps for success. How to find ideas for a business, conduct market research, create your own Web site and select your e-commerce software. How to set up your business.

144 pages, softcover, ISBN 978-1-55270-301-4   CIP
Canada: $24.95 US: $24.95   UK: £15.79

MAKE IT ON YOUR OWN!

How to Succeed in Your Own Business

By: Barrie Jackson

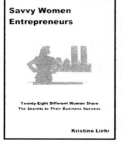

What it takes to run a business and make it succeed. Contains practical, hands-on information, for immediate use. Learn from the author's personal experience and mistakes. Lots of anecdotes from the author's business adventures which make for interesting reading with a "practical punch".

Before his untimely death, Barrie Jackson, forged Cooper Boating Centre into Canada's largest yacht charter company.

212 pages, softcover; ISBN 978-1-896210-37-7   CIP
Canada: $29.95 US: $29.95 UK: £18.99

Savvy Women Entrepreneurs

Twenty-Eight Different Women Share the Secrets To Their Business Success

By: Kristina Liehr

You don't have to go to business school to start a business! Learn how 28 remarkable women entrepreneurs started their own business; many in their garage or kitchen. Read about the steps that they took; the obstacles they overcame and the joy, happiness and success that they achieved. The chances they took and how they learned from their mistakes. Get the confidence and inspiration to start YOUR own business or EARN EXTRA INCOME.

140 pages, softcover; ISBN 978-1-55270-000-6   CIP
Canada: $24.95 US: $24.95 UK: £15.79

For details visit our Canadian Web site: www.ProductivePublications.ca
American Web site: www.ProductivePublications.com
Order securely online or mail the order form at the end of this catalogue
Phone our Order Desk toll-free at: 1-(877) 879-2669

Steps to Starting and Running a Successful Business in CANADA

By: Don Lunny

Managing your own business can be a rewarding experience but survival can be tough in today's economy. This book shows you the essential steps to ensure that your business is profitable.

Author, **Don Lunny**, is an experienced business owner and consultant with many years of experience.

190 pages, softcover ISBN 978-0-920847-85-5   CIP
Canada: $34.95

Checklist for Going into Business

By: Don Lunny

Points to create your own checklist to create a profitable business. Starting it is reality. But, there is often a gap between your dream and reality - that can only be filled with careful planning. You need a plan to avoid pitfalls, to achieve your goals and make profits. This guide helps you prepare a comprehensive business plan and determine if your idea is feasible. **Don Lunny** is an experienced business owner and consultant with many years of experience.

53 pages, softcover; ISBN 978-0-920847-86-2   CIP
Canada: $19.95 US: $19.95 UK: £12.59

A Street Wise Manager's Guide to Success in the Restaurant Business

By: Matthew Lallo

You could have called this book "What they don't teach you at The Culinary Institute". As you know, operating a restaurant is a difficult; even a dangerous business. Competition is fierce and costs keep rising. You are subject to a patchwork of government regulations. You will find it a challenge to succeed in this industry, however, this book can help you to greatly improve your chances. It provides you with a pragmatic view of an industry that is unique and it offers you with unorthodox (but proven) advice on the subtle art of survival.

241 pages, softcover; ISBN 978-1-55270-144-7   CIP
Canada: $29.95 US: $29.95 UK: £16.98

You Can Be Rich!

Eight Easy-to-Remember Principles You Can Use to Create Wealth and Achieve Financial Independence

By: Stuart Mathews

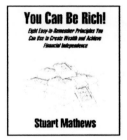

This book is not a get rich quick scheme. It offers an introduction to practical systems of making money. It contains over 20 years of close study into the subject of attaining and holding on to financial wealth. Anyone can become rich or financially independent, but not everyone will. Becoming wealthy will depend on your willingness to identify, learn, and follow financial guidelines and principles. Stuart Mathews shows you how to do this.

174 pages, softcover; ISBN: 978-1-55270-255-0   CIP
Canada: $26.95 US: $29.95 UK: £16.99

For details visit our Canadian Web site: *www.ProductivePublications.ca*
American Web site: *www.ProductivePublications.com*
Order securely online or mail the order form at the end of this catalogue
Phone our Order Desk toll-free at: 1-(877) 879-2669

Entrepreneurship and Starting a Business

Confederation College Entrepreneurship Series

Entrepreneurship and Starting a Business provides a comprehensive introduction to entrepreneurs and what they do, and is a must-read for anyone who has aspirations to start and run their own business. The book examines entrepreneurs, their values and behaviour, and factors that contribute to their success and failure. It also takes an in-depth look at how they spot business opportunities or come up with business ideas.

110 pages, softcover; ISBN 978-1-55270-090-7 CIP
Canada: $24.95 US: $24.95 UK: £15.79

The Entrepreneur and the Business Idea

Confederation College Entrepreneurship Series

If you ever wondered what entrepreneurs are like; where they look for business ideas and opportunities, and what kinds of thinking and tools some of them use in their approach to a possible business start-up, then this introductory book should prove very helpful to you. It includes both a self-assessment and a business opportunity assessment tool, and advocates a "damage control approach" to getting into business.

50 pages, softcover; ISBN 978-1-55270-089-1 CIP
Canada: $14.95 US: $14.95 UK: £9.49

Business Planning and Finances

Confederation College Entrepreneurship Series

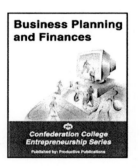

Business Planning and Finances takes a pragmatic and hands-on approach to business planning and financial management, and is written in straightforward language free of technical jargon. It includes a thorough review of the role of planning, the benefits to be realized from planning, and the use of a plan as a management aid.

174 pages, softcover; ISBN 978-1-55270-091-4 CIP
Canada: $34.95 US: $34.95 UK: £21.99

Small Business Finance

Confederation College Entrepreneurship Series

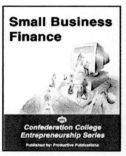

Small Business Finance was designed with the start-up business owner/manager in mind and provides a detailed overview of the organization and operation of a business from a financial perspective. Developed as a combination textbook and workbook, it takes the reader step-by-step through each element of a company's finances from pre-startup costs all the way to record keeping and financial monitoring for an established business.

136 pages, softcover; ISBN 978-1-55270-092-1 CIP
Canada: $29.95 US: $29.95 UK: £18.89

**For details visit our Canadian Web site: *www.ProductivePublications.ca*
American Web site: *www.ProductivePublications.com*
Order securely online or mail the order form at the end of this catalogue
Phone our Order Desk toll-free at: 1-(877) 879-2669**

Youth Entrepreneurship

**Confederation College
Entrepreneurship Series**

Some of North America's most successful businesses have been started by people between the ages of 15 and 25. If you are a young person with a business idea or a desire to start your own business then this informative and practical book should be a "must-read" for you. Learn from the experiences of others and improve your prospects for success.

108 pages, softcover; ISBN 978-1-55270-094-5 CIP
Canada: $24.95 US: $24.95 UK: £15.79

**Business Relationships –
Development and
Maintenance**

**Confederation College
Entrepreneurship Series**

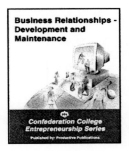

The success of any business hinges on the effective management of three critical categories of business relationships. These are a firm's relationships with its customers, with its employees, and with the individuals and organizations that supply it with essential goods and services. This book outlines the nature and role of each type of relationship, and identifies a variety of best practices and operating tools to be employed in the successful development and maintenance of these relationships.

78 pages; softcover; ISBN 978-1-55270-093-8 CIP
Canada: $19.95 US: $19.95 UK: £12.59

Becoming Successful!

**Taking Your Home-Based
Business to a New Level**

By: Don Varner

Strategies for getting great results in your home-based business! How to turn any type of business into a SUCCESSFUL business!

- Self-Improvement
- Handling Rejections
- Management Skills
- 16 Ways to Prospect
- Designing Great Ads
- Self-Motivation
- Hiring Tips
- Motivating Employees
- Closing Sales
- No-Cost Ways to Advertise

338 pages, softcover; ISBN 978-1-896210-87-2 CIP
Canada: $39.95 US: $39.95 UK: £25.19

**Start Your Own Business:
Be Your Own Boss!**

**Your Road Map to
Independence**

By: Iain Williamson

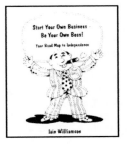

Learn from someone who has done it! What it takes! Where to get ideas and how to check them out. How to research the market. Calculate how much money you will really need and where to get it. Growing pains and managing employees... plus lots more. Iain Williamson has run his own businesses for over 35 years and is a consultant. He'll help you with a Road Map to Independence!

208 pages, softcover; ISBN 978-1-896210-96-4 CIP
Canada: $29.95 US: $29.95 UK: £18.99

For details visit our Canadian Web site: *www.ProductivePublications.ca*
American Web site: *www.ProductivePublications.com*
Order securely online or mail the order form at the end of this catalogue
Phone our Order Desk toll-free at: 1-(877) 879-2669

Can You Make Money with Your Idea or Invention?

By: Don Lunny

- Can you exploit it?
- How to produce it.
- Can you make money?
- Where to get help.
- Industrial Design.
- Copyright.
- Points of caution.
- Patent applications.
- Sample licensing agreement.
- Is the idea original?
- How to distribute it.
- Can you protect it?
- A word about patents.
- Trademarks.
- First steps.
- Possible problems.
- What are your chances?

99 pages, softcover; ISBN 978-0-920847-65-7   CIP
Canada: $24.95 US: $24.95 UK: £15.79

The Canadian Business Guide to Patents for Inventions and New Products

By: George Rolston

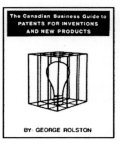

This is your complete reference to patenting around the world. The key elements in the patent process. When to search for earlier patents. When you should file patent applications. The importance of your patent filing date. Understand the critical wording of patent claims. Getting the best out of your patent agent. What the patent office will do for you. What to do if your patent application is rejected. How to go about patenting in foreign countries and how to negotiate a licence agreement. **George Rolston**, is a barrister and solicitor who has specialized in patents for over 30 years.

202 pages, softcover; ISBN 978-0-920847-13-8   CIP
Canada: $48.00

Protect Your Intellectual Property

An International Guide to Patents, Copyrights and Trademarks

By: Hoyt L. Barber & Robert M. Logan

An abundance of information on step-by-step procedures to obtain exclusive protection for unique ideas, inventions, names, identifying marks, or artistic, literary, musical, photographic or cinematographic works. Hoyt Barber is an executive with extensive experience in intellectual property protection. Robert Logan is a practicing U.S. attorney.

305 pages, softcover; ISBN 978-1-896210-95-7   CIP
Canada: $59.95 US: $59.95 UK: £37.79

Evaluating Franchise Opportunities

By: Don Lunny

Although the success rate for franchisee-owned businesses is better than for many other start-up businesses, success is not guaranteed. Don't be "pressured" into a franchise that is not right for you. Investigate your options. How to evaluate the business, the franchisor, the franchise package, and yourself. Author and business consultant, **Don Lunny**, shows you how to avoid the pitfalls before you make a franchise investment.

75 pages, softcover; ISBN 978-0-920847-64-0   CIP
Canada: $19.95 US: $19.95 UK: £12.59

For details visit our Canadian Web site: www.ProductivePublications.ca
American Web site: www.ProductivePublications.com
Order securely online or mail the order form at the end of this catalogue
Phone our Order Desk toll-free at: 1-(877) 879-2669

Basic Beancounting

**Learn to Ape
a Professional
Bookkeeper**

By: T. James Cook, CA

This book is intended to help
non-accountants understand
basic bookkeeping principles
and procedures so that they can
maintain a simple set of accounting records for a small
business. The benefits are up-to-date financial records plus a
cost savings by doing a portion of the work that would
otherwise be performed by a professional accountant.

121 pages, softcover; ISBN 978-1-55270-204-8 CIP
Canada: $26.95 US: $26.95 UK: £16.99

Gorilla Accounting

**How to Survive in a
Jungle of Numbers**

By: T. James Cook, CA

Designed to teach the small
business owner or manager to read
and understand financial
statements, and use financial
management tools including
trend, ratio, and break-even
analysis to get maximum
information from financial records. Financial and cash flow
forecasting are explained and how to use the financial
statements effectively. Easy to read, easy to understand, and easy
to put into practice.

113 pages, softcover; ISBN 978-1-55270-205-5 CIP
Canada: $26.95

Salary Administration

**By:
Entrepreneurial Business
Consultants of Canada**

Salary Administration Program provides the means for
management to:

- Properly analyse and evaluate positions.
- Provide equitable and competitive remuneration.
- Appraise individual performance in a position.

164 pages; softcover; ISBN 978-1-55270-085-3 CIP
Canada: $39.95 US: $39.95 UK: £25.19

**Shoplifting, Security,
Curtailing Crime -
Inside & Out**

By: Don Lunny

If you are a shopkeeper or business owner, this practical,
hands-on book will alert you to the alarming theft rates you
may be exposed to. From petty theft, bad cheques to armed
robbery, you get advice on dealing with the situation and how
to train staff. Discusses internal theft by employees - how you
can recognize it and how to reduce it. If it alerts you to just one
problem, it could pay for itself many, many times over.

115 pages; softcover; ISBN 978-0-920847-66-4 CIP
Canada: $29.95 US: $29.95 UK: £18.99

For details visit our Canadian Web site: *www.ProductivePublications.ca*
American Web site: *www.ProductivePublications.com*
Order securely online or mail the order form at the end of this catalogue
Phone our Order Desk toll-free at: 1-(877) 879-2669

Marketing for Beginners

How to Get Your Products into the Hands of Consumers

By: Iain Williamson

Covers the basics of marketing for new entrepreneurs. How to make people aware of your products. How to get them to buy. How to get products into the hands of consumers. Traditional channels of distribution versus direct marketing. One-on-one marketing versus mass marketing. Take a look at the Internet as a marketing tool. Ways to promote and advertise your products. After-sales service and the lifetime value of your customers. Sources of marketing information. The author has been marketing products for 20 years.

215 pages, softcover; ISBN 978-1-896210-97-1   CIP
Canada: $29.95 US: $29.95 UK: £18.99

Marketing Beyond 2000

Why You Will Have to Use the Internet to Market Your Goods or Services in the 21ˢᵗ Century

By: Iain Williamson

The Internet will become an awesome marketing tool in the 21st. Century. Learn how its current limitations are being overcome. Take a look at the future of radio, TV and newspapers.

Glimpse at the marketplace of the future. The author says it's up to you to take advantage of this tremendous marketing tool. Find out how!

194 pages, softcover; ISBN 978-1-896210-66-7   CIP
Canada: $27.95 US: $27.95 UK: £17.69

Successful Direct Mail Marketing in Canada

A Step-by-Step Guide to Selling Your Products or Services Through the Mail

By: Iain Williamson

Techniques to make money in the highly competitive direct mail market. Direct mail as an inexpensive way to reach customers. Ways to keep your costs to a minimum. How to save on postage by using bulk rates. How to get the most out of your computer. The author has over 15 years experience selling by direct mail.

114 pages, softcover; ISBN 978-1-896210-39-1   CIP
Canada: $19.95

Jump Start Your New Employees

Get the Most Out of New Hires From Their First Day on the Job!

By: Julie Olley

An organizational tool for various employee transitions with suggested steps to boost initial productivity of new employees from their first day on the job; to minimize the impact on your customers and identify training needs. Also, to professionally handle departing employees while maintaining security and company property. How employee transitions can be used to create a positive impact on your customers.

Olley: 64 pages, softcover; ISBN 1-55270-084-4   CIP
Canada: $12.95   USA: $9.95   UK: £8.19

**For details visit our Canadian Web site: www.ProductivePublications.ca
American Web site: www.ProductivePublications.com
Order securely online or mail the order form at the end of this catalogue
Phone our Order Desk toll-free at: 1-(877) 879-2669**

Page 18

The Six Sigma Toolbox

54 Improvement Tools and When to Use Them

By: Jerry W. Wishes

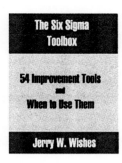

In this book Jerry Wishes provides fifty-four improvement tools. They are focused around two concepts. First, Variation is Evil. Every process has variation but the secret is to restrict it to natural causes and then use improvement tools to "manage" the variation. Second, use of the tools is not optional. Once you embrace them, you do so forever.

306 pages, softcover; ISBN 978-1-55270-258-1 CIP
Canada: $48.95 US: $48.95 UK: £30.99

Quality in the 21ˢᵗ Century

What You Have to Change to Stay in Business

By: Jerry W. Wishes

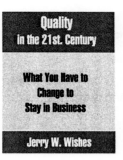

Jerry Wishes says: "If you don't 'get it' soon and start doing things differently, you'll be in a down-cycle and never understand why." His hope is that this book will give you some insight and a direction you can use to conquer the challenges ahead.

202 pages, softcover; ISBN 978-1-55270-259-8 CIP
Canada: $39.95 US: $39.95 UK: £25.19

Seven Sigma

The Pursuit of Perfection

By: Jerry W. Wishes

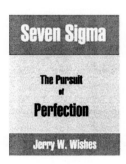

This book makes the case, through the use of a fictional business story, for the rejection of mediocrity in the corporate world. The acceptance of 'things just go wrong' is replaced with the need to raise the bar on expectations. The story takes place at a high-technology start-up.

240 pages, softcover; ISBN: 978-1-55270-260-8 CIP
Canada: $42.95 US: $42.95 UK: £26.99

Modern Materials Management Techniques:

A Complete Guide to Help You Plan, Direct and Control the Purchase, Production, Storage and Distribution of Goods in Today's Competitive Business Environment –Essentials of Supply Chain Management

By: Paula Mackie   **SECOND EDITION**

Covers the entire process of a company's operations relating to the acquisition of goods and services. Written for the public and private sectors as well as college and university educators.

398 pages, softcover; ISBN: 978-1-55270-257-4 CIP
Canada: $74.95 US: $74.95 UK: £47.29

For details visit our Canadian Web site: *www.ProductivePublications.ca*
American Web site: *www.ProductivePublications.com*
Order securely online or mail the order form at the end of this catalogue
Phone our Order Desk toll-free at: 1-(877) 879-2669

Innovate or Perish!

**Seven-Step Innovation
Process to Meet
the Challenges
of Globalization**

By: Richard Sussman Sc.D.

A complete manual for manufacturing companies to produce new products and processes that can enhance their competitive position. The process starts with the creation of a strategic innovation plan and then provides a system to evaluate the current products and manufacturing capabilities of a company. Methods to select and execute the new developments in the most effective manner. Outsourcing and executive management are reviewed. Dr. Richard Sussman was one of the top technical leaders in the steel industry.

242 pages, softcover, ISBN 978-1-55270-253-6   CIP
Canada: $49.95 US: $49.95 UK: £21.49

Effective Management:

**Interpersonal Skills that
Will Help You Earn
the Respect and
Commitment of Employees**

By: Dave Day Ph.D.

Ten key interpersonal skills for the manager... from choosing a leadership style to the day of completing annual performance evaluations. Contains practical suggestions to increase the productivity and commitment of all employees. Essential reading for all new managers and a resource for existing managers. Dave Day has over 35 years experience as a manager, consultant and Professor of Management at Columbia College.

180 pages, softcover; ISBN 978-1-896210-99-5   CIP
Canada: $27.95 US: $27.95 UK: £17.69

**Critical Analysis
in Decision-Making:**

**Conventional and
"Outside the Box"
Approaches to
Developing Solutions
to Today's Business
Challenges**

By: James Briggs

This book examines why some people make good business decisions more effectively, more often, than others. Great leaders in the public service, business, and the non-profit sectors, remind us that an effective decision-making process is the key to solving problems for any organization. Effective organizations search for leaders who have good problem solving skills.

234 pages, softcover; ISBN 978-1-55270-116-4   CIP
Canada: $48.95 US: $48.95 UK: £30.99

**Project Management:
Welcome Opportunity
or Awesome Burden?**

By: Robert G. Edwards

This concise, how-to, self-help guide will help both aspiring and practicing project managers. Its content was developed during the author's forty-four years in professional engineering and project management. The principles and practices that he describes are based on his personal experience and can easily be applied to most simple or complex projects.

170 pages, softcover; ISBN 978-1-55270-086-0   CIP
Canada: $26.95 US: $26.95 UK: £16.99

**For details visit our Canadian Web site: *www.ProductivePublications.ca*
American Web site: *www.ProductivePublications.com*
Order securely online or mail the order form at the end of this catalogue
Phone our Order Desk toll-free at: 1-(877) 879-2669**

Cooperative Time Management

Get More Done and Have More Fun!

By: Chance Massaro & Katheryn Allen-Katz

Contains the wisdom of the last fifty years of research and writing about time management together with eighteen years working in organizations helping people get the most satisfying results. It is intended for people who have goals and want to achieve them. It is interactive and easy to use. The authors are time management experts. Follow the steps which they outline in this 224 page workbook and YOUR RESULTS WILL BE REMARKABLE!

224 pages, softcover; ISBN 978-1-896210-86-5   CIP
Canada: $34.95 US: $34.95 UK: £21.99

THE LEAN OFFICE

How to Use Just-in-Time Techniques to Streamline Your Office

By: Jim Thompson

This book is for everyone who works in an office. Find out how to foster and nurture employee involvement and put excitement back into continuous improvement. Get the tools needed to improve office productivity. Most importantly, reduce employee stress and frustration, while improving productivity. Find out how this happens <u>with</u> employees, not <u>to</u> employees! Jim Thompson is a lean production consultant who studied these systems first-hand while with GM and Toyota in California.

138 pages, softcover; ISBN 978-1-896210-41-4   CIP
Canada: $24.95 US: $24.95 UK: £15.79

LEAN PRODUCTION

How to Use the Highly Effective Japanese Concept of Kaizen to Improve Your Efficiency

By: Jim Thompson

Learn specific techniques and behaviours to improve your effectiveness. Find out about a system that has been used very effectively at the organizational level for over forty years. Author, **Jim Thompson** has held senior management positions with General Motors and the Walker Manufacturing Company.

146 pages, softcover; ISBN 978-1-896210-42-1   CIP
Canada: $24.95 US: $24.95 UK: £15.79

LEAN PRODUCTION FOR THE OFFICE

Common Sense Ideas To Help Your Office Continuously Improve

By: Jim Thompson

More ideas for everyone who works in an office:

- ‣ Be idea-driven
- ‣ Reduce frustration
- ‣ Add value
- ‣ Let others benchmark you

How to use employees' creativity and ingenuity. Employees' feelings **do** count! Author, **Jim Thompson**, is the guru of applying lean production to the office environment.

136 pages, softcover; ISBN 978-1-55270-025-9   CIP
Canada: $24.95 US: $24.95 UK: £15.79

For details visit our Canadian Web site: *www.ProductivePublications.ca*
American Web site: *www.ProductivePublications.com*
Order securely online or mail the order form at the end of this catalogue
Phone our Order Desk toll-free at: 1-(877) 879-2669

Speak Up!

Helpful Tips for Business People who Need to Speak in Public

By: T. James Cook, CA

Helps business people improve their speaking skills and become good oral communicators. Includes an assessment of present skills together with practice sessions. Better speaking skills will lead you to more responsibility, authority, and material benefits. Confidence in your speaking skills will result in reduced stress levels when you know that you are going to have to speak, or when you are in a potential speaking situation. Ideas that are well articulated are always given more weight and make you more successful.

110 pages, softcover; ISBN 978-1-55270-256-7   CIP
Canada: $24.95 US: $24.95 UK: £15.79

Quick Fixes for Business Writing

An Eight-Step Editing Process to Find and Correct Common Readability Problems

By: Jim Taylor

Breaks down the editorial process into a series of tasks which are designed to improve the readability of the final product. It will be invaluable to you; regardless of whether you are a novice or a proficient editor. Author, Jim Taylor, has taught Eight-Step Editing for 18 years and clients for his workshops include the Editor's Association of Canada and the Ontario Cabinet Office.

156 pages, softcover; ISBN 978-1-55270-252-9   CIP
Canada: $24.95 US: $ 24. 95 UK: £15.79

Training Your Board of Directors

A Manual for the CEOs, Board Members, Administrators and Executives of Corporations, Associations, Non-Profit and Religious Organizations

By: ArLyne Diamond, Ph.D.

For more than ten years now the author has been training boards of directors of organizations of all kinds, from religious organizations to fast-growing high tech companies. This manual is different from most board training books. It is a combination of short informative pieces and a series of interactive exercises designed to enable the participants to actively reach the desired conclusions rather than being lectured to, or corrected by "the expert."

350 pages, softcover; ISBN 978-1-55270-207-9   CIP
Canada: $39.95 US: $39.95 UK: £25.19

Leadership with Panache

52 Ways to Set Yourself Apart as a Dynamic Manager

By: Jeff Jernigan

This book cuts to the underbelly of leadership in the modern organization. Divided into 52 "Ways" so that you can select one topic each week of the year for group discussion with your management and supervisory associates. Poses hard hitting questions for consideration. Author, **Jeff Jernigan**, has over 25-years experience as an organizational development specialist providing companies support in creating, continuing and capitalizing on change. He is the recipient of numerous industry awards.

180 pages, softcover; ISBN 978-1-55270-081-5   CIP
Canada: $29.95 US: $29.95 UK: £18.99

**For details visit our Canadian Web site: *www.ProductivePublications.ca*
American Web site: *www.ProductivePublications.com*
Order securely online or mail the order form at the end of this catalogue
Phone our Order Desk toll-free at: 1-(877) 879-2669**

How to Deliver Excellent Customer Service

A Step-by-Step Guide for Every Business

By: Julie Olley

A pre-designed workbook approach for businesses that wish to develop, implement, analyse and follow-up customer service projects. Step-by-step "HOW TO:" ideas and sample formats are included. The suggestions can be implemented over time. Author, **Julie Olley**, was formerly National Manager of Quality Assurance with a major international travel organization. She has designed several curricula for The Canadian School of Management and International Business.

160 pages, softcover; ISBN 978-1-55270-045-7   CIP
Canada: $26.95 US: $26.95 UK: £16.99

Anybody Can Sell!

Sales Strategies to Increase Your Business Profits

By: Don Varner

Written for those who have started a business and have limited selling experience.

- Covers creative marketing and sales presentations.
- Hints on self-motivation and how to handle rejection.
- Discusses different kinds of buyers and how to handle them.

102 pages, softcover; ISBN 978-1-55270-004-4   CIP
Canada: $18.95 US: $18.95 UK: £11.99

Secrets of Successful Advertising and Promotion

Practical Steps to Growing Your Business

By: Don Varner

- Covers all the basics of advertising and promoting for business.
- How to prospect for more customers.
- How to increase the average size of your sales.

Author, **Don Varner**, is an expert with many years of experience in this area.

158 pages; softcover ISBN 978-1-55270-002-0   CIP
Canada: $24.95 US: $24.95 UK: £15.79

Timeless Strategies to Become a Successful Entrepreneur

By: Lawrence Scott Troemel

This book is all about starting, building, and managing a small business. The approaches covered in this book have been successfully implemented for decades and will continue to be viable well into the future. Every entrepreneur will benefit from the advice in this very readable book. It is also full of interesting anecdotes.

208 pages; softcover; ISBN 978-1-55270-046-4   CIP
Canada: $29.95 US: $29.95 UK: £18.99

For details visit our Canadian Web site: *www.ProductivePublications.ca*
American Web site: *www.ProductivePublications.com*
Order securely online or mail the order form at the end of this catalogue
Phone our Order Desk toll-free at: 1-(877) 879-2669

The Glass Slipper

Smart Steps for Every Businesswoman's Success

By: Shelley Peever and Layla Didmon

The Glass Slipper is a functional business guide specifically geared toward women in small and medium sized businesses. Each chapter is an integral part of an overall guide that will assist women in gathering information to apply to businesses of their own. A case study section appears at the completion of each chapter. This provides a physical example of the tools and resources offered throughout the book.

110 pages, softcover; ISBN 978-1-55270-262-8   CIP
Canada: $24.95 US: $24.95 UK: £15.79

How to Buy or Sell a Business

Questions You Should Ask and How to Get the Best Price

By: Don Lunny

The decision to buy or sell a business requires careful consideration. It may affect the course of the participants future lives. Yet a surprising number of owners rush into transactions without adequate preparation. Find out how to set the price, locate prospects, evaluate offers, close deals and finance purchases. Author, **Donald Lunny**, has many years of business experience and has been involved with the purchase and sale of many businesses.

134 pages, softcover; ISBN 978-1-896210-98-8   CIP
Canada: $24.95 US: $24.95 UK: £15.79

Tips for Entrepreneurs

How to Meet the Challenges of Starting And Managing Your Own Business

By: Henry Kyambalesa

This book is the culmination of a 3-year research study into the challenges faced by entrepreneurs when they become their own boss. Tips for those about to start a business & tips for those already in business. Decide whether self-employment is for you. Practical advice on getting started. The skills you will need. Henry Kyambalesa is a tenured lecturer in Business Administration. He holds B.B.A., M.A., and M.B.A. degrees.

194 pages, softcover ISBN 978-1-896210-85-8   CIP
Canada: $26.95 US: $26.95 UK: £16.99

Work from Your Home Office as an Independent Contractor

A Complete Guide to Getting Started

By: Chantelle Sauer

An independent contractor is someone who works from his or her home or home office e.g., consultants, entrepreneurs, business owners, freelancers and outsourcers. Learn about the advantages and disadvantages as well as the legal obligations. Also get many ideas on how to become an independent contractor. Author, **Chantelle Sauer**, has spent four years as an independent contractor. She knows from first-hand experience how to get work.

166 pages, softcover; ISBN 978-1-55270-077-8   CIP
Canada: $24.95 US: $24.95 UK: £15.79

For details visit our Canadian Web site: *www.ProductivePublications.ca*
American Web site: *www.ProductivePublications.com*
Order securely online or mail the order form at the end of this catalogue
Phone our Order Desk toll-free at: 1-(877) 879-2669

The Basics for Sales Success

An Essential Guide for New Sales Representatives, Entrepreneurs and Business People

By: Bill Sobye

An introductory book which covers the basic points on how to:

- Find customers
- Study your prospects
- Dress for success
- Handle "the butterflies"

- Set goals
- How to include humour
- Success and rejection
- Business versus pleasure

Bill Sobye has 28 years of experience as a Sales Manager.

157 pages; softcover; ISBN 978-1-896210-65-0 CIP
Canada: $24.95 US: $24.95 UK: £15.79

Bulletproof Salesman

A Lively Guide to Enhance Your Sales Techniques

By: Steven Travis Smith & Bruce D. Seymour

Strategies to Help You Bridge the Gap Between Textbook Training and the Real World

A humorous, yet practical guide written using a tag-team approach between the authors. It explains how they've completely screwed-up over the years avoided making the same mistakes again. Learn from their failures as well as their victories. They explain how to reach absolutely anyone, evade the traps constructed to keep salespeople out, and how to instantly detect deception during negotiations.

231 pages, softcover; ISBN 978-1-55270-209-3 CIP
Canada: $29.95 $US: $29.95 £18.99

Software for Small Business 2011 Edition

Windows & Vista Programs to Help you Improve Business Efficiency and Productivity

By: Iain Williamson

Reviews of 240 programs for new and experienced users. Covers operating systems, word processing, desktop publishing, voice dictation, graphics, digital photography, digital video & audio, spreadsheets, accounting, databases, contact management, communications, Internet software, security and virus protection.

372 pages, softcover; ISBN978-1-55270-405-9 CIP
ISSN: 1492-384X Canada: $79.95 US: $79.95 UK: £50.49

Learn UNIX in Fifteen Days

By: Dwight Baer and Paul Davidson

This book was written out of the need for a text which presents the material which is actually taught in a typical UNIX course at the college level. It is not intended to replace a comprehensive UNIX manual, but for most students who have not yet spent five years learning all the "eccentricities" of the UNIX Operating System, it will present all they need to know (and more!) in order to use and support a UNIX system.

176 pages, softcover; ISBN: 978-1-55270-087-7 CIP
Canada: $34.95 US: $34.95 UK: £21.99

For details visit our Canadian Web site: *www.ProductivePublications.ca*
American Web site: *www.ProductivePublications.com*
Order securely online or mail the order form at the end of this catalogue
Phone our Order Desk toll-free at: 1-(877) 879-2669

Management During an Economic Crisis

Best Practices for Small Business Survival in a Recession

By: Robert Papes

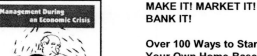

Best practices which are vital to every small business to help them survive the current recession because "hope" of better times is not a viable strategy. This book is all meat and potatoes with no filler. Author, Robert Papes, is a consultant with many years of experience in helping businesses in difficulty.

182 pages, softcover; ISBN 1-55270-384-7 CIP
Canada: $29.95 US: $29.95 UK: £18.99

MAKE IT! MARKET IT! BANK IT!

Over 100 Ways to Start Your Own Home-Based Business

By: Barbara J. Albrecht

This book is about starting your own home-based business. It's also about earning extra money when your wages don't stretch far enough. Money for vacations and education often fall through the cracks in your financial plans and you may find that you need a second income. Newspaper columnist, Barb Albrecht, has assembled these 100 great ideas to help you put cash into your "money jar". If you're looking to run your own part-time business or start a new career as owner of your own enterprise....you must read this book.

144 pages, softcover; ISBN 978-1-55270-145-4 CIP
Canada: $24.95 US: $24.95 UK: £15.79

Your Homebased Business Plan

-Also-

Working With Your Banker

By: Donald Lunny

SECTION I - The Business Plan
for Homebased Business: a step-by-step guide to writing it.

SECTION II - Working with your Banker: the fundamentals of borrowing and how they affect you.

Donald Lunny: an entrepreneur and consultant with many years experience in organizing and restructuring companies.

52 pages, softcover; ISBN 978-0-920847-35-0 CIP
Canada: $14.95 US: $14.95 £9.49

THE NET EFFECT

Will the Internet be a Panacea or Curse for Business and Society in the Next Ten Years?

By: Iain Williamson

Are you ready for the greatest change to business & society since the Industrial Revolution? Examine the world ten years from now when entire sectors of the economy may be eliminated and others will be born. Find out who will be the winners and losers and how it will affect you. Prepare for the dramatic changes that are coming!

244 pages, softcover, ISBN 1-896210-38-4; CIP
Canada: $29.95 USA: $21.95 UK: £18.99

For details visit our Canadian Web site: *www.ProductivePublications.ca*
American Web site: *www.ProductivePublications.com*
Order securely online or mail the order form at the end of this catalogue
Phone our Order Desk toll-free at: 1-(877) 879-2669

Death by Food

Why More People in North America Die By Food Poisoning than Were Murdered in 9/11

By: Iain Williamson

If you've ever had food poisoning, you're certainly not alone. 76 million Americans and 12 million Canadians suffer from a foodborne illness **every year**. Food poisoning is now one of the leading causes of illness in both Canada and the United States. Deaths due to foodborne pathogens total about 5,000 **annually** for the US. This no-nonsense book claims that the food you eat may be neither safe nor healthy and suggests what you can do about it.

156 pages, softcover; ISBN 978-1-55270-383-0 CIP
Canada: $24.95 US: $24.95 UK: £15.79

Yoga for Mind, Body and Spirit

Details of Practices That Will Help Your Health, Psychological and Spiritual Well-Being

By: Dr. John R.M. Goyeche

Detailed descriptions of certain yoga practices for physical, mental and spiritual development; for different-aged people; for different situations and for people with certain health concerns. Dr. Goyeche has studied and taught yoga on three continents and in many settings for over 30 years.

188 pages, softcover; ISBN 978-1-55270-056-3 CIP
Canada: $24.95 US: $24.95 UK: £15.79

Winning Over Depression

Bio-Energetic Therapy to Overcome Sadness, Fear and Anger

By: Dr. John R.M. Goyeche

A straightforward book that discusses the causes of depression. Offers practical answers to overcome it. Written for the general public and also practitioners of psychiatry, medicine and health care. Dr. John R.M. Goyeche has 25 years of clinical experience in hospitals, mental health centres and rehabilitation clinics..

130 pages, softcover; ISBN 978-1-55270-051-8 CIP
Canada: $24.95 US: $24.98 UK:£15.79

Benefit From Hypnosis, Hypnosis by Telephone and Self-Hypnosis

How to Improve Your Self-Esteem, Creativity and Performance as well as Your Spiritual, Physical and Mental Well-Being

By: Dr. John R.M. Goyeche

Hypnosis can help you with:
Habits & Addictions   Fears & Anxieties
Self-Esteem & Depression   General Medical Problems
Creative Activity   Spirituality
Memory Retrieval   Performance Enhancement

Dr. Goyeche is a member of the Canadian Society of Clinical Hypnosis, a Fellow of the International College of Psychosomatic Medicine, a member of the International Institute for Bio-Energetic Analysis.

212 pages, softcover; ISBN: 978-1-55270-050-1 CIP
Canada: $21.95 US: $21.95 UK: £13.89

**For details visit our Canadian Web site: www.ProductivePublications.ca
American Web site: www.ProductivePublications.com
Order securely online or mail the order form at the end of this catalogue
Phone our Order Desk toll-free at: 1-(877) 879-2669**

Slot Machines: Fun Machines or Tax Machines?

A Technician Reveals the Truth About One-Armed Bandits

By: Ian B. Williams

How slot machines work and how to play them. Covers the pay-out systems. Helps you have a better casino experience. Also examines the social implications of slot machines in our society; both the positive and negative. **Ian B. Williams** is a certified electronics technician and a trained slot technician, who worked for several years in the casino industry.

134 pages, softcover; ISBN 978-1-55270-049-5 CIP
Canada: $24.95 US: $ 24.95 UK: £15.79

Dollars to Donuts

A Personal Wealth Management Model for Canadians

By: Daniel Kesselring

Five Easy Steps that Can Change Your Financial Direction Today

This book provides a unique unbiased perspective from outside the financial services and wealth management industries. It is a product of research, personal observation and a lifetime of trial-and-error experience that led to a system of money management that has served the author extraordinarily well over the years.

157 pages, softcover; ISBN 978-1-55270-208-6 CIP
Canada: $24.95

Make Money Trading Options

How to Start Immediately

By: Jason Diptee

Want to invest in an expensive stock, the Japanese Yen or the DOW but only have $200- $300 to invest? Option trading allows you to enter these markets to take advantage of investment opportunities that would otherwise require thousands of dollars. This book will teach beginners how to participate in the largely untapped and unknown area of investing that can generate profits in a matter of weeks. Jason Diptee holds an MBA and is an experienced seminar leader on the subject of option trading.

116 pages, softcover; ISBN 978-1-55270-148-5 CIP
Canada: $24.95 US: $24.95 UK: £15.79

"You're Hired.... You're Fired!"

A Manager's Guide to Employee Supervision

By: Deborah L. Whitworth

This book is a great read if you are a manager or a supervisor; even if it is only being in charge temporarily for a day. It will provide you with a step-by-step method of acquiring practical human resource management skills.

Author, Deborah L. Whitworth, has been a human resource manager for over 20 years. She believes that management isn't rocket science but a process. You want to do the right thing. Unfortunately, nobody has told you what the right thing is. Deborah acts as a role model and shows you how to manage yourself, so you can be free to manager others.

144 pages, softcover; ISBN 978-1-55270-146-1 CIP
Canada: $24.95 US: $24.95 UK: £15.79

For details visit our Canadian Web site: *www.ProductivePublications.ca*
American Web site: *www.ProductivePublications.com*
Order securely online or mail the order form at the end of this catalogue
Phone our Order Desk toll-free at: 1-(877) 879-2669

So, You Wanna Be a Millionaire...

By: James P. Johnson

This book provides you with a step-by-step guide to developing a personalized financial plan that will help you build wealth. The techniques are very simple to understand and the author has done a great job in explaining the basic concepts in a straightforward way. He has included many tables that you can immediately use in creating your own wealth-building plan.

200 pages, softcover; ISBN: 978-1-55270-088-4 CIP;
Canada: $36.95 US: $36.95 UK: £23.29

Short Cut to Easy Street

How to Get Money in Your Mailbox Every Day, Plus Automatic Income for the Rest of Your Life

By: Stephen W. Kenyon

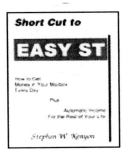

A great book on self-motivation, direct mail, self-publishing, marketing/advertising/promoting and network marketing. Study and learn the details of Stephen Kenyon's fascinating system for attracting wealth and success. He shares with you the inside trade secrets and techniques which he learned over a 30-year period.

244 pages, softcover; ISBN 978-1-55270-057-0 CIP
Canada: $37.95 US: $37.95 UK: £23.99

How to Write a Million Dollar Adventure Novel

Novel Writing as a Profitable Profession

By: Dr. Ray Mesluk

A structured approach to writing your novel quickly and easily. Master the techniques of novel writing and turn them into a profitable career.

304 pages, softcover; ISBN 978-1-55270-001-3 CIP
Canada: $34.95 US: $34.95 UK: £21.99

The "Please" & "Thank You" of Fundraising for Non-Profits:

Fifteen Essential Ingredients for Success

By: ArLyne Diamond, Ph.D.

This book will show you how to successfully raise funds for non-profits; whether you are a member of a national organization, or a small community association. The author, Dr. ArLyne Diamond, has many years of experience with non-profits. She says raising money is an art form rather than a science. Her book shows you how to do it.

126 pages, softcover; ISBN 978-1-55270-261-1 CIP
Canada $24.95 $US: $24.95 UK:£15.77

For details visit our Canadian Web site: *www.ProductivePublications.ca*
American Web site: *www.ProductivePublications.com*
Order securely online or mail the order form at the end of this catalogue
Phone our Order Desk toll-free at: 1-(877) 879-2669

ORDER FORM

Qty.	Title	Price
	ADD Postage: $9.95 first title within Canada or $12.95 to USA	
	ADD $2.25 Postage per title thereafter in Canada or $3.75 to USA	
	SUB-TOTAL	
	ADD 5% HST - Canadian Residents Only (others EXEMPT)	
	TOTAL	

Name_____

Organization_____

Street_____

City/Town_____State/Prov_____ Zip/Postal Code_____

Phone_____Fax_____

☐ Cheque ☐ VISA ☐ MasterCard ☐ American Express

VISA **MasterCard** **AMEX**

Credit Card Orders: can be faxed to: + (416) 322-7434

Card Number_____

Expiry Date(Month/Year)_____

Cardholder Signature_____

Mail to: **Productive Publications**
PO Box 7200, Stn. A, Toronto, ON M5W 1X8 Canada
Order Desk toll-free: 1-(877) 879-2669 Fax: (416) 322-7434
Order Securely Online at: www.ProductivePublications.ca